Shakespeare's adolescents

Manchester University Press

Shakespeare's adolescents

Age, gender and the body in Shakespearean performance and early modern culture

Victoria Sparey

MANCHESTER UNIVERSITY PRESS

Copyright © Victoria Sparey 2024

The right of Victoria Sparey to be identified as the author of this work has been asserted in accordance with the Copyright, Designs and Patents Act 1988.

Published by Manchester University Press
Oxford Road, Manchester, M13 9PL

www.manchesteruniversitypress.co.uk

British Library Cataloguing-in-Publication Data
A catalogue record for this book is available from the British Library

ISBN 978 1 5261 6819 1 hardback

First published 2024

The publisher has no responsibility for the persistence or accuracy of URLs for any external or third-party internet websites referred to in this book, and does not guarantee that any content on such websites is, or will remain, accurate or appropriate.

Typeset
by Deanta Global Publishing Services, Chennai, India

Contents

Acknowledgements	*page* vi
Introduction – misunderstood teens: examining early modern ideas about puberty	1
1 'A rose by any other name': flowering adolescence and the gendering of puberty	40
2 Beards and blushes: fertile complexions in Shakespeare's plays	74
3 Voicing adolescence: the heated words of puberty	102
4 The maypole and the acorn: body growth and disparities in height in Shakespeare's plays	157
Conclusion – spot the difference: symmetry, difference, and gender in early modern constructions of adolescence	192
References	205
Index	223

Acknowledgements

I am so happy to have written this book about Shakespeare's vibrant and complex adolescent characters. It has, however, taken a lot of time, patience, and effort to get the book over the finish line. I am acutely aware that I could not have completed this project, in simply being able to find the time to do so around teaching and childcare commitments, without the kindness and generosity of supportive family, friends, and colleagues. I am also thankful to my students for their unwavering enthusiasm for the material that I teach.

I am grateful to all my colleagues who are part of the research and teaching community at the University of Exeter. For their support and advice over the years, I would like to thank Kristen Brind, Chris Campbell, Chris Ewers, Jana Funke, Jason Hall, Vike Plock, Joe Kember, James Lyons, Ellen McWilliams, Sinéad Moynihan, Gwen Morris, Benedict Morrison, John Plunkett, Jane Poyner, Mark Steven, Angelique Richardson, Andrew Rudd, Jules Warner, Ed Whiteoak, Paul Williams, Paul Young, and Tricia Zakreski. I feel especially fortunate to work in an environment that is enriched by scholars who specialise in early modern and medieval literature, including: Pascale Aebischer, Niall Allsopp, Karen Edwards, Jo Esra, Marion Gibson, Felicity Henderson, Naomi Howell, Eddie Jones, Elliot Kendall, Nick McDowell, Ayesha Mukherjee, David Parry, Henry Power, Chloe Preedy, Philip Schwyzer, Caroline Spearing, Naya Tsentourou, and Elizabeth Williamson. Special thanks are due to Andrew McRae and Sarah Toulalan, who supported my early postgraduate journey in supervising my thesis on Shakespeare's mothers and early modern reproductive theory. Through Sarah and Andrew's guidance, I developed research skills and knowledge that I have used in writing this book about adolescence. Likewise, the invaluable advice I received from Elaine Hobby and Lesel Dawson on my doctoral research has carried forward into my use of medical history in *Shakespeare's Adolescents*.

More recently, Pascale Aebischer, as my colleague and friend, has had a pronounced impact on me as a researcher and the thinking I have used in writing this book. Having worked closely with Pascale on teaching modules and collaborative research over the last few years, Pascale's influence and expertise have informed my interest in theatre history, which has become a key component in my research methodology. Pascale's feedback on early drafts of chapters has been vitally important to the book's development, and I am grateful for the generosity that Pascale continues to show in giving time and thought to my research. Perhaps most importantly, in showing confidence in my work, Pascale has helped me trust in the contribution that my research can make to Shakespeare scholarship.

My warm thanks also extend here to Karen Edwards who has always expressed faith in my ability to write a good book. Jo Esra likewise receives my sincerest gratitude for her wise words, solidarity over teaching contracts (and reimagined research timelines), and a friendship forged over coffee and cake. The support I have received from colleagues at the University of Exeter has a long history and individuals who have made their mark, but no longer reside in Exeter, deserve acknowledgement. I continue to value conversations had with Jen Barnes, Briony Frost, Johanna Harris, Shona McIntosh, and Margaret Yoon; these colleagues always added humour and interest to working days. Jennifer Evans's longstanding enthusiasm for my work has also been greatly appreciated (and reciprocated), and it has been wonderful to collaborate on recent research, as our critical thinking once again finds intersections. I am grateful for conversations I have had with Harry McCarthy; Harry's research excellence has helped inform my own examination of collaborative staging and the acting skills of adolescent performers in this book.

Some parts of *Shakespeare's Adolescents* have appeared in print before. Chapter 2 is developed out of an article that appeared in *Shakespeare Bulletin* (Sparey, 2015). The article first appeared in *Shakespeare Bulletin*, Volume 33, Issue 3, Fall, 2015, pages 441–67, and I am grateful to Peter Kirwan, the current editor of *Shakespeare Bulletin*, for granting permission to re-use this material. This article was really the starting point for my interest in the symmetry and difference at work in early modern representations of male and female puberty.

I am also thankful to the anonymous readers who provided considered feedback on chapters and the final manuscript of this book. I am indebted to these readers for their thoughtful and enthusiastic engagement with the book's content. Matthew Frost and Jen Mellor, my editors at Manchester University Press, and Lillian Woodall and her team at Deanta, also have my gratitude for their patience, skill, and humour in guiding me through the publication process.

The cover image to this monograph, Arthur Rackham's illustration of Hermia and Helena, is reproduced by permission of the British Library (Shelf mark original source: Cup. 410.bb.55, facing page 12). I was first drawn to Rackham's work when I was a teenager, when I purchased a very battered 1930s edition of *Gulliver's Travels* from a sale in my school library. Rackham's illustrations, which captured my own adolescent attention some decades ago, I think continue to convey vitality, without sentimentality, and allude to the complexity of Shakespearean adolescent figures that I strive to illuminate in this book. I am grateful to the British Library for permitting my use of Rackham's striking image.

My final but most important thanks go to friends and family. I am lucky to have the support of many friends (from school friends, Fastest Cookies, and the J300/Morley Road girls). I would struggle to navigate day-to-day challenges without my school-run network of support! My mum, dad, and sister have been the source of life-long encouragement and love, for which I am truly thankful. I appreciate the belief that my parents have always shown in me, and I know this book will have pride of place on their bookcase. I am also grateful to my parents-in-law, Paul and Maureen, for the confidence they have shown in me, and the time that strategic trips with grandchildren provided so that I could work. As I write these acknowledgements to recognise the influence and support I have been fortunate to receive, Maureen is deeply missed.

My husband, Philip, has been my partner in life for over twenty years. His support and collaboration in all life decisions have made writing this book – and much more – possible, in terms of practicalities, emotional support, and fun! I will always be thankful for my kitchen counsellor who offers pragmatic advice, excellent meals, and steadying reassurance when I most need it. Our children, Henry and Bea, bring joy, witty commentaries on almost anything, and much love, all of which lift any day. For Philip, Henry, and Bea I am eternally grateful: they are my everyday that is my everything.

Introduction – misunderstood teens: examining early modern ideas about puberty

> I would there were no age between ten and three-and-twenty, or that youth would sleep out the rest; for there is nothing in the between but getting wenches with child, wronging the ancientry, stealing, fighting – Hark you now! Would any but these boiled-brains of nineteen and two-and-twenty hunt this weather? (Shakespeare, *The Winter's Tale*: 3.3.58–64)

The Shepherd's words in *The Winter's Tale* rehearse what, in many ways, have become familiar ideas when considering the representation of adolescence in early modern culture. Firstly, the Shepherd describes behavioural characteristics that he suggests are typical of unchecked adolescence: begetting illegitimate children, disrespect for elders and authority, crime, and violence. Adolescence, which most early modern commentators saw as lasting until somewhere between twenty-two and twenty-five years of age, is aligned with disorderly words and actions. In his *Touchstone of Complexions*, for example, Levinus Lemnius provides a telling description of 'wyllfull and slypperye Adolescencie which endedth at xxv' (1576: 29[v]). Ideas of 'wyllfull' words and actions certainly seem to fit with easily performed traits of masculine 'swaggering' adolescence that crossdressed heroines regularly claim to adopt in Shakespeare's plays, in gestures to a stereotype that initially assists the audience in understanding the age and gender appropriate to a theatrical disguise. Rosalind's claim 'We'll have a swashing and a martial outside' (1.3.116) in *As You Like It*, and Portia's description of 'fine bragging youth' (3.4.69) in *The Merchant of Venice*, make use of this construction of masculine adolescence.

Secondly, as realised in the Shepherd's derisory comment about 'boiled brains', the erratic behaviour of adolescents is understood to result from a heated bodily condition appropriate to age. In the early modern life cycle, which generally presented ageing as a process of cooling and drying out, adolescence was framed as hot and dry. Adolescents became disassociated from the excessive moisture thought to characterise early childhood but still possessed surplus heat that promoted the heat-fuelled acts of sex, argument, and violence that the Shepherd includes in his account. Thirdly, as words spoken by a father, the Shepherd provides a parental reaction to adolescence, which is characterised by concern and anxiety in response to hazardous behaviour typical of this age. Figured as a difficult time for parents, adolescence is recognised as a stage of life that would be happily avoided, and Shakespeare's Shepherd articulates his parental wish that 'no age' existed between childhood and adulthood at all.

In these ways, the Shepherd promptly takes us to some well-known approaches to adolescence in studies of early modern culture, which have generally upheld ideas about adolescence being a precarious age that must be endured until the stability of adulthood is achieved. Alexandra Shepard's discussion of adolescence, in *Meanings of Manhood*, for example, notes that in early modern culture the traits of the adolescent male included 'disruption, excessive drinking, illicit sex' (2003: 94). In a similar vein, Coppélia Kahn's analysis of 'Coming of Age' in *Romeo and Juliet* observes the extremes of adolescent actions in Shakespeare's teenage tragedy, revealing 'phallic violence and adolescent motherhood, typical for youth in Verona' (1978: 20). Expressions of adolescent masculine bravado in *Romeo and Juliet* are manifested as a destructive form of family loyalty. One representative moment occurs when Tybalt, upon seeing his 'enemy' Romeo at his family celebrations, swears 'by the stock and honor of my kin, / To strike him dead I hold it no sin' (1.4.169–70). The scene illustrates the fraught framing of adolescent fervour in households: Tybalt's fury is represented as being both in support of his family as he seeks to defend his kin's honour, and also against what is honourable, as Capulet berates Tybalt for his intent to 'make a mutiny' (1.4.191) at the celebrations. Capulet demands decorum from the 'saucy boy' (1.4.194). Under the influence of the 'ancient grudge' (Prologue, 3) of an older generation, early modern adolescents and their experiences of growing up can, as Kahn and others have shown, be understood as being shaped by restrictive patriarchal familial bonds (1978; Roberts, 1998; Potter, 2002). It is against such bonds that Romeo, Juliet, and all adolescent characters in Shakespeare's play must try to define themselves. Seen through this model of intergenerational tension, adolescence is understood as unruly and disordered in contrast to the ordered, and domineering, state of adulthood.

However, as I demonstrate across the chapters in this book, the changes that took place during adolescence were not only thought to threaten physical harm and the destruction of families. Early modern constructions of adolescence were also about expected and desired changes that enabled the individual's growth and development. The volatility of adolescence is not always at the centre of Shakespeare's adolescent characters, and, while early modern culture and Shakespeare's plays do appear fascinated by the disorderly side of adolescence, such fascination was part of a two-sided image, where adolescence was recognised as an energised and mutable state that was greatly esteemed. The promise ascribed to adolescents in Shakespeare's plays will be explored in this book as pronounced; even as commentators lament the misdeeds of adolescent characters, as in the Shepherd's misgivings about his son, Shakespeare's plays continually hint at, and often overtly showcase, the exceptional activities that 'Would any but' (3.3.62) the early modern adolescent achieve.

Even in Verona, where Capulets and Montagues fight in the streets in actions easily identified as the misguided behaviour of adolescence, characters evoke sympathy, and even praise, as well as derision. Capulet, for example, observes that Romeo is widely acknowledged as 'a virtuous and well-governed youth; / I would not for the wealth of all this town / Here in my house do him disparagement' (1.4.179–81). A positive model of adolescence, one that resists challenge or violent assault, is identified in the hostile setting of Verona. The prized reputation of the Capulets must relegate ancient grudges to the reverence given to a venerated figure of adolescence. Though the violence between Romeo and Tybalt is delayed rather than prevented, and the adolescent who-does-not-want-to-fight finally gets drawn into the fray, Capulet's words identify a respected image of adolescence that can exist and be exalted in early modern communities. The loss of what is valued in adolescence is, after all, surely at the heart of the play's tragedy.

Similarly, in *Measure for Measure*, the potentially fatal consequences for adolescents who have sex outside of marriage are explored through Claudio. Having 'got a wench with child' – to use the Shepherd's words once more – Claudio finds himself in prison, awaiting execution. Placed under the restraints provided by the Provost, Claudio characterises his crimes as those of unrestrained passions: 'A thirsty evil, and when we drink, we die' (1.2.119). Claudio confesses to exercising 'too much liberty' (1.2.114) in his courtship of Juliet, and the Provost likewise regards Juliet as tainted by her actions. By 'falling in the flaws of her own youth', Juliet 'Hath blistered her report' (2.3.11–12). Shakespeare clearly makes use of negative stereotypes about rash adolescent behaviour that were available in early modern culture. Nevertheless, Claudio, as an example of an adolescent whose lustful appetites have destabilised his position in society, receives more sympathy in *Measure for Measure* than other characters. Angelo and the Duke are figures of authority whose own questionable actions have the greatest influence over whether the adolescent lives or dies in the play.[1] The Provost in *Measure for Measure* might provide the physical restraints that hold Claudio accountable to Vienna's laws, but he also tellingly provides an account of 'a young man / More fit to do another such offense / Than die for this' (2.3.13–15). Vitality and continued activity, even if such activities are adolescent misdeeds, are identified as fitting attributes of Claudio's age in contrast to ideas of recrimination and death.

Notorious and also admired, the characters I discuss in *Shakespeare's Adolescents* are examined as the heroes, heroines, and victims in Shakespeare's plays. In the chapters of this book, I use early modern medical writings to explore how the bodily transformations of puberty could both derail and enable adolescent subjectivities that are represented in Shakespeare's works. The Shepherd's speech about adolescence from *The Winter's Tale*, which began this introduction, can perhaps more appropriately be seen to engage with familiar negative stereotypes about adolescence in order to introduce the 'age' that an audience is being invited to consider in more expansive ways across the rest of the play. After all, the Shepherd's words about 'boiled brains', shortly followed by his son's arrival, seem to express affection between father and son rather than serious concern. In a play that includes shipwrecks, accusations of adultery, and the abandonment of an infant, the Shepherd's words and presence (as a more typically 'comic' character) provide relief. His arrival and his speech contribute to the oft-noted generic shift from tragedy to comedy in *The Winter's Tale* (Bristol, 1991), as the bear exits the stage, and attention is shifted from the anxieties of the older generation to the hopes of a younger one.

Moreover, although ostensibly a commentary on his son's adolescent misdoings, the Shepherd describes an 'age' that also begins to highlight important symmetry across the adolescent developments of girls and boys: the young men who 'swagger' encounter 'wenches' who will entertain them. By including the sexual ruin of 'wenches', the Shepherd's speech acknowledges that adolescence includes implications for girls as well as boys. The Shepherd's description recognises that this seemingly regrettable age is undergone by both sexes. This speech is, after all, interrupted by the Shepherd's discovery of the infant Perdita who is moments later, with the instantaneous passing of sixteen years, transformed into an adolescent who is firmly within the age-range that the Shepherd berates. Shakespeare's Shepherd, in a sense, remains unchanged despite the passing of time in that he continues to fulfil the role of the 'father' of an adolescent. The Shepherd helps begin to signal the play's turn to a preoccupation with this adolescent age, moving from a commentary about adolescent males and wenches to a focus upon the fate of an infant who swiftly becomes a sixteen-year-old girl. While restrictive, gendered ideas are inscribed upon the activities of the males and females recorded in the Shepherd's speech – the female is, after all, identified solely as the sexual partner of the adolescent male she encounters – the movement of the play's plot attests to there being more to this adolescent age than the Shepherd initially claims. For if adolescence were 'no age' at all, as in the Shepherd's fanciful musings, or even if it were an age that could only be accessed through the limited and negative stereotypes that are noted, then the action of the play would be decidedly limited. While gender difference is a crucial part of the picture, so too is the idea that adolescence is something that unites boys and girls in the experience of an 'age'. Indeed, in *Shakespeare's Adolescents*, I explore how placing characteristics pertinent to age ahead of gender can help us identify how and where gendered differences (and biases) are specifically promoted in early modern constructions of adolescent bodies and behaviours.

To date, scholarly discussions of adolescence have tended to approach constructions of age in relation to gender, situating gender as the concern that directs analysis. By this means, Shakespeare studies have illuminated stark differences evident in the experiences of early modern boys and girls. For example, parental anxieties regarding 'disorderly' developments that take place during female adolescence have been fruitfully examined in the respective works of Helen King and Ursula Potter (2004; 2013). King and Potter have observed the way in which restrictive checks upon the behaviour of girls were underpinned by the early modern cultural understanding of female puberty as characterised by a certain disease: greensickness. Although broadly understood as a condition that was considered a 'disorder predominantly with virgins' (King, 2004: 29), greensickness posed particular concerns about sexual maturation in girls. By the sixteenth century, discussions about greensickness became centred upon ideas about orderly and disorderly menstruation. The cause of greensickness focused upon the retention of menstrual blood in the body, although excessive menstrual flux might also be included in a diagnosis. A girl's perceived inability to regulate her body was, in turn, thought to lead to ill health, unruly behaviour, and even death (Potter, 2013: 421).

Work on greensickness as a female affliction has importantly shown how the pubescent female, in being deemed unable to regulate herself, could be identified – with medical sanction – as requiring intervention from others around her who might manage her 'unwell' state. Bodily and behavioural changes that accompany puberty, viewed through the template of greensickness, become particularly volatile changes that 'could challenge parental skills, threaten domestic harmony, and, worst of all, culminate in the tragic death of a daughter by suicide or by disease' (Potter, 2013: 421). Greensickness was, moreover, thought to be relieved through sexual intercourse. Sexual activity was understood to encourage the release of retained menstrual blood by directing 'heat' to the genitals that would widen the passages through which the menstrual blood would flow (King, 2004: 83–8). Author of a midwifery guide, Jane Sharp, describes greensickness in terms of the girl's body being compelled towards sexual activity: '[greensickness] is more common to maids of ripe years when they are in love and desirous to keep company with a man' (1671: 256). This 'cure' of sexual intercourse, however, further heightened parental concern for, and legitimised control of, their daughters' sexual development.

In this way, how old Juliet is clearly matters in *Romeo and Juliet* (down to the hour, for the Nurse). Juliet's being 'a pretty age' (1.3.11) of almost fourteen promotes discussions about her readiness for marriage and shapes hostile reactions to Juliet's rejection of her family's choice of Paris as a husband. Cultural ideas surrounding Juliet's age, which align adolescent disobedience with symptoms of an unhealthy puberty, see Juliet defamed by her father as 'you green-sickness carrion' (3.5.156). Used as a rationale for overbearing parenting, whether well-intended or otherwise (parents feared that their greensick daughters might die, after all), concerns about greensickness meant that parents could intervene in their daughters' lives to prevent them from succumbing to pubescent bodily imbalances and reputational ruin. Greensickness offered a way to frame a girl's own expression of will during her sexual maturation as a symptom of disease, and this has been identified as a gendered modelling of puberty, and a source of intergenerational tension (King, 2004; Potter, 2002, 2013).

Such studies of gendered bodies helpfully set early modern girlhood in relation to womanhood, where we can trace how a misogynistic fashioning of menstrual and uterine disorders is used to restrict female behaviour across the life cycle. For example, discussions of women's health in relation to wombs and menstruation have long established how reproductive health and fertility was a key component of early modern womanhood (Mendelson and Crawford, 1998: 23–9; King, 1998; Crawford, 2004: 24–6; Peterson, 2010). Puberty sees changes in bodies that are in many ways bound to a cultural emphasis upon reproductive ability in gendering the futures of individuals and evaluating their social value. In Konrad Eisenbichler's edited collection, *The Premodern Teenager* (2002), for example, representations of adolescence are used to address a wealth of issues where gender is a prominent concern, sometimes bringing the sexes together, largely to examine and demonstrate sharply gendered differences in the experiences of adolescence in medieval and early modern society. It is in Eisenbischler's volume, after all, that Potter's important discussion of greensickness in relation to girlhood in *Romeo and Juliet* can be found.

Several gender-focused studies have also begun to tease out constructions of adolescence that realise positive and multi-faceted formulations alongside the more familiar negative ones. Such studies usually consider girls and boys in separation, discussing one or the other in depth. Despite touching on girlhood apprenticeships in one chapter (1994: 133–55), Ilana

Krausman Ben-Amos's examination of *Adolescence and Youth*, positioned in the context of apprenticeships and other work-related relationships, has primarily situated male adolescence beyond the structure of the family and helped highlight the considerable influence adolescent males had in early modern societies. Katie Knowles's *Shakespeare's Boys* (2013) similarly suggests ways in which representations of boyhood in Shakespeare's plays, from early modern through to modern incarnations, realise wide-ranging identities. Paul Griffith also identifies positive representations of adolescence, observing that 'Youth was a tempestuous age that required careful taming, but it was also a hopeful age of promise and the quickening of physical and mental faculties' (1996: 19). While Griffith suggests that positive framings of adolescence were largely to do with male promise (1996: 46–7), work by scholars including Jennifer Higginbotham (2018), Deanne Williams (2017) and Kate Chedgzoy (2013, 2019) has suggested similar scope for variety in the transition between childhood and womanhood. Higginbotham's *Shakespeare and Girlhood*, for example, has analysed the discursive complexities surrounding girlhood to illuminate the ways in which 'girls' featured prominently in early modern discourses (2018: 20–61). Furthermore, Williams has illuminated a tradition of children's performances in civic pageants, and courtly and private entertainments that included admired female performers (2017). Likewise, Chedgzoy's examination of records from the Mildmay-Fane family has demonstrated an example of 'a familial context that promoted girls' education and cultural engagement' (2013: 272), where girlhood intellectual and creative abilities were valued. Chedgzoy's work suggests a broader sense of understanding how Humanist education may have worked within elite families that 'formed girls as readers *and* writers' (2013: 272).

The burgeoning arena of childhood studies has begun to show how ideas about childhood and adolescence could underpin experiences that destabilised more rigid constructions of gender identity as conditioned, for example, by the tenets of chastity, silence, and obedience (Chedgzoy, 2013; Williams, 2014, 2017; Chedgzoy, 2019). *Shakespeare's Adolescents* develops findings in these influential studies to offer fresh insight into cultural representations of puberty by drawing out the ways in which male and female pubescent bodies were understood to realise aspects of symmetry *and* difference. While studies about childhood can often place male and female children together in collected works, these collections largely draw together works by scholars that help illustrate the multifaceted meanings of children in early modern culture and drama (Immel and Witmore, 2006; Chedgzoy et al, 2007; Miller and Yavneh, 2011; Preiss and Williams, 2017; Higginbotham and Johnston, 2018). The introduction to *Literary Cultures and Medieval and Early Modern Childhoods* explains how this approach serves the purpose of putting child subjectivities at the centre of historical analysis that seeks to 'explore a very wide range of topics in their collective and coordinated efforts to locate the marginalized figure of the child in earlier cultures' (Miller and Purkiss, 2019: xxiv). Such collections, therefore, do not necessarily aim to draw out specific connections between boys and girls of the same age per se, although broad parallels might be observed in the wide-ranging examples that are used. Indeed, as noted above, existing collections tend to be key in highlighting observations about gender difference, rather than age-specific similarities, in relation to experiences of childhood and adolescence.

In this book, however, I analyse early modern ideas about pubescent bodies to discuss adolescent boys and girls together in order to engage more fully with aspects of sameness, which, in turn, help illuminate aspects of ascribed difference. By placing age ahead of gender in this examination of adolescence, *Shakespeare's Adolescents* examines in detail the perils and promise attributed to an age where gender is not solely seen to be at work, or even always privileged, in constructions of identity. There is evidence to suggest that early modern culture did not always prioritise gender in constructions of pre-adult identities and bodily concerns. For example, Hannah Newton's study of 'children's physic' (2012: 32) has shown that early modern medical practices depended on evaluations of an individual's age and physique, where Newton notes a 'comparative lack of "gendered" diseases in both sexes [that] is at odds with medical understanding of the diseases of adult women, which were almost always linked to gender' (2012: 47). Age, on the other hand, appears to have always been used to differentiate between pre-adult conditions and adulthood itself: 'Older children differed from infants, medical writers did not believe that older children were identical to adults' (Newton, 2012: 39). Puberty, understood as the age-specific alterations in the adolescent's body, is, therefore, suggestive of both the individual's pre-adult state, where age is the key determining factor behind bodily concerns, and the very process by which the individual's sexual maturation is observed and the body becomes more conspicuously gendered. For most critics to date, then, adolescence has been discussed primarily as 'a site where the gendering of childhood comes into particularly clear focus, revealing that not only the experience of childhood but the stages of life themselves may be different for boys and girls' (Chedgzoy et al, 2007: 23). In *Shakespeare's Adolescents*, I attend to adolescence as an age, in the first instance, and gender as an additional concern, to examine how and where models for expansive and more limited subjectivities become imagined in constructions of early modern boyhood and girlhood.

Issues of gender difference remain a useful and appropriate means to organise the focus of age-specific research in single-authored texts, as their titles often suggest, for example: *The Girlhood of Shakespeare's Sisters* (Higginbotham, 2013); *Shakespeare and the Performance of Girlhood* (Williams, 2014); *Shakespeare's Boys* (Knowles, 2013); and *Shakespeare and Girls' Studies* (Balizet, 2019). In each of these works, there is a logical rationale for the approach they adopt, but notably these approaches compound the separation of male and female in historical studies that use adolescence as a component of identity.[2] Body-focused studies also tend to replicate this emphasis upon either male or female (Paster, 1993; King, 1998; Schoenfeldt, 1999; King, 2004; Potter, 2013). Sara Read's analysis of menstruation in early modern culture, for example, focuses upon the female in a way that is clearly appropriate to Read's tracking of 'transitional bleedings' (2013: 3) across women's lives. Yet, as this book will show, there is also value in considering developing male and female bodies together. For example, as I discuss in the second chapter of this book, the onset of menstruation and the accompanying growth of pubic hair in adolescent girls was understood in ways that drew parallels with the pubescent changes that simultaneously marked the adolescent male, in this instance, the development of facial hair. Difference in terms of sex and gender, which can offer rich ground for individual scholarly studies, can also be usefully understood alongside ideas of sameness in terms of shared ages and stages of sexual development.

Adolescence was a lengthy and somewhat fluid age of development that in many ways exceeded the body, as studies about education and employment have highlighted (Ben-Amos, 1994; Jewell, 1999; Chedgzoy et al, 2007; Lamb, 2018). However, in this book I illuminate the ways in which early modern ideas about adolescence were specifically shaped by an understanding of the physical changes that took place during puberty. I therefore disagree with Griffith's assertion that, in early modern culture, 'there does not seem to have been any clear and considered medical opinion about sexual development' (1996: 38). As I show in the chapters of *Shakespeare's Adolescents*, the bodily changes of puberty underpinned early modern ideas about adolescent promise and problems. Physical and humoral developments, affecting bodies, minds, and identities, can be seen to intersect with discussions about other features of early modern adolescence. The 'body/mind overlap' that more generally underscores humoral philosophy (Wynne Smith, 2008: 463) includes age-specific formulations that offered scope for individuals to navigate gendered restrictions in their articulation of adolescent subjectivities. For example, the pubescent female body, so often used as a means of inscribing misogyny (Paster, 1993; King, 2004; Potter, 2013), could also be framed as a vibrant site of resistance and negotiation. Bodies that are fashioned as 'heated' and adolescent, we will see, did not inevitably re-inscribe patriarchal hostility towards female subjectivities in only imagining bodily instability.

Shakespeare's Adolescents, then, places male and female together in order to examine how far 'being a particular age', when certain bodily changes were expected, informed the cultural framing of young men and women. In their overview of the findings presented in *The Routledge History of Sex and the Body*, Kate Fisher and Sarah Toulalan articulate a need to attend more fully to age 'as a category of analysis' (2013: 11) when examining historical constructions of the body. As I address in the next section of this introduction, scholarly interpretations that have considered pubescent bodies, to date, have often been influenced by a particular take on early modern humoral theory that again privileges ideas of gender over age. Moreover, studies about the body of the 'boy actor' have especially concentrated on a somewhat limited modelling of early modern ideas about gendered humoral heat. As I explain in the next section, age features in nuanced ways in early modern ideas about humoral bodies. A fuller understanding of these age-specific aspects will help unpack the ways in which cultural ideas about adolescent bodies are at work in the representation of theatrical characters on Shakespeare's stage.

An important convergence in childhood and performance studies deserves recognition here. Crucial work about children on early modern stages has been done in relation to children's theatre companies (Munro, 2005; Busse, 2006; Bly, 2009; Lamb, 2009; Witmore, 2007; van Es, 2017; Packard, 2019; McCarthy, 2022). Through these studies, the childhood of performers on public stages has become a central part of analysing early modern theatre. Many observations made across this book's chapters acknowledge a debt to the work of scholars working in this area. Research into children's companies is, however, often framed as importantly distinct from discussions about adult companies like the Lord Chamberlain's/King's Men that performed Shakespeare's plays. Edel Lamb, for example, has highlighted how children's companies drew upon a greater use of props (in number and emphasis) than adult companies (2009: 18–19), while attention has also been paid to the distinct repertory that children's companies appear to have cultivated (Munro, 2005; Bly, 2009; Lamb, 2009). Lamb observes pronounced contrasts between adult and children's companies, because of the 'disparity between the child and adult role' (2009: 21) in the children's companies' performances. Likewise, Lucy Munro observes the 'age-transvestism' (2009: 2) at work in performances by the Children of the Queen's Revels.

Furthermore, Bart van Es has suggested different power relations and processes of fetishising children in the relationships between adults and child players in the different companies. Such differences are proposed to result from 'the disturbing reality of impressment' in children's companies, as opposed to adult companies 'where child actors were apprenticed to lead

Introduction – misunderstood teens 11

players and thus voluntarily pursuing a trade' (van Es, 2017: 105). As I discuss across the third and fourth chapters of *Shakespeare's Adolescents*, an awareness of debates surrounding the apprenticeships and supportive training structures in the Lord Chamberlain's/King's Men helps inform representations that involve adult/adolescent interactions, as well as the interactions *between* adolescent characters and actors, in Shakespeare's plays.

As works about children's companies attest, care must be taken not to conflate too readily the theatrical practices and cultural understanding of child actors in children and adult companies. By distinguishing themselves from work on adult companies, however, age-focused studies of children's companies can, however, unintentionally underscore the idea that the adolescent actor's role in adult companies is already understood. Shakespeare's playing company and its 'boy actors' have seemingly been 'intensely analysed' and so adequately covered when compared to children's companies (Lamb, 2009: 12). Such claims are made by citing an admittedly lengthy list of scholars whose work, discussed in the next section of the introduction, was produced to consider performances of gender rather than age (Lamb, 2009: 12). A somewhat oppositional framing of children and adult companies may not, moreover, always be appropriate if interactions and theatrical crossovers between companies become underplayed. For example, evidence of the circulation of boy actors from children's companies to adult companies (McCarthy, 2020a) records young and talented actors being 'borrowed' for acting seasons. What is more, adult and children's companies could merge, as was permanently the case with Lady Elizabeth's Men and the Children of the Queen's Revels in 1613 (Simpson, 2019: 119–33). Crossovers between adult and children's companies indicate that there were intersections in the theatrical and cultural value that companies placed upon their adolescent players.

For the purposes of this book, cultural and theatrical fashioning of bodies *as* adolescent on early modern stages will see consideration of practices at work in children's companies as well as the 'adult' company that performed Shakespeare's works, but which included its own adolescent 'boy' players as key members. Characters with adolescent physicalities, identifiable through the performable, culturally recognised signs of puberty, which are used to organise the 'anatomising' chapters of this book, were regularly represented upon early modern stages. Sometimes boy actors performed these adolescent roles, sometimes older actors. 'Real' physicalities of the bodies onstage will be examined as sometimes manipulated, disguised, or utilised in performances of adolescence in Shakespeare's plays. The boy player in Shakespeare's company, almost certainly an adolescent by early modern calculations of age, could be made visible in moments of metatheatre that invited audiences to situate play content in the context of the player's own ongoing maturation. Conversely, the physicalities and ages of actors could be theatrically re-contextualised in performances of adolescence, as seems to have regularly been the case for the star adult actor of Shakespeare's company, Richard Burbage.

Burbage, born in c. 1567, regularly performed male adolescent roles in the first half of his career with the Lord Chamberlain's Men/King's Men. Many of these representations of adolescence, when the actor was in his late twenties and thirties, are tracked across the mid-1590s and early 1600s in this book. Burbage was, for example, around the age of thirty when he first performed the role of Romeo, and the actor's stardom seems to have been grounded, at least in part, in a particular talent for performing adolescent male characters. In each of the book's chapters, while I discuss the significance of acknowledging the adolescent actors in several Shakespearean female roles, I also often pay attention to the likely casting of Burbage in Shakespeare's plays. Burbage's age and life, though understood through somewhat sketchy details, offer comparatively well-documented aspects around theatrical roles compared to other actors. Burbage's position in a play, especially as an adolescent character, offers a means of unpacking consistent tropes as well as developments in the construction of adolescent characters in Shakespeare's drama. The gendering of adolescence in plays, for example, often places Burbage as an adolescent male character opposite one or more boy players, who perform female adolescent roles. The formula is suggestive of a theatrical styling of comparative age-related physiques that, as I examine across *Shakespeare's Adolescents*, become inscribed with gender identities. Observing a trajectory for Burbage's performances of adolescence allows for some tentative conclusions to be drawn about the different representations of adolescence in Shakespeare's plays across the mid-1590s into the 1610s, when Burbage is more often cast as the father to an adolescent, rather than an adolescent himself in the latter part of his acting career.

Consideration of how a 'star' actor like Burbage features in performances of adolescence can also help map emphases in Shakespeare plays and indicate the prominence of adolescent concerns in the stories being told in early modern culture. Representations of adolescents in Shakespearean drama, while fictive constructs, offer valuable ways of thinking about the cultural fashioning of early modern adolescence, providing different outlooks, plots, and settings for the examination of age to take place.[3] Burbage's presence in relation to boy players, moreover, can indicate the particular 'life cycle' of the playing company, which seems to have been either training or showcasing an adolescent actor by producing either supported or expansive female roles for these key young members of the company (Power, 2003; McMillin, 2004). In this sense, the attention I pay to Burbage is about illuminating the prominence of the adolescent actors around him, actors whose pre-adult state may misleadingly suggest their inconsequential position in the theatre company or play narrative. Indeed, the 'adult' and 'star' presence of Burbage can often seem less striking than the boys with whom he works, and the examples I discuss in this book suggest how Burbage's adolescent character forms part of the company's collaborative representation of adolescent concerns through its plays, where the skills of adolescent players were often actively showcased.

Fuller understanding of how early modern adolescent bodies, actions, and minds were understood and represented theatrically will help develop our understanding of the boy players who represented female characters on Shakespeare's stage, as well as the fictions they created. While this may not identify the player behind a role, and 'rescue the names of boy-players from oblivion' (Kathman, 2004: 2) in the way that David Kathman's diligent study has begun to do, the analysis I provide in *Shakespeare's Adolescents* aims to illuminate the cultural and theatrical value attributed to adolescents as mutable and admired individuals. This may go some way in reassessing the idea that adolescent growth was largely regarded as a problem, especially in theatrical contexts, where the boy actor has been presented as 'fairly low on everyone's list of priorities' (Belsey, 2005: 53), and then completely 'devalued, when they grew up' (Wiebracht, 2020: 351). In *Shakespeare's Adolescents*, I examine how the process of growing up was understood to involve being seen as apt to acquire theatrical skill and perform physical and linguistic dexterity that appealed to theatre audiences.

An enquiry into cultural attitudes towards adolescence helps reimagine the boy actor as an individual whose age offered commendable resources that it was in a company's best interests to support and develop. The adolescent actor in this book is not only the oft-imagined theatrical liability whose body and voice behaves in an unpredictable and solely problematic fashion. As I discuss in the next section, theatre studies has sometimes silently accepted the femininity or genderless nature of the boy actor as a cultural given without fully exploring the theatrical efforts, and individual acting skills, that were required to signify age and gender on the early modern stage. After all, theatrical contexts can differ from wider cultural contexts when the unbroken voice or beardless face can be set up in a way that is made to *appear* feminine. Early modern theatrical practices could work with or against ideas about pubescent bodies in interesting ways, depending on the character that was being performed. Boy actors, who would have been adolescents for the years that they performed female roles, were not culturally positioned as possessing an ungendered, child-like humoral condition. However, the player's adolescent state was thought to underpin physical and mental agility that playwrights may well have taken advantage of in the writing of parts. As I explain in the next section, the idea that the pre-adult state of a male player was interchangeable with a theatrical female character has come under significant pressure as the result of important revisions in our understanding of early modern constructions of adolescent bodies and gender. These revisions have left room to investigate how age, as a performable identity, is crucial in shaping representations of gender in early modern drama.

In this book, I provide a complementary contrast to the customary emphasis on difference and division of the sexes (and, to a lesser degree, division of the acting companies) when dealing with issues concerning early modern representations of adolescence. Throughout this study, 'sex' refers to biological difference that was used to distinguish between male and female, and 'gender' refers to cultural expectations and stereotypes that were attached to the sexes (masculine and feminine). While, as Mark Dooley observes, 'it is important not to simply fall back into reading the biological sex of the actor as an essential truth behind what are much more complex issues of representation' (2001: 63), I examine representations of the pubescent characters constructed in Shakespeare's plays as well as pointedly metatheatrical moments that invite the inclusion of the boy player's own culturally fashioned male adolescence in interpreting meaning. Metatheatre sets girl characters alongside boy actors in ways that can particularly illuminate how and where ideas of sameness and difference become culturally inscribed upon bodies.

Through approaching these intricacies surrounding adolescence, I aim to open up the ways in which this stage of the life cycle held particular importance in early modern constructions of identity. While the adolescent subject remains elusive in early modern evidence, I explore the cultural and theatrical contexts in which adolescent subjectivities would have been understood, experienced, and, indeed, celebrated.

Misunderstood adolescents: gendering adolescent bodies, 'boy actors', and the legacy of Laqueur's 'one-sex' theory

Literary critics and historians who have addressed ideas of gender in relation to age have encountered difficulties in unravelling how early modern culture understood the stages of life prior to adulthood. For a long time, studies of early modern adolescence worked under the assumption that adolescence was gendered feminine, and there appear to be several reasons for this. The first reason seems to be based upon the way life cycle models, outlined in some depth in the next section of the introduction, allow for the notion that until a male is an adult (in the Aristotelian model, 'Childhood' lasted until the age of twenty-five) he might be regarded as emasculated and incomplete. This 'incomplete' and 'imperfect' physicality could, in turn, be interpreted as a feminised state, because historically women have often been framed as less perfect than an idealised male state.[4] Such a reading that equates adolescent masculinity with femininity is not the full picture, as this section highlights, but the rationale recognises that an insult to adult manhood *could* infantilise the subject by projecting him backwards along the trajectory of the life cycle, as demonstrated in Aufidius's infamous slight upon Coriolanus when he calls him a 'boy of tears' (5.6.98). Boyhood is contrasted with manhood to articulate the protagonist's loss of power. Such emasculation, as the adult male is disarmed of his authoritative position and reimagined as a boy, might appear similar to depictions of female subordination to (adult) male power.[5]

Early modern life-cycle models are structured around an adult centre, and this notion of adolescent incompleteness, or still-to-be-achieved adulthood, when viewed as a condition of lacking, can be likened to the female's position in early modern culture. Adolescence and its formative qualities, where, for example, the tempered, self-control of manhood is still to be acquired, might be deemed an effeminate stage of life. Likening the state of childhood to femininity is thereby grounded in assumptions about both states being subject to disempowerment and negativity when compared to the positively framed adult male. Such assumptions that conflate femaleness (adolescent or adult) with male adolescence will be reworked across the chapters of this book, but a broad model of disempowerment and 'imperfection' could set adolescent boys alongside the early modern female if the adolescent male is seen as distanced from the authority of the revered state of adult masculinity (Shepard, 2003: 94; also see Schoenfeldt, 1999).

Another reason why early modern adolescence is often associated with femininity seems to stem from the gendering of childcare in early modern households. Young males and females spent their early childhood in the company of women. The physical separation of boys from men, and their grouping with women and girls, has helped form the idea that male children were feminised until they were physically and socially placed amongst men. Attention has especially been paid to the cultural ritual of breeching, where a young boy (aged around five to seven years) would be symbolically and overtly gendered as masculine in his exchange of feminine/ungendered skirts for masculine breeches (Buck and Cunningham, 1965; Snyder, 1999; Frick, 2011). With his change in apparel being accompanied by increased interaction with men and engagement in 'manly' accomplishments, a boy experienced the transition from a more female-orientated period of childhood to a period where his masculinity appears conspicuously under construction.

The practice of breeching, however, continues to be analysed for how children were gendered prior to and after the ritual. The transition from coats/skirts to breeches was not as sudden as is sometimes assumed. Carole Collier Frick (2011) has, for example, examined transformations in the history of garments worn before and after breeching, demonstrating that prior to the seventeenth century, the 'unbreeched' child's undergarments could be gendered and sometimes include light fabric codpieces. Frick's findings have suggested that the un-breeched stages of childhood may be less about signalling the ungendered or feminised state of the young, and more about recognising a way in which anxieties about demonstrating the masculinity of young children – through additions of fabric codpieces – became more or less pronounced at different points in history. Simply put, a boy in a skirt could well have been happily understood as a boy in a skirt where gender is unthreatened by age-related garments. When a young boy's masculinity did seem threatened and required demonstration, clothing for the young responded accordingly.

Studies about the gendering of early childhood continue to reveal nuanced conclusions. Female care-givers may well have gendered their interactions with children prior to breeching. As Miller and Yavneh observe in the introduction to *Gender and Early Modern Constructions of Childhood*, 'there were probably cultural norms that distinguished sex-specific treatment even of infants and toddlers' (2011: 7). Certainly the arrival of either a boy or a girl anticipated a 'sexed' future to some extent, whether it be in responses to secured inheritance rights in the birth of a boy, or the provision of appropriate spiritual and social guidance in the rituals of early modern baptism. The sex of a child determined the provision of godparents, for example, with typically two godparents being of the same sex as the child and one of the opposite sex (Cressy, 1997: 150).

The gendering of children's bodies in medical writings and Puritan diaries has also been discussed in Newton's examination of medical practice in the treatment of child patients (2012). As was highlighted in the previous section, Newton's work identifies how young patients were treated and grouped together in terms of age rather than sex in the records that we have from physicians and caregivers (2012: 47). Notably, ambiguity generally persists in gendering the treatment of the body prior to adulthood, especially in the prepubescent body. Wendy Churchill, for example, suggests that children were regarded as unsexed until puberty (2013: 19–20). With puberty, however, girls and boys were also thought to continue to share features of their age, as they had in earlier childhood, but specific bodily transformations start to have distinctly 'sexed' implications for the pubescent body, placing ideas about adult reproductive bodies in sight.

Therefore, although the Aristotelian life cycle saw 'Childhood' last until twenty-five, early modern commentators identified bodily changes in adolescent boys and girls as being markedly different from those that took place in early childhood. Puberty marked a transitory state between childhood and adulthood, which carried its own age-specific features, including a more pressing concern for inscribing gendered identities that were bound to the reproductive function of the 'sexed' body. That bodies and behaviours could be less conspicuously gendered in earlier childhood indicates how early modern identities did not have to be centred upon ideas of reproductive/genital-efficacy across the life cycle. This is not to say that prepubescent experiences were ungendered, rather that the experiences of puberty stressed sexual difference between young males and females through meanings being insistently ascribed to the body. Rather than simply suggesting a shift from ungendered childhood to a gendered adolescence, therefore, early modern representations of puberty demonstrate most clearly how symmetry and difference could both be observed in early modern age-gender formulations, and where the cultural meaning of bodies in constructions of gender identities is contingent upon constructions of age.

Henry Cuffe, author of the popular *Different Ages of Man* (1607), for example, makes use of Aristotle in his thinking, and so saw adolescents as children, but Cuffe also distinguishes between early childhood and adolescence by noting that it is in adolescence that particular bodily changes, those of puberty, become significant. Early childhood is characterised by simple bodily growth, whereas later 'childhood', when sexual maturation begins, is discussed as a time when 'budding and blossoming' takes place (1607: 118). Will Greenwood, similarly, differentiates between 'childhood' states, describing 'the *vehemency of Adolescency*' as being 'betwixt the age of 14 and 28',[6] extending the pre-adult timeline further still (1657: 82). When discussing adolescence, then, we should be relatively confident in recognising distinction between early modern framings of adolescent femininity and masculinity.

However, in studies of early modern theatre, assumptions about the feminised 'boyishness' of adolescent actors can persist. One key reason for this is the unique circumstances of the theatre that saw female parts performed by 'boy actors'. In the context of early modern theatre, the adolescent actor is, after all, purposely conflated with the fictional female figure he performs onstage. In the theatre, the boy in the skirt *was* expected to be understood as feminine. The adolescent actor has been discussed in much compelling scholarship regarding gender identity and eroticism on the all-male early modern stage (Howard, 1988; Jardine, 1989; Stallybrass, 1991; Orgel, 1996). Stephen Orgel's influential *Impersonations*, examines the boy actor's 'boyishness' as the focus for erotic desire that is directed towards a sexual identity that seems to exist between male and female. Orgel observes that 'eroticized boys appear to be a middle term between men and women' (1996: 63), and suggests that the actor's age is largely understood in relation to this gender ambiguity, which itself is erotically charged. Juliet Dusinberre similarly frames the boy actor's body as 'a blank page on which gender, as opposed to biological sexual identity, can be written' (1998: 2). Such scholarship is formative in Shakespeare studies: a reading of *As You Like It* or *Twelfth Night*, for example, cannot (and should not) ignore the ambiguous gendering that is explored in relation to the plays' crossdressed heroines. However, while theatrical practice seems to have manipulated the erotic potential of boys-playing-girls (who then sometimes also play boys, as with Rosalind's performance as Ganymede), the actual bodies of the adolescent actors who performed these roles were not culturally framed as effortlessly 'blank' and genderless. Therefore, performances of gender ambiguity that previous scholarship has illuminated in Shakespeare's plays can, as I explore across the chapters of this book, be re-examined for how these adolescent stage identities might have been performed. Rather than a 'blankness' that is effortlessly based on somewhat misleading cultural assumptions about early modern adolescent bodies, verbal cues, as well as the physical and material means that were available in performance, would be used to construct gender ambiguity that would sit at a distance from, and perhaps deconstruct, early modern ideas about the boy actor's 'sexed' adolescent body. Management of the body of the adolescent actor, and the implications of the adolescent male's presence in roles that make him pointedly visible, I suggest, carry repercussions for interpretations of gendered power relations in early modern culture. Shakespearean drama often highlights its boys 'beneath' (Stallybrass, 1991) its female roles, and these moments can carry altered meanings once eliding adolescent boyhood with femininity comes under conspicuous tension.

The assumption made in much important Shakespeare scholarship about boy actors' bodies being easily perceived as 'blank' (Dusinberre, 1998: 2) registers the seismic influence of Thomas Laqueur's reading of a 'one-sex' model for the early modern body. In his book *Making Sex: Body and Gender From the Greeks to Freud* (1990), Laqueur suggests that in the early modern period male and female were differentiated through degrees of humoral heat. The (adult) male was envisaged at one end of the spectrum, exhibiting greater heat than the (adult) female, whose humoral coolness typically placed her at the opposite end of the spectrum. Orgel's observation about boys being 'the middle term between men and women' can likewise be seen to assess where identity (here, a 'boyish' identity) fits within the markers of sex identity that are used in a 'one-sex' framework. According to Laqueur, difference in sex was imagined as fluid, based upon a sliding scale of heat, where 'heated' behaviour in females was identified as masculine, and where extremes in such behaviour might even warrant a change of sex. Gender, being also understood through properties of masculine heat/

feminine coolness, was thus set alongside understandings of sex in Laqueur's model, where the 'masculine' heated behaviour of a female also suggested a physical state that moved the female body towards that of the male. Indeed, Laqueur posited that early modern culture understood male and female bodies as structurally the same, where differences in heat altered the situation of body parts. As such, the penis/womb is regarded as an equivalent organ, where wombs are inverted penises that remain internalised because they lack the influence of masculine heat that drives the genitals out from the body.

Some early modern texts endorse the 'one-sex' model that Laqueur observes. For example, Nathaniel Wanley's *The Wonders of the Little World* includes a chapter on 'Of such Persons as have changed their Sex' (1673: 52–3), and Juan Huarte's *Examen De Ingenios, or, The Tryal of Wits* marvels at the workings of Nature, where 'after she has made a Woman, she had a mind to convert her into Man, she need no more than turn out her Genitals' (1698: 404). Such fascinating material, alongside Laqueur's argument in *Making Sex* (1990), piqued academic interest during the 1990s in a way that showed its prominence in interpretations of early modern bodies, and especially their representation upon the early modern stage. As Helen King observes in *The One-Sex Body on Trial*, Laqueur's ideas have been 'By far the most influential work on the history of the body, across a range of disciplines' (2013: 1). For example, Stephen Greenblatt's analysis of different-sex twins in *Twelfth Night*, in his widely read *Shakespearean Negotiations* (1988), in a chapter bearing the wonderful name 'Fiction and Friction', argues for the fluidity of sex identity in early modern culture, and in Shakespeare's play. Greenblatt makes use of the case of 'sex change' for Marie Germain, who allegedly experienced a change of sex due to the 'heated' action of chasing a pig around a yard. The example of Germain was certainly used by early modern medical writers. Greenblatt quotes the anecdote's use in an English translation of Ambroise Paré's work, *On Monsters and Marvels* (1665), and the chapter helps explore fascinating cultural anxieties about sex identity. However, the sources used by Greenblatt (and Laqueur) can also be considered in the context of how their writers present the cases they describe: as atypical and uncommon. Paré is relaying reported marvels, and though he accepts the validity of the accounts, the title of his book articulates the uncommon nature of the events that are recorded. Similarly, in Nathaniel Wanley's text, *The Wonders of the Little World*, the chapter on sex change is preceded by one about 'Persons as have renew'd their Age, and grown young again' (1673: 51–2). The implicit assumption in a book about 'wonders' is that sex is usually to be regarded as stable, and ageing typically occurs along a predictable trajectory. While such works remain fascinating and, indeed, telling about cultural anxieties in their 'one-sex' features, these texts do not provide evidence of a dominant 'one-sex' framework by which early modern bodies were understood.

Indeed, broadly speaking, Laqueur's 'one-sex' model is now treated with caution in early modern studies, because clear challenges and expansions have been made to the conclusions that his study presented (Harvey, 2002; Park, 2002; Stolberg, 2003). The existence of a 'two-sex' anatomical model of the early modern body has, for example, been highlighted to resist the stress upon fluid sex identity at work in Laqueur's 'one-sex' model (Stolberg, 2003). Katherine Park has shown how the assumption that male and female bodies are the same, and only differentiated by degrees of heat, presents an inadequate representation of early modern anatomical knowledge (2002). In particular, Park demonstrates how a 'one-sex' model disregards the recognised existence of the clitoris in early modern culture. If the cool and inverted womb is the feminine equivalent of the externalised penis, what, then, is the anatomical extra of the clitoris? A one-sex model for the body provides only part of how early modern people understood their bodies.

Most early modern writers did not, for example, see the womb as interchangeable with the penis. Anatomical difference was recognised between the two organs that extended beyond an understanding of each organ's location in the body. Seventeenth-century writer on midwifery Sharp was both aware of 'one-sex' modelling for the body and also clear in her rejection of such ideas: 'The parts in men and women are different in number and likeness, substance, and proportion; the cod [scrotum] of a man turned inside outward is like the womb, yet the difference is so great that they can never be the same' (1671: 67). For Sharp, as with many early modern writers, an awareness of the reproductive properties of male and female as necessarily different underpins an understanding of a two-sex model, where 'we cannot be without ours no more than they can want theirs' (1671: 32). Sharp, therefore, mainly shows the influence of one-sex thinking when discussing the formation of an infant's sex *in utero*, where heat (albeit from several possible generative components) is more simply understood as a determining factor (1671: 37). Jacques Ferrand, in *Erotomania* (1640), is perhaps especially pointed in his refutation of the possibility that individuals may experience a spontaneous change of sex. Ferrand suggests that a woman might only be mistaken for a man if the signs of a prolapsed womb 'was so great [...] it resembled a mans yard' (1640: 15). Ferrand's explanation, like Sharp's observations, demonstrates both an awareness of 'one-sex' ideas and the rejection of them, here, because Ferrand does not equate even the externalised womb with a penis.

As King points out in *The One-Sex Body on Trial*, 'none of the many challenges made to [Laqueur's] theory has dented its popularity' (2013: 1). Laqueur's presentation of a one-sex body has 'dominated thinking about sexual difference from Classical antiquity to the end of the seventeenth century' (King, 2013: 25). According to King, solely working with a 'one-sex' theory in mind misses the nuances at work in both classical and early modern sources that draw upon 'one-sex' and 'two-sex' features (2013: 29–70). As King notes in her study of the Hippocratic writings about women's health that underpinned early modern medicine, a two-sex distinction between men and women existed in humoral theory itself. Women were not simply imagined as 'cold men' (1998: 11). Recognising how the humoral properties of heat and moisture that differentiate women from men were themselves thought to underscore fixed bodily manifestations, such as menstruation and beard growth, helps illuminate the distinction that was made between male and female bodies, and suggests more materialised difference than a sliding scale of heat might otherwise suggest. A woman's moister and cooler body was thought to result in a physicality that was clearly distinct from that of the male, which included a woman's experience of menstruation, a generative seed that was materially different from a man's seed, and body tissue that was not as dense as that of a man. For the purposes of this book, it is notable that these bodily distinctions between male and female that King highlights in this two-sex *humoral* model result from the changes of puberty. The focus upon menstruation in identifying a female body, as the clearest foundation for the notion that female bodies are moister than male bodies, particularly highlights how it is with puberty that the hot/cold and moist/dry humoral distinctions between the sexes especially come into play.

While some early modern commentators did accept reports of sex change, such events were regarded as unusual, and the 'heated' actions of puberty were typically seen to be more about the production of bodily signs that offered confirmation of sex, and, more specifically, the individual's developing sexual maturity. While such signs might themselves be part of a fraught life-stage, for most the alterations of adolescence were not deemed precarious *because* it threatened to alter an individual's sex. If we return to reports of changes of sex in early modern texts, it is perhaps telling that most accounts concern adolescents, apparently on the brink of puberty. Paré, for example, discusses a boy who 'being taken for a gi[r]l until the fifteenth year of his age' is ascribed the sex of a girl 'because there was no sign of being a man seen in his body' (1665: 652). With the advent of puberty, such signs became evident and the 'girl' became recognised as a 'boy'. The phrasing of this example is particularly interesting, because it also seems to imply that the boy's sex was perhaps simply imperceptible *until* puberty rather than being changed with puberty. Yet a boy might, here, be 'taken for a gi[r]l', and understand themselves as such, until the signs of puberty are deemed recognisable through the body.

Signs of difference between male and female, even in these extreme examples of fluid sex identity, are noted as being apparent on an adolescent body. When the boy player of early modern theatre began his career in representing female characters on stage, between the ages of twelve and fourteen (Kathman, 2005), let alone several years into that career as an older adolescent playing complex female parts, the culturally recognised signs of his 'sexed' body would most likely already be apparent or becoming so. Making the signs of male or female puberty recognisable on the early modern stage in representing characters, therefore, becomes part of theatre's concerted efforts in selectively making bodily signs of a gendered adolescence clear (and in instances of crossdressing, pointedly unclear) in ways that would have required the management of the actor's own body. Therefore, with all the challenges that have been made to a 'one-sex' framing of early modern bodies (including King's book on the matter), it seems timely for discussions about boy players to return to the strategies that must have been involved in either using or re-signifying the meaning of the adolescent actor's body.

The performance of bodily states has been considered in some depth in relation to theatrical constructions of gendered adulthood. Gail Kern Paster's examination of humoral fluidity in *The Body Embarrassed* (1993), for example, provides a notable model for discussions about gendered bodies in early modern drama. Paster focuses her attention upon adult reproductive bodies, setting processes of menstruation, childbirth, and lactation of the 'leaky' female body in opposition to the comparatively contained male body. While Paster's work has instigated vibrant debate about this comparative 'leakiness' and containment to which adult men and women were subject, along the humoral spectrum (Schoenfeldt, 1999; Pomata, 2001; Wynne-Smith, 2011), our understanding of theatrical bodies beyond this adult-centredness is in need of development. We find, for example, that Laqueur's model, or Paster's, cannot fully accommodate age when we ask: what is to be done with the adolescent male? The adolescent who has not achieved full manhood (one end of the 'one-sex' spectrum) struggles to find a place between (heated) maleness and (cooler) femaleness. In the 'one-sex' model, the adolescent male is identified as an 'incomplete' male and becomes a feminised individual as he slides down the humoral scaling of sex. But the adolescent male was understood to experience *excess* heat during this particular point in his life cycle, sitting at odds with the heat-based rationale of the 'one-sex' humoral framework. Likewise, the 'heated' adolescent female becomes strangely masculinised during puberty, a time where signs of emergent fertility would, as I demonstrate across this book, more logically attach themselves to cultural associations with emergent 'womanliness'. Models of humoral containment and fluidity are useful when viewing developmental stages of the early modern life cycle, but activity and change is not always synonymous with unruly 'leakiness' (although it can be). As I discuss across the chapters of this book, the early modern adolescent's bodily mutability and excesses in heat could underpin valued physical and mental attributes.

Therefore, in the next section of the introduction, I aim to carefully outline the humoral modelling of adolescence in the context of the early modern life cycle in order to tease out the humoral ideas that gendered adolescence in early modern culture. In so doing, I draw attention to the way in which symmetry was recognised in discussions about male and female adolescents. Alongside such broad symmetry, however, the discussion begins to unpick where gender difference was also embedded in the modelling of puberty as a stage of life for young men and women. As such, I endeavour to show the value of understanding depictions of humoral heat in relation to age *and* gender, where aspects of sameness and difference could be helpful, rather than problematic, in gendering adolescent characters, and where the physical manifestation of the signs of puberty were a key part of recognising these representations in early modern theatre.[7]

Adolescence as a stage of life in the early modern life cycle

Various models were used to map the early modern life cycle (see Garber, 1997: 1). Henry Cuffe's popular book, *The Different Ages of Man* (1607, 1633, 1640), for example, happily makes use of several models, including Pythagoras's four ages, Aristotle's three ages, and the seven ages used by many medieval theorists. Cuffe does not express consternation about differences across theoretical models and makes selective use of them all. Across his treatise, Cuffe, like other early modern commentators, imagines the life cycle in natural terms that seem to offer flexibility in accommodatingly loose categories. Agricultural language of growth and ripening is used to explain bodily alteration, where the passing of time during human life is likened to the seasonal changes of the natural world. In describing the Pythagorean four stages of life (Childhood, Youth, Manhood, and Old Age), for example, Cuffe likens childhood to 'the *spring*, wherein all things together with a pleasant verdour and greenenesse flourish' (1607: 116). Youth is associated with '*Summer*, for that growen strength of the body and minde', and manhood is compared 'vnto the *Autumne* or *Haruest*' in being the time when 'the good giftes and indowments of our minde (as we see it fall out in the fruites of Nature) receiue a kind of seasonable and timely ripenesse' (Cuffe, 1607: 116–17). Meanwhile, Pythagorean old age, Cuffe observes, 'resembleth vnto the colde and troublesome *winter season,* very fitly thereby expressing the cumbersome coldnesse of the latter end of our life' (1607: 117).

As with many early modern writers, Cuffe's age divisions are not constant in all the models that he uses, numeric ages often being loosely applied.

Stages of life are more consistently recognised through changes that are registered upon the body. When citing the three-age model of Aristotle (Childhood, Manhood, and Old Age), childhood – here lasting until the individual is twenty-five – is associated with the spring, largely because this encompasses various ideas about bodily growth. Cuffe calls the lengthy Aristotelian stage of Childhood the 'growing age' and sees fit to subdivide it into further categories to differentiate between childhood, where 'our bodies grow bigger and taller', and the *'budding and blossoming age* [...] when our cheekes and other more hidden parts begin to be clothed with that mossie excrement of haire' (1607: 118). This *'blossoming age'* lasts until the age of eighteen, while 'Youth' provides a final pre-adult stage of life. For Stephen Batman, sexual maturity was achieved across one life stage 'called *Adolescentia*, for because it is the full age to get children' (1582: 70). The body grows, demonstrating 'might and strength' as well as flexibility 'yet in this age the members are softe and tender, and able to stretch' (Batman, 1582: 70). Although Cuffe uses different categories to Batman, he similarly moves his attention from observations about general growth of the body in its 'flourishing' to concerns for specific signs of emergent sexual maturity during puberty. For example, Cuffe particularly highlights the appearance of body hair ('that mossie excrement') as a development that is different from the body growth of earlier childhood (1607: 118). Cuffe suggests an appreciation of differences, especially in 'body and mind', that distinguish the prepubescent individual from the pubescent one (1607: 118).

Early modern writers regularly conflate the terms 'adolescence', 'puberty', and 'youth'. Henry Cuffe, for example, sometimes identifies 'youth' as a life stage that follows the 'budding and blossoming age' (118) of adolescence/puberty, but where adulthood is to be achieved several years later. In *Touchstone of Complexions,* Lemnius likewise seems to differentiate between puberty and adolescence (1576), stating that puberty lasts from fifteen until eighteen, suggestive of a three-year time frame during which sexual capability is particularly achieved (1576: 29^v). Adolescence is then described as the 'slypperye' age characterised by unsettled humoral heat and moisture, lasting between eighteen and twenty-five (1576: 29^v). However, in other writings, Lemnius expresses concern about the sexual immaturity of young men, noting that a male's seed remains unsuitable for producing offspring until age brings reproductive strength: 'when his age is growen to ful ripenesse, & is come to the perfect strength of a man' (1592: 170). As I will discuss below, such notions of fully-achieved growth and sexual maturity were commonly associated with the constitution of the male in his early-mid-twenties, as he left the long age of Childhood and entered Manhood (Paré, 1665: 624). For the purposes of this book, which attends to growth and changes in the body that were initiated with puberty, and were understood to finally stabilise once adulthood was achieved, I use the term 'adolescence' for consistency, doing so in line with the broader sense of bodily development that is observed in early modern writings. For example, Thomas Elyot's popular book, *The Castel of Helthe*, identifies adolescence as an age that lasts from thirteen until twenty-five, characterising this age as a stage during which particular forms of bodily development took place 'in the whiche tyme the body groweth' (1539: 10–11) towards adulthood. These changes, we will see, remained tied to alterations associated with puberty, as Lemnius' observations suggest.

While early modern writers are inconsistent in categorising ages in the life cycle (Cuffe uses the Aristotelian and Pythagorean life cycle model to formulate at least two different categories of 'Youth'), the humoral logic that is used to understand the human body as it ages is generally consistent across observations. As is characteristic of early modern understandings of age, Cuffe's description of the life cycle uses humoral theory that framed ageing as the cooling and drying of the body's substance. Heat and moisture possessed by the human body at birth, which underpinned its vitality, was understood to be gradually lost across the life cycle. Cuffe, for example, describes how infancy is 'ful of moisture' and youth 'bringeth a farther degree of solidity' (1607: 114). Adulthood is described by Cuffe as 'ever te[m]perate', while with old age 'declineth our body unto colde and drinesse' (1607: 114). Left unexamined for its implications in each stage of life, however, this familiar description of ageing, as being hot through cold, wet through dry, and centred about a humorally balanced, 'te[m]perate' adulthood, threatens to flatten the significance that writers attributed to adolescence and the importance that the bodily changes of puberty held within individuals' lives. The relationship between individual life stages and the whole trajectory of life, with its epicentre of 'te[m]perate' adulthood, were understood in more nuanced terms than this model initially suggests.

When identifying 'a further degree of solidity' in relation to adolescence, Cuffe speaks broadly, observing the loss of moisture from childhood. Only hinted at in the depiction of adulthood as 'temperate' in comparison to the youthful stage of life it follows is the implication that 'solidity' in adolescence (probably quite literally the density of the flesh) is not the same as humoral stability. Indeed, the adolescent body, in its loss of moisture, bucked the other overarching trend of the humoral life cycle that saw progressive ageing accompanied by humoral cooling. The loss of cooling moisture was instead understood to have the consequence of dramatically increasing the heat of the body. An adolescent male or female was understood as more prone to heated humours than they had been as infants, when they theoretically had more vital heat within the body but where excess moisture helped temper its effects. It was this excess in heat that particularly enabled the specific growth and bodily developments of adolescence. Of adolescents, Batman observes: 'they grow by vertue of heate that hath masterye in them, euen to the perfection of complement' (1582: 70). Elyot similarly attributes the growth of adolescent bodies to a particular humoral constitution that was 'hotte and moyst' (1539: 10–11).

It is here that the importance of dwelling upon the specific implications of humoral changes within life-cycle stages becomes evident. As medical historians, such as Toulalan, have stressed: 'each stage of life [...] had its own physical characteristics and brought particular kinds of disorders according to its humoral condition' (2013: 282). To be an adolescent, therefore, involved keeping sight of the adult one was to become, but it also meant attending to the particular experiences that puberty was understood to inscribe upon the body. How, then, were the physical changes of puberty understood and represented as part of adolescence in early modern culture? One key point seems to be that while bodily developments that took place during puberty were considered significant, these changes were not approached as sudden, where the individual's humoral disposition would be reinvented beyond recognition overnight. Humoral changes associated with a particular stage of life, and the accompanying developments such changes incurred upon the body, took time (often seven years). Changes would become gradually discernible in the ageing body across an entire stage of life. Francis Bacon's description of the life cycle in *Historie Naturall and Experimentall*, for example, suggests how the physical signs of ageing were significant but gradually produced across each seven-year long 'age':[8]

> The *Ladder* of *Mans Bodie*, is this [...] To bee *Borne*; To *Sucke*; To be *Weaned*; To *Feed upon Pap*; To *Put* forth *Teeth*, the First time about the Second yeare of Age; To *Begin to goe*; To *Begin to speaks*; To *Put forth Teeth*, the Second time, about seven years of Age; To come to *Pubertie*, about twelve, or fourteene yeares of Age; To be *Able* for *Generation*, and the *Flowing* of the *Menstrua*; To have *Haires* about the *Legges*, and *Arme-holes*; To *Put forth* a *Beard*; And thus long, and sometimes later, to *Grow* in *Stature*; To come to *full years* of *Strength* and *Agility*. (1638: 369–70)

Puberty might begin at around twelve or fourteen, but achieving all the signs of 'full years' (identified by Bacon as the ability to generate seed, produce body hair, grow to an appropriate height, and achieve physical strength) required time. Notably, the ability to have sex and produce reproductive materials of seed and menstrual blood were not, in themselves, enough to demonstrate an adult physicality. As the French physician Paré observed, reproductive seed might be produced at fourteen, but it was thought to lack generative potency until the man was twenty-one: 'although the seed be genitable for the most part in the second seventh year, yet it is unfruitful until the third seventh year' (1665: 624). Likewise, in Bacon's model, seed production initiates puberty, but the development of that seed was understood to accompany, and underpin, the strengthening and growth of the rest of the adolescent body, which was recorded in other notable physical manifestations, most of which are my focus in the chapters of this book (beard growth, heated cheeks, changes to voices, and growth in height). Bacon's terminology, where being '*Able* for *Generation*' is described as relatively early in the developmental framework is a little misleading in linguistically conflating the initial production of reproductive seed (and possibly the ability to have sex) with the seed's efficacy in its ability to produce offspring. As Toulalan has observed: 'neither girls nor boys were yet hot enough to breed seed for conception; the increasing heat at puberty precipitated the ripening of the seed [...] a gradual process that took place over a period of time' (2013: 284). Achieving sexual maturity was understood as a protracted process of 'ripening'.

Marrying before bodies were 'ripe' would prevent the production of fruit (offspring) from seed that itself had not fully matured. Lemnius, for example, warned against 'those that be little elder then boyes, apply[ing] thēselues to the procreation of Children' (1592: 171). To marry too soon and strive to reproduce, before the adolescent body was itself fully developed, could harm the male who would become 'very weak and feeble in their loynes and shancks, and all their vitall iuice [...] so exhausted and consumed' (Lemnius, 1592: 170–1). Early modern medical, religious, and popular writings make clear that such sexually active futures should not be rushed for fear that this would result in the reproductive deficiency of inadequately heated seed. Protestant minister William Gouge similarly observed in *Domesticall Duties* that although marriage might legally be permitted at the age of twelve (for girls) and fourteen (for boys), physical 'ripenesse', achieved later than these ages, should be considered necessary for 'successful' marriage (1622: 180). All parties should 'forbeare some yeares longer' in establishing marital unions (Gouge, 1622: 180). Reproductive futures were expected for the adolescent male and female who would otherwise 'not [be] considered fully adult' (Oren Magidor, 2017: 54). Using the linguistic framing of most early modern commentators, Gouge observes how puberty is recognisable for signalling growth but not the achievement of full maturation: 'Child-hood is counted the floure of age. While the floure of the plant sprouteth, the seed is greene, vnlfit to be sowen' (1622: 180). The 'ripening' that took place within the adolescent body depended upon the development of generative seed, the full strength of which could be gauged by viewing the whole body.

Early modern writings identify cultural sensitivity to the pubescent body's gradual maturation that appears to have been upheld to some degree in social and sexual practices. Historical studies set the average ages for first marriage in early modern England as somewhere between an individual's early-mid-twenties, where regional and social contexts may have sometimes seen marriages take place in late teens (Ingram, 1987: 129). Although aristocratic marriages tended to take place at a younger age than in other social ranks, it was extremely rare for individuals to wed in their early teens. When this did occur, marriages were accompanied by stipulations that meant young husbands and wives did not cohabit until a suitable time when consumption would be deemed acceptable (Laslett, 1965: 96–9). In short, sexual acts were postponed in a marriage until ripening bodies were deemed ripe.

Early modern commentators often underline the need for a model of timely maturation for adolescents. As numerous examples used in this book will show, connections between untimeliness and puberty incurred connotations of medical disorder and threatened behaviours that warranted concern. For example, precocious menarche in girls could present medical challenges, being linked to diseases like greensickness and pica (Evans and Sparey, 2024). However, while cases of girls younger than the age of thirteen experiencing menstruation were regarded as unusual in the medical writings of English writers, travel narratives from this era emphasise a normative model of 'early' menarche and an accompanying sexual awakening for girls from countries with warmer climates than the Euro-centric template used to construct medical norms in England. Assessed in terms of geo-humoral logic that related a hot climate to excesses in humoral temperaments, girls of colour are often subjected to hypersexualisation in early modern accounts. For example, in *The Anatomy of Melancholy*, Robert Burton relates records of African girls being sexually experienced at an early age: 'in *Africke* a man shall scarce finde a maide at 14, yeeres olde, they are so forward' (1621: 541). Burton's word choice of 'forward' is telling; African girls are understood as premature/early in their sexual development and they also become aligned with ideas of sexual aggression/forwardness. As Caroline Bicks notes, Burton, and other early modern writers that underscore these racialised assumptions, contributed to the construction of damaging racial stereotypes that carry a disturbing legacy, and 'foregrounds the precociously overheated temperaments of African girls who can't wait until fourteen to give their bodies away' (2021: 25; Also see Karim-Cooper, 2023: 259). Across this book, we will see that ideas about female chastity are recurring points of tension in early modern constructions of female puberty, about which girls might achieve negotiated agency. It is worth highlighting, then, that the ability to make use of ideas of revered chastity in girlhood suggests double standards based on racial identities when early modern commentators assume a lack of, or at least a smaller window for, chaste innocence as a feature of maturation in adolescent girls of colour.

Early modern English medical writings repeatedly represent 'normative' adolescence as a time during which the ageing process was not marked by progressive cooling but by a gradual and necessary increase in generative heat. This occurred in both sexes and was crucial in underpinning the individual's progression towards 'ripe' adulthood. Transitions between and across ages, moreover, appear to have been drawn-out and fluid. In *Coming of Age in Shakespeare* (1997), Marjorie Garber's analysis of maturation in Shakespeare considers more absolute distinctions between ages. According to Garber, whose work is influenced by psychoanalytic theory, physical and emotional maturation is sudden and 'traumatic' for the individual, being experienced on the threshold between ages (1997: 6). Garber focuses, therefore, on familiar ideas about climacteric ages that act as thresholds between life stages, which can be mapped out in terms of the seven-year stages of the early modern life cycle: seven, fourteen, twenty-one, etc. Here changes that are understood in relation to entering a life stage are examined as producing an especially vulnerable state, where anxieties are envisaged as more acute through the transition between ages. Garber's approach has helpfully expanded notions of maturation beyond bodies in its discussion of the properties required in achieving independent 'adult' minds. However, Garber's work and similar approaches that do not aim to analyse 'the condition of being in any given stage' (1997: 6) leave a great deal of room for attention to be paid to the way early modern culture understood ageing bodies that were situated within a particular life stage.

Changes that occurred in these life 'stages' were treated as significant but not immediate. Sara Read's consideration of menstruation in early modern England has, for example, demonstrated how young women were understood to mature gradually across their reproductive lives. Read has shown that the 'transitional bleeding' (2013: 14) of menarche typically preceded reproduction by ten years, indicating a modelling of the relationship between 'threshold' moments in the life cycle and their relationship to broader ideas about ongoing sexual maturation. Although Read suggests that this model of gradual development was likely different for the maturing male, which Read describes as 'a sudden affair as the production of seed proved that the boy was sexually mature' (2013: 39), it appears that a degree of symmetry between the female's lengthy maturation was also observed for the male. Seed production was at the centre of the bodily changes that took place for both sexes during puberty, and the appropriate heat and moisture of such seed usually only signalled full maturity several years after its initial production. As medical writers observed, like Lemnius and Paré cited above, adolescent males were understood to initially produce seed that was not ready to produce children, but such seed would attain heat and efficacy by the male's early twenties (Lemnius, 1592: 170; Paré, 1665: 624). As with adolescent girls, adolescent boys were thought to take time to develop in order to reach sexual maturity.

For both the adolescent male and female, evidence that their seed's efficacy had been achieved depended upon several bodily changes that took place during adolescence being observed. As we have seen, these bodily alterations went beyond an initial production of generative materials in the menarche for adolescent girls, and the production of 'cold' seed for adolescent boys. These bodily changes in themselves were, however, regarded as noteworthy and promising in being symptomatic of the early stages of puberty that typically took place in the early teens. Most early modern medical writers generally differentiated between the function of a female's blood as 'seed', which was required to join with a male's seed in order to conceive, and the menstrual blood she produced. Menstrual blood did not itself create life; it was this blood that was redirected to nourish the foetus once conception had taken place. However, writers do tend to identify the female's onset of menstruation as primary evidence that the process of ripening towards a generative maturity had begun. Menstruation demonstrated that excess moisture was being removed from the body and that a subsequent rise in the body's humoral heat (needed for generative seed) was being achieved. Most early modern medical writings adopted two-seed Hippocratic and Galenic models for reproduction, rather than the Aristotelian one-seed model. For example, Sharp's *The Midwives Book* from 1671 happily repeats theories presented in earlier midwifery writings, especially those of Nicholas Culpeper, in describing an accepted two-seed model for generation (68–9).[9] Sharp goes on to discuss the distinct reproductive function of the mother's menstrual blood as nourishment for the developing foetus, observing how menstruation begins at 'twice seven years', accompanied by other signs of puberty, including unruly behaviour, swelling breasts, and lustful thoughts (1671: 69).

On their fourteenth birthdays, then, boys and girls were not abruptly deemed mature men and women, nor were these pubescent boys and girls indistinguishable from each other. Bacon's model of ageing bodies, cited above (Bacon, 1638: 369–70), is especially useful in suggesting how a sense of symmetry in terms of ageing was observed across developing male and female pubescent bodies, while difference was also importantly marked in this stage of life. Notably, it is only when boys and girls 'come to *Pubertie*' that sex-specific aspects of ageing are observed upon the body in an account of the life cycle. Prior to puberty, shared features of emerging teeth and speech development characterise childhood. For Bacon, the 'sexed' signs for pubescent bodies are menstruation and beard-growth: 'the *Flowing* of the *Menstrua* [...] *To Put forth a Beard*' (1638: 369–70). Bacon does not, however, explicitly allocate menstruation to maturing girls or the emergence of beards to boys, probably because such clarification is not thought necessary. There is, in a sense, an assumption that readers will understand this trajectory of the life cycle that includes both sexes.

Some of the changes of puberty were less gender-specific than others. The experience of sexual desire in both adolescent males and females was itself considered a sign of humoral excesses that originated from a body that no longer required such heat and moisture for simple body growth. Having been fully augmented (including the production of generative seed), the body had heat to spare, which, as *Aristotle's Masterpiece* observes, could then influence the mind to encourage sexual activity: 'the Blood, which no longer taken to augment their bodies, abounding, incites their minds to Venery' (1684: 5–6). Based on such logic, Ferrand in *Erotomania* observed how love melancholy was especially evident in pubescent adolescents of both sexes, reasoning that the humoral excesses of heat and the retention of seed could 'corrupt within the body, and so by sending up divers noysome vapours to the Braine' (1640: 132). For Ferrand, love melancholy is understood as a complaint particular to adolescents, because 'some diseases are more appropriate to certaine ages, and seasons, then others are' (1640: 132). Lusty thoughts, love melancholy and the giddiness of 'boiled brains', as Shakespeare's Shepherd in *The Winter's Tale* (3.3.62) attests, were characteristic of humorally hot male and female adolescents.

While burgeoning desires were recognised as part of adolescence for young men and women, other signs of adolescence were more sex-specific. Although symmetry was observed in the way the production of seed and its intensified humoral heat incurred changes in young men and women, the physical changes observed upon the adolescent male and female body were differentiated. Ferrand, for example, may see love melancholy as an adolescent ailment, experienced by all sexes, but his observations also note that the condition is often the result of puberty, which is otherwise marked differently upon the male or female body:

> the most received opinion is, that men and women are subject to this disease of Love-Melancholy, as soone as ever they are entred into those yeares, in which they begin *Pubescere,* to come to their Puberty: which appeares in men chiefly by their voice, which at that time growes greater and harsh withall, and in women it may be knowne by observing their breasts, which about this time begin to swell and grow bigger, and that for the most part, about the age of twelve, or Fourteene: And this is now the generall Rule, by which their Puberty is knowne. (1640: 135)

The changes of puberty seem to be recognised as a shared stage of protracted transition for males and females, but where similar timing and some shared humoral traits of excessive heat (and by extension, comparable experiences of heated thoughts) were also accompanied by divergence between female and male experience, where bodily maturation becomes especially 'sexed'. Ferrand identifies the deepening voice of the male and the development of breasts in the female, noting that the pubescent male and female who share a humoral disposition prone to lovesickness also exhibit other bodily developments that mark sexual difference.

Such details help develop persistent questions about where gender and sex fit in early modern models of the life cycle. Some research has suggested that there is little evidence of a formalised female life cycle that specifies sex-specific distinctions in every stage of life. Jennifer Higginbotham, for example, concludes that clear representations of the 'seven ages of woman', and particularly the gendered terminology that accompanied such a model, did not emerge until the mid-late seventeenth century (2013: 35). Higginbotham's study of the language used to depict a variety of ideas about girlhood across the seventeenth century has helped show the confused nature of specifically feminine language in relation to age before the late seventeenth century in the use of terms such as 'maid', 'girl', 'damsel', and 'wench'. It should be borne in mind, however, that this does not mean that early modern culture was inattentive to the particular changes that ageing held for female lives before this time. The evidence I use in this book from the late-sixteenth through to the late-seventeenth centuries suggests that young men and women were widely understood as exhibiting both shared and distinct characteristics during adolescence.[10]

As I have shown in this section, after fourteen (and sometimes as early as nine), early modern bodies were understood to be involved in a process of maturation that involved gradual humoral change, which was itself often accordingly gendered, in its journey towards adulthood. Alterations in the heated adolescent body, during what Henry Cuffe termed the '*budding* and *blossoming*' age (1607: 118), were largely specific to males and females as the emergent signs of sexual maturity became registered upon the body. Writers repeatedly observed that adolescent boys began to grow facial hair, and their voices would deepen, while adolescent girls began to menstruate and develop breasts. For example, Peter Chamberlain's list of physical alterations that took place during puberty, in *Midwife's Practice*, differentiates between the bodies of the pubescent male and female: 'About that time young men begin to grow hairy, to change their voice, and to have lustfull imaginations, maidens paps begin to swell, and they to think upon-&c' (1665: 69). Alterations in the body were not rigidly aligned with numeric age (menstruation, usually thought to begin sometime between the age of nine and fourteen, was considered the start and not the end of the female's bodily changes), and, as Churchill notes of distinctions between girlhood and womanhood, 'these categories depended on the fact that aging was accompanied by an expected set of physiological changes in the "sexed" body' (2013: 105). The influence of humoral heat was notably understood as a necessary and expected part of a girl's maturation, as it was for a boy's progression towards manhood. While a girl might be cooler than a boy of the same age, her adolescence meant that her own humoral disposition would also be regarded as exceptionally heated in relation to her life cycle trajectory. Indeed, humoral heat underpinned the gendered manifestations of bodily change during puberty. Such symmetry and difference during puberty seems to have sat together within early modern models of age and gender. What is more, these discernible signs of female and male puberty, as I examine in the chapters of this book, were readily understood and incorporated in representations of adolescent characters in early modern theatres.

Shakespeare's adolescents: performing puberty

Across the chapters of *Shakespeare's Adolescents*, I draw into focus how female and male puberty could be performed as part of theatrical constructions of age on the early modern stage. Chapters are structured around the anatomised features of the pubescent body that medical writers regularly use in discussing puberty, and which provide culturally recognised signs that could be used in theatrical performances of adolescence. All the chapters of this book keep sight of life-cycle models set out above and, where appropriate, consider features attributed to the male and the female alongside each other. *Shakespeare's Adolescents* examines how early modern culture understood puberty and the extent to which the age of adolescence was used as a category that grouped males and females together, as well as offering a means through which differentiation between its representations of the sexes was achieved.

In the first chapter, I examine the use of seasonal and agricultural metaphors in the linguistic framing of early modern adolescence as a crucial starting point for teasing out the way cultural motifs about adolescence were utilised in Shakespeare's plays. The early modern body, its parts and processes of maturation, are often described in seemingly figurative terms. Yet the language of agricultural and horticultural growth was connected to an understanding of real developments that were understood to take place in adolescent bodies, and these developments could consequently be alluded to in theatrical constructions of adolescent characters. Two key strategies in conceptualising adolescence emerge in the first chapter: the widespread use of body-related metaphors of ripening and flowering for representing *both* male and female adolescence in early modern writings, and the setting of such imagery in stark contrast with the threat of decay. In the opening chapter, I consider how floral representations of adolescence in Shakespeare's plays are used in relation to gender to reveal nuances at work in the gendered application of age-specific language. I examine Hermia's representation in *A Midsummer Night's Dream* (c. 1595/6) to demonstrate how the adolescent female and male are situated in a different way when facing the threat of 'cankered blooms', which both might experience, but where floral imagery is situated differently in relation to the humoral changes imagined to be at work inside the adolescent's body. Moreover, in analysing the pairing of the elderly Adam with the adolescent Orlando in *As You Like It* (c. 1599), I explore how the cultural pairing of adolescent promise and its threatened decline might be physically and visually realised on stage in representing the comparative ages of certain characters. Such theatrical strategies could contextualise the representation of a male adolescent character, like Orlando, in a way that masked the maturity of Burbage, while celebrating the skills of an actor who, by the late 1590s, had a record of performing adolescent protagonists.

In the second chapter, I turn from this broader linguistic and emblematic fashioning of 'heated' and 'ripening' adolescence, to the physical changes of puberty. Specifically, I examine how the 'heated' changes of puberty were interpreted through an understanding of adolescent faces and facial adornments. In exploring the representation of adolescent beards and blushes in early modern medical and cultural discourses, I discuss how a shared sign of puberty in males and females (heat rising to adolescent faces) suggested continued symmetry in the maturation of the sexes. Such symmetry, however, left room for difference to be marked upon male and female bodies (while pubescent girls blush, boys produce beards). Moreover, these features were utilised in theatrical performances of adolescence. Playful allusions to absent beards, growing beards, or unseen pubic beards are discussed as part of Shakespeare's construction of adolescent identities through detailed analysis of *Much Ado About Nothing*, *Measure for Measure*, *As You Like It*, *Coriolanus*, and *Twelfth Night*. In this analysis, I engage with relevant scholarship relating to early modern beards (Fisher, 2001; Johnston, 2011; Rycroft, 2019), but my readings especially develop Will Fisher's work on beards and his formulation of age/gender models. By examining how Orlando's 'little beard' (3.2.190) relates to Burbage's resituated adult complexion and, presumably, his partially shaved face, I highlight how an adolescent's anticipated beard did not inevitably have to be shaped as a 'lack' in constructions of masculine identities. While Burbage is theatrically styled as a promising adolescent male character, whose beard growth is underway rather than fully achieved, his partially 'bearded' state is used in comparison to the theatrical styling of 'beardless' female adolescent characters who would have been played by boy actors, who may well also have had to have shaved to perform their parts. Moreover, I highlight how allusions to absent feminine facial beards, but inferred pubic 'beards', recognise intersecting issues of symmetry and difference in early modern ideas about male and female maturation that aided theatrical representations of adolescent femininity.

In the third chapter, I investigate the attributes of adolescent voices in Shakespeare's plays. Here, I explore the much-discussed topic of the male adolescent's breaking voice, and its implications for the boy actor on the early modern stage. By situating changes of voice in the context of all the changes experienced within the maturing body, however, I suggest how understanding 'adolescent' voices in Shakespeare's plays may be less about vulnerability of vocal pitch (Bloom, 2007: 25) and more about verbal styling in relation to cultural ideas about the 'heated' and agile minds, and words, of adolescents. I draw upon works from childhood studies, including discussions of educational practices for boys, which have helped establish some recognisable features of speech in relation to age (Lerer, 2017: 17; Munro, 2017; McCarthy, 2021). Moreover, Blaine Greteman's analysis of work by John Milton has mapped the qualities of children's voices, demonstrating how ideas about early modern 'childish' voices were complex, realising qualities of mimesis, liberty and licence, resistance and obligation, as well as consent and politicised agency (2013). I develop Greteman's analysis of 'the relationship between childish mimesis and adult subjectivity' (2013: 3) by placing the speech of boy actors in the context of cultural framings of adolescent speech as an admired manifestation of heated bodies and minds. Adolescent agency, I argue, could be articulated through a certain mode of controlled speech that made the character/actor recognisable as a figure whose adolescent 'heat' had been harnessed in the qualities of their commendable, and often dazzling, vocal performance.

Although adolescent male voices more notably 'break' in a way female ones do not, I investigate how the heated activity of the adolescent's maturation that altered male voices is also observed in the way female voices were understood and represented in early modern culture. The third chapter, therefore, again considers how symmetry was recognised in the pubescent vocal changes that took place for the early modern male and female. Heat, which rose to significantly alter male vocal chords, also rose in the adolescent female body to similarly influence the mind and manner of speech. Although I acknowledge how familiar models of feminine virtue that connected silence with chastity and obedience needed navigating, I illuminate the contexts that allowed, and even deemed it appropriate, for the adolescent female to be talkative and witty in her use of words. Controlled and versatile verbosity, I argue, could avoid associations with shameful bodily 'leakiness' (Paster, 1993: Chapter 1) and need not always be understood as evidence of unruliness that was symptomatic of greensickness (King, 2004; Potter, 2013). My analysis in this chapter complements Bicks's recent work on the 'brainwork' of early modern girls, and recognises similarly positive representations of the mental and linguistic dexterity of Shakespeare's adolescent female characters (2021). Like Bicks, I perceive in adolescence a 'cognitively agile period' (2021: 28), although I ascribe these applauded features of mind and voice to female and male adolescents, specifically drawing out the commercialised eloquence of the adolescent boy player.

In the third chapter, therefore, I attend to the similarities and differences attributed to male and female adolescent voices to rethink the implications of well-known, and pronounced, moments of metatheatre on Shakespeare's stage. I examine how meta-theatrical moments work to re-inscribe patriarchal authority, if the eloquence that is applauded in a female character becomes resituated as the distinct, rather than paralleled, skill of the male adolescent actor. Critical works that register moments of empowerment for the fictive female *and* boy performer have tended to elide character with performer when the boy 'upstages' his master through his commanding performance (Newman, 1991: 45; Dusinberre, 1993). I argue that such readings are available, most clearly when metatheatre is *not* encouraged or when age-specific parallels retain cohesion between boy player and girl character. However, I highlight how elision between boy and female character has depended upon assumptions about theatrical hierarchies that position female character (regardless of the character's age) and boy actor as similarly disempowered in early modern culture. While my reading acknowledges the complexity of boy players' positions in theatrical cultures, where abuse and exploitation, as well as structures of support, appear to have been at work, I suggest how readings of vulnerability, especially vocal vulnerability, offer a limited view on the accomplished boy actor, and the compellingly 'heated' vocality with which he was regularly accredited in early modern theatrical cultures.

In the book's fourth chapter, I explore how the body growth of puberty could be used in performances of adolescent height upon Shakespeare's stage. I consider how what Francis Bacon's notes as the symptom of puberty that saw adolescents '*Grow* in *Stature*' (1638: 370) formed part of early modern theatrical production. Hamlet's exchanges with a boy player, who is told 'your ladyship is nearer to heaven than when I saw you last' (2.2.351) suggest concerns for how an actor's changing height might be disguised or used in early modern drama. A change in height may undermine theatrical representation. Yet, as I show in the chapter, acting companies seem to have manipulated the staging of age and gender by taking advantage of theatrical illusions that were made possible through the comparable physicalities of its players. Scripted dialogue often pointedly highlights differences in height between characters and, I suggest, uses cultural ideas about maturity, maturation, and gender to fashion characters and inform a play's core thematic concerns.

In my analysis of *A Midsummer Night's Dream*, I examine the comparative staging of the heights of the boy players performing the roles of Helena and Hermia. This comparison *between* boy players, one tall and one short, is contextualised in relation to early modern accounts of adolescent growing bodies. By reworking existing critical viewpoints that identify the child actor as small when compared to the adult actor or audience member, the chapter explores how the *growing bodies* of adolescents were utilised in performances, and could actively help in the representation of difference between girl characters as well as the boy actors who played them. Moreover, in this chapter, I suggest how locating Burbage as Lysander (Grote, 2002: 229) in the earliest performances of the play helps illuminate the support structures in place for the adolescent actors performing the roles of girls and indicates Burbage's own development of adolescent roles in his early years with the Lord Chamberlain's Men. In the early performances of *A Midsummer Night's Dream* (c. 1595/6), Burbage's representation of the adolescent Lysander involves less complexity and stage time than the adolescents that the actor would subsequently portray in his career, such as Romeo or Orlando. I suggest how Burbage's likely role in the adolescent love plot of *A Midsummer Night's Dream* correlates with the play's emphasis upon a narrative of adolescent growth, as well as the play's efforts to use, support, and showcase the energetic performances by the adolescent players performing the roles of Hermia and Helena.

In this fourth chapter, I also return to *As You Like It* to consider how adolescent height appears to have been used by the company as a reusable resource in a play from c. 1599, suggesting a trajectory for the way in which Shakespeare was experimenting with representations of adolescence across the 1590s. I show how, in *As You Like It*, Shakespeare seems to both reuse and expand the theatrical representations of adolescence that involve the staging of comparable heights. The 'more than common tall' (I.3.111) actor who plays Rosalind in *As You Like It* (c. 1599) is, I suggest, set in contrast with her shorter colleague who plays Celia (in ways that echo the model used in *A Midsummer Night's Dream*), but Rosalind/Ganymede is also more explicitly set against Burbage's Orlando. In his early thirties by 1599, and with several adolescent male roles under his belt, Burbage's representation of the adolescent Orlando would have needed to convey an age-appropriate masculinity that was nuanced enough to not be undermined by the tall *and crossdressed* Rosalind's representation of Ganymede in the play's narrative. In comparison with the earlier play of *A Midsummer Night's Dream*, notions of age and gender are more expansively manipulated in the staging of *As You Like It*, and character/actor height features in the management of the fictions that are created. It is not, I argue, that the adolescent boy playing Rosalind/Ganymede was immediately or easily like a girl, but that his adolescent physique was artificially contextualised to signify both female and male adolescence alongside the somewhat complex and comparative staging of other actors' bodies as also adolescent.

Through the chapters of *Shakespeare's Adolescents*, I offer an in-depth historical analysis of early modern cultural and medical representations of adolescence in order to suggest ways in which Shakespeare's plays engage with and explore those ideas in theatrical contexts. By recognising how puberty was understood as a discernible physical process that was normalised, and so not only associated with bodily uncertainty, I seek to examine how female and male puberty could be, and often was, staged and even celebrated in Shakespeare's plays.

Notes

1 For discussion of the questionable actions of the Duke and Isabella against Angelo, see Pascale Aebischer (2008). On morals in *Measure for Measure*, see Jonathan Dollimore (1994).
2 A shift towards discussing the sexes together may be discernible in works from the last few years. Charlotte Scott's *The Child in Shakespeare* (2018) notably considers children of both sexes across its chapters about early childhood. The book explores Shakespeare's use of children in relation to powerful feelings of love, loss, and regret. Edel Lamb's *Reading Children* (2018) also considers male and female children as young readers, considering the nature of material designed for the young as well as more gendered material for boy and girl readers.
3 Chedgzoy makes a similar case for using fictional constructions of adolescent identities as a means of examining cultural understanding and possibilities for imagined age-related selves in her introduction to *Shakespeare and Childhood* (2007: 19).
4 Medical writers certainly retain the language of 'perfection' in their discussions of reproductive bodies, where the male is imagined as perfect. However, such ideas are also clearly problematic. Thomas Raynalde, for example, grapples with this notion of 'perfection' and sex in *The Birth of Mankinde*, first published in 1545, where 'seed, as we said before, is nothing so firm, perfect, absolute, and mighty in woman as in man, and yet can you not call this any imperfection or lack in woman. For the woman in her kind and for the office

and purpose wherefore she was made, is even as absolute and perfect as man in his kind' (Raynalde, 2009: 47).
5 A compelling but problematic argument that conflates women and boy players in terms of subordination to adult, male power is provided by Juliet Dusinberre in '*The Taming of the Shrew*: Women, Acting, and Power' (1993: 67–84). Dusinberre's reading, which centres upon a character's and actor's lengthy speech, will be discussed in the third chapter of this book.
6 Throughout this book, italicised content in quoted works replicates the original presentation of the text unless a parenthetical note indicates otherwise.
7 Humoral bodies were complex bodies, and studies of this feature of early modern culture are widespread. While this book focuses upon the particular intersections between adolescence and gender in ideas relating to humoral heat and moisture, early modern humoral theory has also been shown to have been central to ideas about subjectivity, race, and gender. See works by Gail Kern Paster (1993); Helen King (1998); Michael Schoenfeldt (1999); Karen Harvey (2002); and Mary Floyd-Wilson (2003).
8 A Latin edition of this text, *Historia Vitae & Mortis*, was printed in 1623.
9 On Sharp's use of Culpeper's *Directory for Midwives*, see Elaine Hobby's (1999) detailed introduction and accompanying footnotes for her modern edition of Sharp's book. Mary Fissell's *Vernacular Bodies* (2004) also gives a helpful overview of reproductive theories used across the late sixteenth and early seventeenth centuries.
10 The early modern medical writings I use in this study range from texts published in the early sixteenth century through to publications from the late seventeenth century. As Karen Harvey (2002: 202–23) has shown, the humoral reasoning used in medical literature persisted into the eighteenth century. Writers from across the century borrowed from each other (Fissell, 2004), as Elaine Hobby (1999) documents in her edition of Sharp's *Midwives Book*. Originally published in 1671, Sharp's book particularly reworks material from Nicholas Culpeper that was published in the 1650s. Texts from across the seventeenth century are used in *Shakespeare's Adolescents* to demonstrate the pervasive nature of the humoral ideas used to understand the body. In my conclusion, moreover, I note where certain emphases in medical writings have been suggested by looking across a wider historical period than Shakespeare's works, where we can also see similar alterations in the 'afterlife' presentations of Shakespeare's adolescent characters.

1

'A rose by any other name': flowering adolescence and the gendering of puberty

> And so from hour to hour we ripe and ripe,
> And then from hour to hour we rot and rot,
> And thereby hangs a tale. (Shakespeare, *As You Like It*: 2.7.26–8)

> AS the Spring is the onely fitting seede time for graine, setting and planting in Garden and Orchard: So youth, the *Aprill* of mans life, is the most naturall and conuenient season to scatter the Seeds of knowledge vpon the ground of the mind. (Henry Peacham, 1622: 21)

As shown in the quotations from Shakespeare's *As You Like It* (c. 1599) and Henry Peacham's *Compleat Gentleman* (1622) above, early modern depictions of age commonly made use of horticultural and agricultural imagery. Ageing was observed as a trajectory of growth and 'ripening' towards adulthood, followed by the decline of older age, which – carrying the metaphor forward – could be described as a process of rotting. Moreover, the line notations provided by editors of *The Norton Shakespeare Comedies* (1997) suggest that, in performances of *As You Like It*, there would have been scope for bawdy humour in slippage between rot/rut in the cited lines, because of uncertainties surrounding early modern pronunciation. This might well have been the case, seeing as the play repeatedly casts overviews upon the human life cycle, as in the famous 'seven ages of man' speech, and then returns its audience's attention to the 'rutting' exploits of the adolescents at the centre of its comic love plots.[1]

As the examples from Shakespeare and Peacham suggest, adolescence was contemplated both as a discernible age with its own distinct features, where the characteristics of 'ripening' could be expected, and also part of the whole life cycle where connectivity between ages was assumed and links were drawn. In the quotation from *As You Like It* (even with pronunciation aside), we can observe the semantic connection between the 'Ages of Man' because the stages of life are discussed using an agricultural model that only really makes sense in relation to the rest of the model's components: at its simplest level, images of ripening anticipate ripeness that, in turn, set up the expectation of over-ripeness/rotting. In Shakespeare's usage above, and in many other early modern writings that I use in this chapter, there is notably scope to collapse the predicted trajectory of ageing and blur the transition between ripening and rotting in a way that displaces the imagined 'ripe' adult centre of the life cycle.

How and why adolescence might be understood through this comparative framing with decline and old age is the focus of this chapter: why is adolescent ripening promise so regularly set alongside descriptions of decay? As I will show, such an imagistic strategy of merging adolescence prematurely with old age could be used in different ways. Ideas about premature ageing could provide a threatening image that demonstrated the harmful effects of adolescent exploits upon an adult state and be used to encourage caution during adolescence. In *As You Like It*, however, the witty lines show a different slant on this relationship between adolescence and old age that was also available: the upward and, here, the more appealing trajectory of human life is identified in adolescence ('ripe and ripe'). Adulthood as an age – here hyperbolically fleeting, if not absent – signals not the pinnacle of life but the downswing of life's trajectory ('rot and rot'). Adolescence as a time of peril, excitement, and development meant that early modern representations of this age, including theatrical representations, regularly positioned adolescence as the age that mattered most in shaping how human life would run its course, and this fashioning of adolescence within the life cycle appears to have excited much cultural interest.

After all, early modern life-cycle modelling situated particular activity in the 'ripening' age of adolescence that could understandably shift focus from an adult centre. Bodies and minds were understood to undergo palpable change during adolescence that had lasting effect. Depictions of the alterations that took place during adolescence often, therefore, kept sight of later stages of the life cycle. It is, for example, during the 'Spring' of adolescence that Peacham sees fit for seeds of knowledge to be sown for the individual so that the individual can benefit from their growth and continued development into adulthood. The important *formation* of selfhood, where alterations, impressions, and experiences solidified into a state that under pinned subsequent experiences, was understood to occur during the age of adolescence. In Peacham's advice to young gentlemen, the ripeness of adulthood per se is elusive; adulthood is the centre of the trajectory of human life that is suggested, but it is the process of ripening, and the maturation of the 'Seeds' planted during adolescence that receives greatest attention. Adolescence, as a stage of life, was especially worthy of attention *because* it was here that the determinants of an individual's adult future could be founded. Consequently, the process of pubescent 'ripening' that was associated with adolescence depended greatly upon how bodily maturation was imagined in relation to the oft-decentred state of 'ripeness' and fertility that the adolescent's 'ripening' condition anticipated.

Taking as its starting point these early modern metaphors of agricultural growth used for human ageing, I use the first section of this chapter to unpack uses of ripening and floral imagery in Shakespeare and early modern culture more broadly in order to understand the nuanced ways in which this linguistic and imagistic framework of agricultural growth was used to depict adolescence. I outline how the language of 'ripening' and 'flowering' adolescence informed cultural and theatrical understanding of this life stage, and suggest why imagery of rottenness so often accompanied representations of male and female puberty. The extended reading I provide of the pairing of the elderly Adam and Orlando in *As You Like It* demonstrates how the cultural tendency to collapse the trajectory of the life cycle and associate 'ripening' adolescence with 'rotting' old age could be a useful motif in theatrical representations of an admired male adolescence. *As You Like It*, as a comedy that focuses its plot upon the adventures of 'ripening' adolescents, especially in the anticipation of pairing Orlando with Rosalind, tellingly begins by pairing the adolescent character of Orlando with the elderly character of Adam. My analysis of *As You Like It*, in this chapter, considers how this performative pairing helps establish Burbage-as-adolescent in his representation of Orlando, demonstrating how early modern cultural associations of 'rutting' with 'rotting' could take on physical representation in the comparative theatrical construction of age for Orlando and Adam.

In the first section of this chapter, I lay a foundation for considering the relationship between age-specific imagery and the gendering of adolescence in early modern representations, which I consider in depth in the second section. In this chapter, I therefore begin the process of navigating how culturally central images of puberty were used in early modern texts, observing intersections and symmetry in the descriptions of male and female. While I demonstrate how both male and female could be depicted as flowers in relation to age more so than gender, negotiating the taint of rottenness is shown to potentially situate the adolescent male and female differently in relation to the bodily changes that were experienced during puberty. I compare the threatened 'blooms' of Hermia, in *A Midsummer Night's Dream*, to cultural representations of flowering male adolescence, including the depiction of the lovely young man of Shakespeare's *Sonnets*, to explore how age-specific linguistic signifiers of bodily change can become gendered. As ideas of excess humoral heat, appropriate to the age of adolescence, become concentrated upon corporeal sites of contagion, I suggest how gender identity becomes implicated in the manner by which the adolescent's actions are aligned with either self-willed agency or a lack of self-control. Here, the adolescent's assertions of their will must navigate restrictions based on gendered bodies, where the female adolescent is placed at a notable disadvantage when wilful self-expressions are more readily aligned with disease and a dysfunctional reproductive body rather than simply an adolescent one.

Flowering adolescence: misgendering an age?

Although the physical changes of puberty did, in many important ways, assign difference and create distance between boys and girls, early modern adolescent males and females could also be grouped together, and talked about in similar terms, due to their experience of the same 'age' of 'ripening' in the life cycle. Indeed, the linguistic framing of early modern adolescence may be another reason why associations between masculine adolescence and femininity have been regularly highlighted. Agricultural terminology, we have seen, is consistently used in depictions of the early modern life cycle in relation to both male and female adolescent. The adolescent male whom Peacham hopes to instruct is thought of as possessing fertile soil, receptive of seeds (here metaphorical seeds of knowledge) that will begin to develop. Such metaphors work well in a culture that also depicted bodily changes in terms of seed production and development, where narratives about reproduction could also place the female as the metaphorical 'soil' awaiting the male's seed (Sharp, 1671: 32).[2] Notably, the agricultural language of adolescence also includes, as shown in Cuffe's depiction of this 'budding and blossoming age' (1607: 118), the use of flower imagery when describing adolescence, where both young men and women could be styled as flowers.

Floral metaphors have often been associated with feminine qualities when reading early modern literature, and in representations of the body in particular (Stott, 1992: 60; Karim-Cooper, 2006: 17).[3] In her dictionary on *Women in Shakespeare*, for example, Alison Findlay observes only occasional exceptions in observing that 'flowers stand for women' (2010: 'Flowers' 142). Certainly, menstrual bleeding was most often referred to as 'flowers' (Read, 2013: 24), and notions of 'deflowering' are predominantly used in relation to female virginity. However, such floral terminology, though often specific to females in application, are likely to have been informed by language more generally associated with age. Although lengthy debate exists around the etymology of menstrual 'flowers' (Crawford, 1981: 49–51; Green, 2005: 52; Read, 2013: 24–5), scholars suggest that the likeliest root for the term is the familiar proverb that 'fruit follows flowers' (Sharp, 1671: 215). The proverb uses the agricultural language familiar to life-cycle modelling, where menstrual bleeding indicates a landmark in the young woman's life: the onset of menstruation (flowering) promises the likelihood of bearing children (fruit). While menstruation could be, and commonly was, called 'flowers' throughout a woman's reproductive life, and so was used throughout adulthood as well as adolescence (Read, 2013: 24), the proverb seems to be primarily about transitions in a female's life: adolescent flowering is followed by ripeness that allows the production of fruit. This perhaps suggests that certain words used for menstrual bleeding (flowers, menses, terms, courses) might also be influenced by age, even if this were less to do with numeric age and more about the positive associations of still being young and the promise of fruit, as opposed to imagery suggestive of decline. While menstrual 'flowering' is particular to the female, an appreciation that the agricultural linguistic framing of this floral imagery draws upon constructions of the life cycle helps illuminate the language of adolescence. 'Flowers' as menstruation (the onset of which begins and helps characterise female puberty) are identified as feminine through being recognised as a gendered function of the 'sexed' body (early moderns noted that only female bodies would usually menstruate). However, the concept of a 'flowering' stage, and the language used to describe it, is not exclusively applicable to adolescent girls in its early modern usage.

Indeed, it is evident that flower imagery was included in representations of young men, where floral language is not generally associated with femininity but a masculinity appropriate to adolescence. For something to 'flower' in relation to adolescence suggests promise and anticipates future growth. Samuel Crossman, in his spiritual guidance offered in *The Young Mans Monitor*, for example, urged his imagined young male readers to lead godly lives and reject sin 'while it is yet the morning of your life, the flower of your ye[a]rs' (1665: 244). Where young men are addressed in such terms, writers are more clearly imagining males whose 'flowering' state primarily represents their formative, adolescent stage of life rather than their gender. Henry Peacham's advice in *The Compleat Gentleman* is also directed towards male adolescents when he stresses how important the company a young man keeps at university is for his reputation. Peacham uses the metaphor of a garden, with the group of adolescents being depicted as flowers: 'But as in a delicate Garden kept by a cunning hand, and ouerlooked with a curious eye, the least disorder or rankness of any one flower, putteth a beautifull bed or well contriued knot out of square, when rudenesse and deformitie is borne withall, in rough and vndressed places' (1622: 38–9). Here, flowering adolescents can be pleasantly beautiful or rank, depending on the sort of adolescence they enact. In Peacham's garden metaphor, all male adolescents (grouped together at university) are imagined as flowers and are not emasculated through the imagery. What matters for the individual is the untainted sweetness of his flower and the efforts he makes to avoid its contamination in a garden of other flowers.

A similar image is used in *Hamlet*, where Hamlet's lamentations about Denmark describe 'an unweeded garden / That grows to seed; things rank and gross in nature / Possess it merely' (1.2.135–7). Although Hamlet is not using flower imagery to describe adolescence here, the untended garden is observed to be without the promise of flowers and only contains unprofitable seed on plants past flowering ('grows to seed'). The absence of wholesome flowers is clearly understood as negative and, in this case, an especially hopeless condition for the individual and the State. Strength and promise, here as part of a political and philosophical metaphor, can be suggested through pleasing flowers and there is no indication that a floral allusion should be immediately understood as feminine or somehow compromised.

The image of a 'flowering' adolescent in early modern representations is typically suggestive of a promising masculine identity. This especially seems the case when the flower used to describe a young man is the rose. As Peacham makes clear, the rose was highly valued: 'Among flowers, wee most admire and esteeme the Rose' (1622: 1–2). Herbert Cole's discussion of floral imagery used in heraldic emblems concurs in placing the rose at the top of the floral hierarchy: 'By common consent the rose is considered the most beautiful of flowers' (1988: 187). The rose, and flowers more expansively, in the Tudor and Stuart period (where the thistle joined the rose in the Royal heraldic image), were understood as symbols that carried positive associations. In early modern heraldry, floral motifs were common and were related to family honour and influence (Cole, 1988: 128). To be called a rose is usually, at its basic level, a compliment that is associated with promise and, in being an 'indication of health and vitality', often the promise of being young (Thomas and Faircloth, 2016: 'rose').

Being age rather than gender-specific, the floral image of 'budding and blossoming' adolescence can be applied to male and female. For example, in Thomas Lodge's prose romance, *Rosalynde* (1590), the main narrative source for Shakespeare's *As You Like It*, it is worth remembering that the eponymous young heroine is not the only 'rose' of the story. In Lodge's text, Rosalynde's suitor is called Rosader; two 'roses', one male and one female, are the central adolescent figures of the love plot. The appeal of Shakespeare's Romeo is, of course, also famously likened to that of the rose by Juliet. Upon hearing himself associated with a sweet-smelling 'rose' (2.1.85), Romeo evidently recognises praise through which he is encouraged to approach his intended lover. He does not interpret the floral nature of the image as a slight upon his masculinity. Indeed, as Darlena Ciraulo (2015) has shown, rose imagery is repeatedly used in *Romeo and Juliet* to describe young men and women, and such imagery appears appropriate to the linguistic framing of the play's teenage characters. While Kahn (1978) has shown that adolescent masculinity in Verona is also encoded through acts of physical and sexual violence, the age-appropriate language of flowering adolescence is used for both sexes in verbal cues that contribute to the staging of the characters' ages, which remain affiliated with culturally revered qualities of promise.

Hamlet is, therefore, also somewhat tellingly imagined by Ophelia as 'Th' expectation and rose of the fair state' (3.1.149), where the hope of the Nation is articulated through associating the prince with this floral motif. Although debate surrounds the age of Hamlet, arguments about the prince's adolescent features, such as discussion of his ongoing education (1.2.113), seem corroborated in the way that Hamlet's character is repeatedly considered using flowering imagery (Barbara Everett, 1989; Stephen Roth, 2009: 25–38; Lerer, 2017). Hamlet is, for example, associated with violets that are 'emblematic of the spring' (Thomas and Faircloth, 2016: 'violet') and are, like the season in which they are produced, associated with adolescence. The linguistic framing of Hamlet as 'A violet in the youth of primy nature' (1.3.7) as well as a 'rose' contribute to his fashioning as an adolescent character. The growth of individual and State is, however, curtailed by the actions of others who impose a 'rotten' environment in which the play's action is set (1.4.90).

Flowers, while usually considered beautiful and symbols of hope, are, as indicated by several of the examples already cited, also commonly identified as fragile and vulnerable to damage. Flowers were seen to anticipate the next stage of growth, which may be enabled or denied. Ophelia, who had herself described Hamlet as a 'rose' is, for example, also described in floral terms by her brother: 'O rose of May!' (4.2.157). Laertes exclaims his anguish at his sister's madness in terms of the floral promise that has been lost; the exclamation, coming where it does in the play, indicates that Ophelia's growth has been compromised. The scene is centred upon early modern understandings of plants and flowers, with Ophelia famously delivering floral gifts to other characters in her maddened state. These actions have rightly been considered in light of early modern botanical understanding of the herbs and flowers she uses, although the importance of 'flowering' adolescence as a significant context for interpreting the scene has not, to my knowledge, been a significant part of such analysis.

Ophelia's inclusion of rue for herself (4.2.175) has promoted particular scholarly attention, because the herb was one of several 'well-known abortifacients and emmenagogues' (Lucile Newman, 1979: 227) in early modern medicine. Lucile Newman suggests that Ophelia's reference to such substances is shocking in 'a dramatic change in her character from a former state of purity' (1979: 228). Another reading of Ophelia's rue is available, however, if we consider why early modern emmenagogues (substances used to bring on menstruation) might be appropriate herbs for an adolescent female to obtain. Regulated menstrual flux underpinned early modern understanding of healthy reproductive female bodies, and this meant that emmenagogues were commonplace in the treatment of women. Such substances were associated as much with the restoring of health and fertility as with the harmful disruption of pregnancy. As Jennifer Evans observes in relation to these herbs in her study of early modern aphrodisiacs, such 'plants could be used for entirely different purposes. They may have been employed solely to empty the womb without the associated ideas of enhancing procreation, but they were just as likely to be used to promote conception and cure barrenness' (2014: 172). Understanding the likely medical use of a herb like rue thus depended upon identifying the health complaint of the individual.

Plants like rue were understood to have fortifying qualities that acted positively upon the body and these herbs were only deemed hostile through their use in the particular circumstance where the patient was pregnant. Batman's outlining of herbal qualities for rue, for example, included the description of its helpful attributes of sharpening eyesight alongside the instruction: 'but beware women with childe' (1582: 318). Although scholars debate whether Ophelia can be characterised as pregnant in this scene (Neely, 1991; Dawson, 2008: 74–5), this characterisation often uses rue as key evidence of pregnancy, so that rue is primarily understood as an inappropriate and 'unchaste' herb for Ophelia to allocate to herself. As medical writers suggest that rue is *only* harmful during pregnancy, the herb offers an ambiguous means of assessing character; its use could be contextualised as harmless and even as a restorative for reproductive health. Reference to a known abortifacient might well have been interpreted as inappropriate for a virtuous character, but, as a substance that was also geared towards reinstating bodily health and fruitfulness in women, Ophelia's rue also suggests a desire to regulate bodies and remedy unruly desires. For example, greensickness, notorious for affecting adolescent females, was thought to be caused by the retention of menstrual blood. As Sharp's midwifery guide notes, applying the same logic as Batman nearly ninety years later, greensickness in maids might be treated using emmenagogues, such as 'juyces of Rue' (1671: 198). Ophelia's provision of rue for herself might then be understood as a chaste means of curing this notorious affliction in adolescent girls.

Interpretations of this floral scene can, it seems, set Ophelia precariously and paradoxically as both greensick adolescent virgin and as pregnant with a despairing need to terminate the pregnancy. The ambiguity surrounding early modern uses of rue makes both readings possible. However, the botanic allusions in this scene stress the adolescent characterisation of Ophelia, as in Laertes's observations about this 'rose of May!' (4.2.157) that seem to direct the audience's response to the character. The audience is pointedly reminded that Ophelia is to be regarded as a flower. If we follow Laertes's cue to identify Ophelia as a 'Rose' whose condition of 'flowering' has been stilted, and her adult promise left unrealised, her need for rue 'for me' (4.2.175) painfully suggests the desire to restore a 'rose' to its flowering potential. This heightened awareness of Ophelia's adolescence provides a context that particularly supports readings of Ophelia's maddened state as indicating the symptoms of the greensick adolescent, where the call for rue suggests a disordered 'flowering' body in need of treatment.

An age-orientated approach to Ophelia's botanics may, moreover, also help explain why rue is given to others onstage, probably Gertrude and/or Claudius, to be worn 'with a difference' (4.2.176). Rue, though used in the treatment of young women's health, was, in being evergreen, also associated with winter and old age. Polixenes, in *The Winter's Tale*, thus commends the adolescent Perdita for selecting rue to bestow upon him: 'well you fit our ages / with flowers of winter' (4.4.78–9). What is more, we can observe the broad parallels between Ophelia's herb and flower-giving and this scene from *The Winter's Tale*, which also sees an adolescent girl character onstage with armfuls of flowers and herbs. Perdita's appearance suggests similar associations between flowers and age but offers an inversion of the lamentable fragility of 'flowering' adolescence and its potential loss that we see in *Hamlet*. In Perdita's association with spring and adolescence, her botanic stage properties underline the character's connections with the Proserpina myth, where the girl's floral gifts represent the celebrated return of a 'lost' character and spring's return through the shepherds' feast. Proserpina's return was understood to be marked with the bringing of 'springtime flowers' (Findlay, 2010: 332), and this is recalled through the performance of Perdita, whose adolescent age is appropriate and especially prominent in the seasonal scene. With such suggestively age-specific coding of botanical components in Shakespeare's plays, it seems likely that the 'difference' in the meaning of rue in *Hamlet* is generational, and that early modern audiences would have been better equipped to assess the appropriate uses of the herb (with its many uses) when contextualised against the age and gender of certain characters.

In *Hamlet*, the floral imagery of Ophelia's performance is set, at least in part, in the context of the play's broader representation of its characters' adolescent conditions that are compromised in the play. Ophelia's primary association with flower imagery in the play is connected to her age. Like the violets that Ophelia laments have 'withered' (4.2.177) – flowers that, as has been shown, were 'emblematic of the spring' (Thomas and Faircloth, 2016) – the promise of Ophelia's adolescence is transformed into a representation of decline. In the end, violets in Elsinore are *only* imagined as thriving upon Ophelia's grave (5.1.219). The giving of particular flowers in Act 4, Scene

2 carries layered and potentially ambiguous meaning, but the power of the scene seems to arise largely from acknowledging the futility of the floral gifts.[4] It seems that what is yearned for in this tense scene about loss is the restoration of flowering promise, where vitality might override a confrontation with death (rue is also a funereal herb). With all their symbolic value, performed in connection with an adolescent character's maddened state, the cut flowers as the stage properties in a tragedy perhaps also remind us that the bloom that is cut will wilt rather than continue to grow. In *Othello*, Desdemona's death is described in this way, as the plucking of the rose from its life force: 'When I have plucked the rose, / I cannot give it vital growth again: / It needs must wither' (5.2.13–15). To 'rue' is, after all, to regret and grieve what has already been lost.

Desdemona and Ophelia, both young Shakespearean characters that suffer premature deaths, are connected by further age-related botanic imagery: each girl is associated with the willow.[5] Desdemona sings a song about 'a green willow' in the Folio's version of *Othello* (4.3.39), and, in *Hamlet*, Ophelia famously falls to her 'muddy death' from the snapping branch of a 'willow grows askant' on the riverbank (4.4.182; 165). The willow was 'known as the crack willow from the readiness of its twigs and branches to break without warning', and had properties of 'soft, smooth, pliable wood', which made it useful in basket making and fencing (Faircloth and Thomas, 2016: 'willow'). These pliable/fragile properties also made the willow emblematic of adolescence, although it was also often noted for being a tree that did not bear fruit. Being associated with mourning and 'with contraception and reduced fertility', the willow suggests significant, and therefore not coincidental, connections with the meanings of rue (Faircloth and Thomas, 2016: 'willow'). These meanings, moreover, seem powerfully apt for constructions of each of Shakespeare's tragic adolescent girl characters.

The promise attributed to Ophelia and Desdemona is articulated as a marred maturation that never achieves fruition. While the early modern use of the adolescent-as-rose image carried positive associations with beauty and vitality, the use of the metaphor clearly lent itself to the expression of fears about the loss, frustration, or the contamination of adolescent promise. Ruin here might be sexual ruin through ill advised sex, but ruin can also understood more broadly to indicate the loss of the adolescent's potential, articulated in terms of the flower that is prevented from developing productively across the life cycle. Decline and death intervene so that the fruitfulness of reproduction is denied the 'flowering' adolescent: no fruit follows such flowers.

In a similar vein, Hermia in *A Midsummer Night's Dream* is notoriously threatened with the image of herself 'withering on the virgin thorn' (1.1.77) if her emergent fertility is left unused in the marital union her father has selected. Through comparison with the 'withering' nature of imposed celibacy, Theseus indicates his vision of a better future. According to Theseus, obedience to her father's authority will offer Hermia happiness in enabling the preservation of her adolescent beauty through reproduction: 'earthlier happy is the rose distilled / Than that which, withering on the virgin thorn / Grows, lives and dies in single blessedness' (1.1.76–8). Hermia's resistance to her father's will is framed in patriarchal terms: Theseus insists, 'To you your father should be as a god' (1.1.47). Being applied to an adolescent female character, the rose imagery here perhaps assumes feminine qualities in being somewhat singularly used to stress physical beauty and its reproduction through having children.

Hermia's age as much as her gender, however, becomes a key part of Theseus's rhetoric. Part of Hermia's resistance to her father involves asserting constancy in her love for Lysander in a modelling of virtuous femininity, albeit one that here conflicts with the duty to a father. In response to Hermia's expressions of fidelity, Theseus identifies a counterargument that uses familiar stereotypes about the inconstancy of adolescence to appeal to the sexual appetite that he assumes has been activated by Hermia's heated, adolescent blood. Hermia's punishment of enforced celibacy for refusing to marry Demetrius, her father's choice, will, according to Theseus, be hard for the humorally hot adolescent to bear:

> Therefore, fair Hermia, question your desires.
> Know of your youth, examine well your blood,
> Whether, if you yield not to your father's choice,
> You can endure the livery of a nun,
> For aye to be in shady cloister mewed,
> To live a barren sister all your life,
> Chanting faint hymns to the cold fruitless moon. (1.1.67–73)

The threat seems to be that Hermia, driven by the passions of her adolescent blood, will not get to fulfil her desires to have sex and to have children, and that these age-related desires might exceed her desires for Lysander in particular. Hermia, addressed as 'fair' and imagined as a 'rose', is confronted with a future trajectory of her life, where the flowering rose goes to seed and withers on that 'virgin thorn'. Unusually, Theseus elects to stress the inconstancy of adolescence as a legitimate means for a young lady to relinquish her love of one man for another, apparently sidestepping associations with more hostile depictions of inconstant womanhood. Theseus's 'threat' of celibacy hinges upon the assumption that the adolescent's 'rutting' impulse can be used alongside the fear of unproductive rotting on the vine to coerce Hermia into obedience (*As You Like It*: 2.7.27).

As Valerie Traub has pointed out, Theseus's words assume a heterosexual and male-orientated view on desire, where 'Women's religious vocation is consistently viewed by male characters as a fate worse than death' (2002: 64). That an existence away from sexual intercourse with men *is* thinkable for Hermia, who remains unmoved by Theseus's threat, identifying a viable life-cycle trajectory in the threatened isolation ('So will I grow, so live, so die', 1.1.79), indicates continuation for female lives beyond men, as Traub suggests. Hermia's resistance, moreover, challenges assumptions about adolescents and their uncontrollable, heat-driven lust. Hermia revises the future for the withering rose and imagines continued maturation ('So will I grow'), where the ripening process continues, perhaps here enabled by being beyond the body through spiritual contemplation, and where the rotting (and rutting) of the familiar trajectory for life is displaced. The image of the withering rose is rejected as the inevitable consequence of Hermia's resistance to patriarchal authority, and she appropriates the rose image to assert independence in a manner that is itself characteristic of adolescence. Yet, even here, Hermia seems to push back at her father's interpretation of her behaviour as a 'stubborn harshness' (1.1.38) that stems from the thoughtless excesses of adolescence (and her susceptibility to Lysander's influence). In her rejection of Theseus's vision of decline, Hermia demonstrates self-restraint over disordering passions in the calm management of adolescent desires and persists in aligning herself with ideas of growth and vitality over decay.

Roses as images of adolescence are rarely unproblematic or simple symbols of promise when used in Shakespeare's works. The Countess in *All's Well That Ends Well*, for example, finds common ground with Helena when she reflects upon the passions of adolescence in the following terms: 'Even so it was with me when I was young: / If ever we are nature's, these are ours; this thorn / Doth to our rose of youth rightly belong' (1.3.113–15). The rose of adolescence comes with acknowledged thorns as well as pleasing blooms. When Antony describes Octavius Caesar, a figure who became successor to Julius Caesar in his late teens, the use of floral terminology seems to include both praise and an acknowledgement of weakness: 'He wears the rose / Of youth upon him' (*Antony and Cleopatra*, 3.13.20–1). On the one hand, Caesar's bloom is a commended attribute; his youthful masculinity, observed following a military success, appears as a badge of honour and future promise. On the other hand, Antony's comparatively 'grizzled head' (3.13.17) suggests a disposition hardened by military action. A certain naivety and inexperience can be associated with the contrastingly fragile flower imagery used in relation to Octavius. While the comparison moderates the positive nature of the rose image, Antony's own characterisation in the pairing indicates an appreciation of the threat of Octavius's emergent state of development. Antony's position in this scene is described as being 'declined' (3.13.27), which contrasts starkly with Caesar's adolescent framing as a flowering rose, where the linguistic play upon the rose that 'rises' becomes especially evident.

Cleopatra, in the same scene, develops the contrast between generations using the same floral motif. Cleopatra's response to Antony's report constructs an image of herself as the 'blown rose' (3.13.39) that is no longer shown respect by Octavius's messengers: 'Against the blown rose may they stop their nose, / That kneeled unto the buds' (3.1.38–9). Unlike the sweet-smelling rose of applauded adolescence that Juliet admires in Romeo, Cleopatra observes herself as past her flowering prime, where overblown means not only petals that have begun to fall in declining beauty and wavering power, but also indicates that the failing blooms become ill-smelling. Cleopatra's imagery of ageing once again takes the floral language of the life cycle from the anticipated 'flowering' of rosebuds to notions of rotting blooms. Set in the context of military battle and a comparison between generations, one on the rise and the other in decline, Octavius's rose is evidently evoked in a complex manner. Notably, however, the image does not make him feminine; it locates the character within a certain stage of life and aligns this with an appropriate masculinity.

The properties of flowering adolescence, while different for the harangued Hermia and the conquering Octavius Caesar, help illuminate the common means by which early modern culture represented this age: the individual's adolescent state is understood, in part, by being set alongside later stages in the life cycle. The rose of Hermia or Octavius is not yet withered or in decline like the blooms that are also imagined in their representation. The comparison between growth and decay highlights the inevitable continuation of the ageing process, where Octavius will supersede Antony, and Hermia's beauty, as Theseus makes clear, will not last. Cleopatra reminds us that flowering adolescence must, to some extent, always anticipate a future as a 'blown rose' and make the most of the opportunities its own state affords. The fragile rose image thus holds adolescence up as an admired stage of life that is culturally valued, in the same moment that its temporary nature and subsequent state of decline is also considered.

The manner by which such a future is imagined is shaped by how old age is partnered with adolescence for Shakespeare's characters. Octavius's emergent rise to power suggests the inevitable and grandiose motion of history, with the rise and fall of generations mapping onto more naturalised rhythms for the passing of time. The trajectory of rising and declining in *Antony and Cleopatra* is predictable and expected even if it is lamented by Cleopatra. For Hermia, however, Theseus's image of the withered rose is geared to intrude upon her state of flowering and the premature coupling of rottenness with ripening seems key to the threat it contains. Hermia's flowering becomes disconnected from the normalised trajectory of the life cycle because her flowers, Theseus warns, will never come to fruition as she ripens *only* towards rottenness.

A similar pairing of beautiful and festering blooms famously exists in Shakespeare's *Sonnets* that are addressed to the lovely young man. While critics have speculated as to whether the rose imagery used by Shakespeare hints at a particular addressee (especially in 'Sonnet 95' where the 'budding name' is mentioned), little attention has been paid to how flower imagery functions in Shakespeare's depiction of the subject's age (Booth, 1977: 546).[6] Imagery in 'Sonnet 95', for example, is similar to Peacham's all-male garden, where young men retain floral beauty in terms of seemly reputation: 'like a canker in the fragrant rose, / Doth spot the beauty of thy budding name!' (lines 2–3). Addressing the horticultural metaphor that is used for the adolescent's maturation may also help inform an understanding of the renowned final lines of 'Sonnet 20', where the boy is 'pricked […] out' for 'woman's pleasure' (line 13). The line includes the oft-noted pun upon genitals (see line notes in Booth, 1977), but in horticultural terms 'pricking out' is the transference of seedlings to a larger area in which growth will be enabled (Bacon, 1638: 82; Evelyn, 1664: 62, 73). The fetishism of body parts in *The Sonnets* often focuses upon a body that appears to be in the process of achieving maturity, where the male's maturation is placed under scrutiny. The 'procreation sonnets' (Sonnets 1–17) concern themselves with the beautiful adolescent's reproductive future in terms that echo Theseus's treatment of Hermia: 'From fairest creatures we desire increase, / That thereby beauty's rose might never die' (Sonnet 1, lines 1–2). The adolescent of *The Sonnets* is valued, as seen in the application of the rose imagery, but in a way that is conspicuously limited to his pleasing physicality and concerns for his beauty's continuation through the creation of offspring.

The attractive adolescent who is addressed in *The Sonnets* is told that his burgeoning ripeness is not to be wasted and, to help stress the urgency of the speaker's message, the adolescent is repeatedly asked to confront an image of his aged self. In 'Sonnet 5', for example, the speaker shows how the passing of time both constructs the self, enables growth, and then rapidly dismantles the individual who has been created:

> Those hours that with gentle work did frame
> The lovely gaze where every eye doth dwell
> Will play the tyrants to the very same,
> And that unfair which fairly doth excel.
> For never-resting time leads summer on
> To hideous winter, and confounds him there,
> Sap checked with frost and lusty leaves quite gone,
> Beauty o'er-snowed and bareness everywhere. (lines 1–8)

The ageing process, described using the familiar seasonal model, leaves the adolescent's valued beauty subject to the will of Time. The familiar binary of life/death in a culture that included momento mori and motifs like the danse macabre (Neill, 1997) is imagined in more acute terms when the flowering potential of adolescence is starkly threatened with decline. The subject of 'Sonnet 5' is only offered the lifeline of 'summer's distillation' (line 9), where timely advantage must be taken to harvest his adolescent beauty once 'ripeness' is achieved. Through producing offspring, or 'flowers distilled' (line 13), once adolescent maturation is complete and adulthood achieved, the young man can work against the temporary nature of his own adolescence and, as the plant/floral imagery continues, hold off the image of going to seed, or ill-smelling rottenness: 'Leese but their show; their substance still lives sweet' (line 14).

While the threat is less obvious than Theseus's words to Hermia, the young man of the sonnets is subjected to a particularly disturbing self-image, because his silence means he is unable to articulate his own reworking of the plant metaphor. He becomes re-imagined somewhat relentlessly as a failing rose across *The Sonnets*. Moreover, as Alanna Skuse has highlighted, the recurring concept of the 'canker' in *The Sonnets* heightens the threat in the horticultural imagining of adolescence by aligning the metaphor for ageing with images of cancer (2014, 2015). For Skuse, the allusion 'sharpen[s] the imagery of roses and worms with reference to intense corporeal suffering, trading on public fears of a disease with mysterious causes and no effective cure' (2014: 255). Skuse takes her reading further, suggesting that connections to cancer, 'paradigmatically a woman's disease' (2014: 246) due to their cooler, moister bodies, may implicate the male adolescent as feminised. Skuse reads the 'spot' that mars the young man's beauty in 'Sonnet 95' as 'associated with hymeneal or menstrual blood' (2014: 254). The cankered bloom, understood through early modern ideas about bodily cancers, may be seen to take on feminine qualities.

However, the feminising function of the floral-canker language used in the poems may risk being overstated. While the gender ambiguity at work in Shakespeare's *Sonnets* is undeniable and the focus of much compelling scholarship (De Grazia, 1993; Schiffer, 2000; Nelles, 2009), the connection 'between floral and female bodies' that Skuse draws upon was not, as has been shown, an inevitable one (2015: 45). The adolescent's cankered flower in *The Sonnets* fits with Shakespeare's other representations of adolescence, where gender is not immediately compromised in its use. Shakespeare typically uses horticultural canker images, where a 'canker' is a caterpillar, that relate to contemporary concerns about adolescence as an age susceptible to ruin. The image of a cankered bloom, where the tender flower is devoured by a garden pest, especially lent itself to expressing how male and female adolescence could be threatened by rottenness. In *The Two Gentlemen of Verona*, for example, Valentine advises Proteus to take care in his impassioned love suit lest foolish actions mar his progression to adulthood in similar terms:

> And writers say, 'As the most forward bud,
> Is eaten by the canker ere it blow,
> Even so by love the young and tender wit
> Is turned to folly, blasting in the bud,
> Losing his verdure even in the prime
> And all the fair effects of future hopes.' (1.1.45–50)

Proteus is warned not to risk the nature of his 'prime' adulthood by corrupting his budding, adolescent masculinity. Romeo's preoccupation with Rosaline in *Romeo and Juliet* is likewise observed as an unproductive infatuation: 'As is the bud bit with an envious worm / Ere he can spread his sweet leaves to the air / Or dedicate his beauty to the same' (1.1.146–8). In *Hamlet*, Laertes provides a similar age-specific warning to Ophelia: 'The canker galls the infants of the spring / Too oft before their buttons be disclos'd, / And in the morn and liquid dew of youth / Contagious blastments are most imminent' (1.3.38–41). The flower of male adolescence could, like that of female adolescence, be spoiled before it might bloom. Male and female 'flowerings' were imagined as opening buds that could become blown and blasted to a state of rottenness in a way that bypassed the anticipated full bloom and ripeness of pleasing adulthood.

The flowering age of the human life cycle, then, was recognised as both a promising and necessary stage through which the transition into a 'ripe' adult state was achieved and also the stage of life that could circumvent such ripeness altogether, prematurely thrusting the individual into a state of decline. Richard Mulcaster, an early modern educator and instructor to young actors, uses canker imagery to depict the corruption of flowering adolescence that is achieved through rushing a (male) child's educational development and sending him to university before he is ready: 'The cankar that consumeth all, and causeth all this euill is haste, an *vnaduised, rashe, hedlong counsellour*, and then most pernicious when it hath either some apparence in reason that the child is ripe' (1581: 262). Timely and appropriate responses to the age of an individual are advised by Mulcaster: it 'best is to ripe at leasure' (1581: 259). Mulcaster asserts that if due care is not taken over the particular needs of growing children, then the child might expect a spoiled adulthood. Taking advantage of the horticultural metaphor, Mulcaster likens the rushing of a child's education to the picking of unripe fruit that prove unpalatable and must be thrown away: 'The defect to plucke before ripenes, breedes ill in the partie which tasteth therof, and causeth the thing after a bite or two to be cast away' (1581: 259). Once again, the anticipated ripeness of adulthood is re-imagined as ruined; a disturbed process of ripening produces unusable fruit.

Early modern writers could, therefore, manipulate the metaphor of the cankered bloom/ripening fruit modelling of adolescence in different ways: the canker is the adolescent's resistance to a reproductive future in Shakespeare's *Sonnets*, while haste is the disrupting factor in Mulcaster's treatise about education. However, such imagery rested upon the same accepted cultural image of adolescence being the time of flowering, when the potential of an individual can be fulfilled or lost. As such, formulations of the comparative modelling of adolescence against old age, and of cankered blooms, could be used to represent male and female adolescence. The corrupted bloom, cut off in its movement towards an affirmative 'ripeness', and the promise of fruit regularly turned the positive flowering image of adolescence prematurely into one of rottenness.

So far, the comparisons made in early modern culture between adolescent flowers and old age's decline can be seen to create a hostile image, where the comparison between ages threatens the 'rotting' implications of *not* fulfilling the promise of adolescence. However, the example of Octavius, where his 'rose of youth', marks him as the emergent successor to Antony is also suggestive of a means by which adolescence could be set alongside older age in a more positive guise. Although Octavius's rise is not itself a source of celebration in *Antony and Cleopatra*, the normative framing of progressive ageing, where the young follow the path of an older generation, can be reassuring. The pairing of an emergent state of adolescence with declining old age can, as such, be used to suggest life's continuation, and the realisation as well as the ruin of adolescent promise.

In *As You Like It* we find an example of this positive modelling of adolescence against old age. In the pairing of Orlando with his elderly servant, Adam, a stark contrast between characters is made that informs the play's exploration of Orlando's esteemed adolescence. In *As You Like It*, the elderly Adam and the adolescent Orlando typically appear onstage together during the first half of the play (1.1, 2.3, 2.6, 2.7, 3.2), with Adam only really being substituted for, and superseded by, Rosalind as a stage partner for Orlando in scenes that develop the couple's courtship. The regular pairing of Adam and Orlando provides, it seems, a relatively simple and effective way of staging characters' ages in *As You Like It*, where actors and playwrights could make use of cultural motifs about life stages to portray ages on stage that would not have matched their own biological age. Indeed, Burbage may have represented the adolescent Orlando alongside Shakespeare, who was only three years Burbage's senior, seeing as some scholars suggest that

Shakespeare played Adam in this coupling of characters in *As You Like It* (Shapiro, 2005: 216–25).

Orlando and Adam enter and exit the first scene of *As You Like It* together, with the opening speeches establishing Orlando's adolescence quickly: Orlando identifies himself as the youngest brother in his family and complains that he is being denied the 'good education' (1.1.57) and 'exercises as may become a gentleman' (1.1.57–8). Orlando, we might say, desires the kind of education and experiences depicted by Henry Peacham in his advice book for adolescent gentlemen that started this chapter. Adam's old age is likewise verbally stressed in the opening scene through his expressions of familiarity with the rule of Orlando's deceased father (1.1.53–4, 71–2), Oliver's insult of 'old dog' (69), and Adam's own comments about no longer having teeth (70). The image of toothless old age is famously echoed in the 'sans teeth' description from Jaques's speech about the 'seven ages of man', which helps firmly locate Adam in the last stage of the life cycle (2.7.166).

Adam and Orlando, who 'go along together' (2.3.66) for much of the play, indicate a purposeful grouping that draws upon the familiar comparative model for life stages. Adam, for example, positions himself as old in the following way: 'From seventeen years till now almost fourscore / Here lived I, but now live here no more. / At seventeen years, many their fortunes seek, / But at fourscore, it is too late a week' (2.3.71–4). Adam's speech identifies his character as old; he has loyally served Orlando's father for over sixty years. The way the words construct an understanding of Adam's old age also, however, reflects upon Adam's adolescent self, where promise and adventure would, he says, be favourably encountered. Stood next to his adolescent master, who has already expressed his desire to seek his own fortune ('give me / the poor allottery my father left me by testament. With that / I will go buy my fortunes' (1.1.61–3)), the description conflates Adam's reflection upon his own life with what is being viewed onstage in the comparative performance of adolescence and old age. There may even be a gesture towards Orlando in Adam's speech, as the age of seventeen is imagined. That Adam is no longer the adolescent he describes makes Adam's own vulnerability evident in the same moment that his stage partner, Orlando, is identifiable as the old man's adolescent counterpart. Orlando *does* have the ability to make something of an apparently unfortunate state and it is with his character that the adventurous plot of the comedy will lie. Such directive speeches make clear the comparative staging of age, as Orlando as adolescent is positioned, to some degree, in opposition to the elderly Adam. As in La Perrière's poem that accompanies *Emblem XII* from his collection, old age and adolescence are set in a familiar comparative mould, where 'Youth' is 'hote and voyd of care and dread / The aged cold, and full of doubts and feares' (1614: B4ʳ). The presence of Adam, especially early on in the play, helps fashion Orlando's age because adolescence and old age are recognisable companions in early modern culture.

The pairing often, however, also encourages meaning beyond a simple contrast between Orlando's age of promise and Adam's age of decline. After the play's early scenes, Orlando and Adam are also commonly understood through merging the characteristics typically associated with the respective ages of adolescence and old age. For example, Adam vows to continue in loyal service to his master, characterising his old age as a 'lusty winter' (2.3.52). Adam shows an ability to resist and react to assumptions about his physical strength in old age, responding to the demands of his circumstances in a way that shows the potential for adolescent qualities to be retained in older age. As Christopher Martin has observed in his discussion of *King Lear*, images of physical decline can be powerfully accompanied by contrasting depictions of extraordinary strength, for example, where King Lear carries his murdered daughter onstage after killing her attackers (2012: 137–75). Such a moment in *King Lear* can, moreover, signify the resilient strength of an older generation who have 'borne most' (5.3.301) in an action that also registers the tragic nature of the inversion. The demonstration of strength from an older character is a reaction demanded by external injustices that are responsible for the death of Cordelia, a 'young [...] and true' (1.1.104) character. In both the characterisation of Adam and Lear, these moments that resist the framing of old age as a declined physical state are positively presented, and somewhat redemptive in the case of Lear (Martin, 2012: 137–75). The resistance is admirable and goes some way towards undermining hostile depictions of old age. Such resistance in Shakespeare, however, is also unsustainable. Lear's actions are so powerful because they make an older character's demonstrable strength self-referential in recalling, as it subverts, images of physical decline that have also informed the character. In the case of Lear, his actions have resonance because we have only moments before seen the character wearied and battered on the heath: even with such suffering, Lear can muster admirable strength.

Exceptional moments of adolescent vigour do not usually last in Shakespearean depictions of older age. The normalised trajectory of life that sees ageing towards death is typically reinstated. Lear dies moments after his demonstration of physical strength, and Adam, having followed his master with gusto into the forest, lies down onstage ready to die in a comic styling of his decline in Act 2, Scene 6: 'Here lie I down and measure out my grave' (2). Unlike Lear, Adam survives through the physical aid offered by Orlando ('thou liest in the bleak air. / Come, I will bear thee to some shelter' (2.6.13–14)) and then the Duke's men in the Forest of Arden (2.7.166–200). Adam and Lear are not 'made young' by assuming adolescent traits of physical strength, it seems. Such acts, if anything, can even be seen to hasten the subsequent physical decline of a character. It is, however, this willingness to assume 'adolescent' strengths that do not accord with how the character's age has otherwise been performed that seems to broaden the characterisation of old age. By exerting physical strength, the elderly character physically enacts the borrowed mantle of esteemed adolescence to underscore recognisable virtues that persist in old age: valour, spiritual strength, and loyalty, to name a few.

Orlando's adolescence is also articulated in *As You Like It* by appropriating ideas more typically associated with latter stages of the life cycle in the familiar elision of ripening and rotting imagery. Adam is told by his adolescent master that 'thou prun'st a rotten tree / That cannot so much as a blossom yield / In lieu of all thy pains and husbandry' (2.3.63–5). Disruption to Orlando's development in adolescence, here as the result of an obstructive brother, is described using the common metaphor of the plant that is unable to flower. Orlando fears he ripens only towards rottenness due to the compromised circumstances of his maturation. That the elderly Adam is identified as a figure who tends to Orlando's development ('thou prun'st') suggests interdependence between generations. As Nina Taunton observes, representations of old age in early modern literature should be treated 'not only as a bipolar opposite to youth' (2006: 21). Adam is not solely the foil to Orlando's adolescent image; his presence also helps characterise Orlando's adolescence through the pair's shared features that could continue across the human life cycle. Adam's name, which remains the same as that used in Lodge's *Rosalynde*, binds Orlando's articulations of frustrated growth to a companion whose name would likely have reminded an early modern Christian audience of human history as it is outlined in the Bible. Adam, who tended the Garden of Eden, and whose actions introduced mortality to human life, looms as part of the loyal servant's characterisation. That the mortal state is already corrupted through Original Sin can be read in Orlando's image of the rotten tree. Adam's physical representation as old alongside the adolescent Orlando, moreover, could encourage a visual connection akin to the dance macabre, where Man's inevitable mortal fate is part of this pairing onstage.

In this vein, the physical articulation of the connections between adolescence and old age occurs most powerfully in *As You Like It* through the staging of exits and entrances across Act 2 scenes 6 and 7, where Orlando carries Adam upon his back. The pair's re-entry onto the stage takes place following the final lines of Jaques's 'Seven Ages of Man' speech that concludes with the declined image of Man: 'Sans teeth, sans eyes, sans taste, sans everything' (2.7.166). The verbal framing of the pair's entry – literally the actors' cues to enter the scene – encourages attention be paid to the elderly figure's state, most obviously Adam in this moment. By being carried in by his companion, however, an understanding of the elderly Adam also hinges upon the representation of Orlando in the scene. As Philip D. Collington (2006: 163) has suggested, this staging of an older man being carried by a younger one is emblematic, drawing upon the image of Aeneas bearing his father out of Troy, used, for example, in Geoffrey Whitney's *A Choice of Emblemes* (1586). Read as a direct enactment of the emblem, entitled in Whitney as 'Pietas filiorum in parentes', the staging of Orlando and Adam's entrance includes, as Collington argues, 'the traditional image of filial piety' (2006: 186). The emblematic moment suggests an older generation's dependence upon a younger one, which, for Collington, idealises an exceptional model of 'care of youth for old age' (2006: 186). Collington's reading highlights the social interdependence of generations in early modern society and the tensions that surround family interactions (see Semenza, 2011). This treatment of the scene, where adolescence and old age might materially depend on one another, elevates the presentation of adolescence but also keeps adolescence and old age somewhat conceptually separate in the representation.

However, further crossovers are suggested in the emblematic staging of the partnerships between adolescence and old age, because Orlando, our figure of adolescence, must bend his back to carry Adam. Descriptions of old age in early modern culture are suggestive of how an elderly physicality could be performed onstage. One key element that is repeated across early modern images of old age is a bent-back posture. It is common, for example, to hear about 'crooked age' in life cycle models (Cuffe, 1607: 121), and visual representations of old age used recurring motifs, regularly depicting old age through a figure's bent back and need of a stick (Martin, 2012: 137–75). Depictions of Shakespeare's older characters often include the feature of a walking aid. Lady Capulet, for example, mocks her elderly husband's desire to fight in the streets with the adolescents in *Romeo and Juliet* by suggesting that his plea for a 'sword' (1.1.70) be substituted for the 'crutch' (1.1.71). Lady Capulet assigns a literal 'prop', suggestive of a theatrical one, which indicates her husband's old age. Old Gobbo in *The Merchant of Venice* similarly describes his son using the metaphor of the supportive crutch, 'the very staff of / my age, my very prop!' (2.2.59–60), in a scene in which humour is drawn from the physical performance of cultural stereotypes about old age, where the son tricks his father because of his poor eyesight. The property of a walking stick, itself evidence of weak legs rather than a bent back per se, would have probably been most effective on stage when accompanied by the equally familiar image of a bent-back posture as signifiers of old age. The performer playing Adam as being 'almost fourscore' (2.3.71) would undoubtedly have made physical features associated with old age recognisable in the performance. Orlando's entrance with Adam in Act 2.7, moreover, appears to make further use of associations between old age and bent backs. Orlando simultaneously demonstrates adolescent strength by bearing the weight of his servant while he also mimics the stance of the old man he carries, and the final stage of life that Jaques has just ascribed to all men. That all are 'Adams' has Biblical resonance that underpins the 'many parts' that the individual experiences across the life cycle, as well as the parts an actor might perform in the representations of age as part of an acting company. These 'parts' are neatly captured through this emblematic staging of the familiar partnership of adolescence and old age.

The action of Orlando carrying Adam upon his back is potentially overladen with meanings pertinent to the early modern life cycle and, what is more, to the particular performance space of the play's first performance: The Globe. *As You Like It* was one of the first plays, possibly *the* first, staged in The Globe by the Lord Chamberlain's Men following the relocation of timbers of The Theatre (Stern, 2004: 14). The Globe, according to Tiffany Stern, was a space that was set up as a 'living metaphor' through performances that 'draw frequent attention to their own theatrical natures' (2004: 14). As an early play at The Globe, *As You Like It* may well have been used to advertise the company's theatrical skills in a scene that insists upon an ability to stage the Ages of Man in what was also probably a clever handling of the theatre's own motif: Atlas/Hercules carrying the globe (Stern, 2004: 16). Jaques's speech draws attention to its theatrical location by evoking the theatre's motto: 'All the world's a stage', but, as Stern highlights, Burbage as Orlando-bearing-Adam may also have repeated the visual motif that embellished flags for the new theatre. Burbage, who was certainly recognised as the company's 'star' player by 1599, was sometimes referred to as Hercules (Stern, 2004: 16). As an entrance that concludes Jaques's metatheatrical speech, it is likely that the presence of Burbage *as* the adolescent Orlando was made readily available to the audience responding to this moment in the play. Moreover, if scholars are right in suggesting that Shakespeare played Adam (Shapiro, 2005: 216–25), Jaques's speech may additionally advertise the theatre company's array of talent, so that the proficiency of Burbage and Shakespeare in conveying age-based characterisations are highlighted in a moment that applauds the particular skills of the company's star actor and its lead playwright.

The union of the adolescent Orlando and elderly Adam throughout the first half of *As You Like It* culminates and concludes with the physical and visual connecting of characters in Act 2, Scene 7. By the end of the scene, Adam is delivered into the care of the Duke within his forest court. But the pairing has made its mark upon our understanding of Orlando's adolescence. While the partnership of the adolescent and the old man works on a level of contrasts where vitality and decline are set in opposition, the duo also demonstrate how shared characteristics realise continuity across the life cycle. Adam's presence, though perhaps reminding an audience of human mortality, is not a negative influence upon Orlando adolescence: he is no canker-worm to the flower. Adam's old age is positively framed through his loyalty and longevity that supports rather than taints his stage partner's adolescent representation. Adam seeks to help rather than harm the adolescent's plight, and demonstrates that a positive ageing process can be achieved.

Contrasts and connections between adolescence and old age help position adolescence as the stage of life that offered the greatest opportunity for gaining self-knowledge, and where development and improvement underpinned the conditions of later life. As another emblem from Geoffrey Whitney's collection, 'Quere adolescens, vtere Senex', makes clear, the labours of adolescence culminate in the way old age will be experienced (1586: 50). The emblem depicts an old man comfortably housed with goods, while an adolescent labours in the field, accompanied by the words: 'for age thou toyle' (1586: line 2). While the image stresses material wealth and comfort, where the old man may 'vse thy goodes, which thou in yowthe haste wonne' (Whitney, 1586: line 5), the image identifies more broadly that certain models of old age might guide the actions of adolescence, because a 'cause and effect' relationship was recognised. After all, when Adam describes his old age in positive terms, as 'a lusty winter' (2.3.52), he does so with a clear sense of why this is the case: 'For in my youth I never did apply / Hot and rebellious liquors in my blood / Nor did not with unbashful forehead woo / The means of weakness and debility' (2.3.48–51). A well-managed adolescence precedes a comfortable old age. Such sentiment is palpable in the emblematic pairing of Adam and Orlando.

In *As You Like It*, then, a commendable adolescent and admirable old man accompany each other as complementary representatives of normative stages in the life cycle, where one anticipates the other. After all, the young man who can bear the weight of an older one is not an inversion of expected strength as in Lear's carrying of Cordelia. Orlando's physical efforts in striving to aid Adam, moreover, help him resist premature intrusions of decline upon his own maturation because his assumption of an Aeneas-like form indicates a promising future akin, perhaps, to the building of Rome. In *As You Like It*, the pairing of the elderly Adam with Orlando is a strategic one that bolsters a positive and culturally recognisable performance of adolescence. It also, no doubt, helped in the wider comparative staging of age across the play's characters that I discuss across the next three chapters, allowing Burbage to perform his part as an adolescent male, set in comparison with not only Adam but also Rosalind, whose interactions with Orlando feature as part of the play's wider strategic 'adolescent' stage couplings, where the comparative gendering of adolescent experiences come into play.

Gendering flowers and navigating rottenness during puberty

In the above section, I demonstrated that early modern adolescence, as the 'flowering' age, was regularly articulated and understood through a model that collapsed boundaries between 'ripening' adolescence and 'rotting' old age. This comparison between life stages was commonplace and available for use in theatrical constructions of characters' ages. However, this broad appreciation of 'flowers' and 'cankers' as age-specific imagery provides an important foundation, rather than a refined appreciation, for the ways in which such imagery might be put to use in gendered representations. Adolescent boys *could* clearly be likened to flowers without being feminised, and the threat of cankered blooms was not solely the concern of adolescent girls. Even the never truly feared position of Orlando's promising adolescence is articulated using ideas of rotting and hindered growth, where he 'cannot so much as a blossom yield' (2.3.64). And yet, while young men and women might all be budding flowers, the flowering process, which centred on changes to a 'ripening' pubescent humoral body, *was* understood to have significantly different corporeal and behavioural implications for males and females. This meant that a fashioning of gendered flowers could also be produced, particularly through conceptualising the threat of decline differently in relation to the male and female, who were accredited different formulations of agency when asserting control over the pubescent body.

A key point that can be taken from the examples used in the previous section is that boys and girls might be talked about in similar floral terms without gender identity being unclear. Often the context in which the flower imagery of adolescence is used is enough to articulate a gendered representation, as in the cited examples of Peacham discussing 'gardens' (1622: 20) of flowering university students, who would only have been male in the seventeenth century, and Mulcaster's more general fears about hasty harvest in relation to male adolescents' education (1581: 262). Orlando's anxieties about not fulfilling his potential and becoming a 'rotten' tree in *As You Like It* are, likewise, contextualised in relation to his concerns about being denied a gentleman's education and property rights. The 'flowering' promise of early modern male adolescence is often presented in light of discernibly 'manly' aspirations in early modern society.

As Samuel Crossman reminds his reader in *The Young Mans Monitor*, while adolescence may expose vulnerable bodies and minds to untimely decline, the adolescent male can also be duly celebrated as they pave the way for a productive adult future if these threats are circumvented: '*May your youth be as the Spring of loveliness; your riper years as the Summer for real fruitfulness*' (1665: 1). As much as horticultural 'ripening' imagery grouped individuals together by age, the adolescent's experience was bound to an understanding of their anticipated adulthood, their '*Summer*'. As such, the stages of life were subject to gendered features. How far the fruitful futures that are imagined in Crossman's model were deemed in the individual's control, and the extent to which an individual might be given credit for steering their way through adolescent dangers, in the threat of 'cankers', particularly deserves some careful consideration in relation to gender. While the promise and value attributed to adolescence was available to inform the adolescence of girls and boys in early modern culture, the nature of the negotiations required to avoid contamination does not seem to have typically played out in the same way for adolescent males and females.

Concerns about an adolescent's self-control over their pubescent body and the expression of burgeoning desire (underpinned by excess humoral heat in the body), for example, particularly positioned the adolescent female and male in different subject positions in relation to their bodily development. While pubescent males or females could suffer from kinds of love melancholy and be seen to be driven by desires beyond their control, it was female adolescents who were primarily subject to the condition of greensickness, as outlined in the introduction to this book. Understood in proximity to the threat of greensickness, female puberty saw girls' lives threatened by the bodily changes they underwent. Irregular menstrual bleeding, common for girls during puberty, could be interpreted as the retention of menstrual blood and imagined as the festering humours of greensickness. For girls, their 'flowers' of adolescence were very clearly more than metaphor, as menstruation became a physical process to which the language of promise and decline could be specifically ascribed. The broader imagery of 'flowering' adolescence becomes focused upon the adolescent female's menstrual health, and the culturally familiar image of adolescents becoming corrupted flowers achieves an uncomfortable proximity, if not symbiosis, with a physical condition that scrutinised the 'flowers' at the physical centre of female puberty.

Sharp describes how the blocked vessels of the greensick girl 'so spoil the making of blood, nothing but raw and corrupt humors are bred' as corruption spread across the body (1671: 195). As Lesel Dawson observes, the threat of greensickness loomed over female puberty and warned 'how quickly this ripeness will transform into rottenness if the sick virgin will not submit herself to her lover's cure' (2008: 60). Greensickness medicalised female puberty in terms of a disease that heightened the propensity for a female's adolescent promise to collapse into decline by rooting this threat *within* the body. While the adolescent male might commonly be represented as making choices that would taint his bloom, and these ill-considered actions were seen as manifestations of adolescent humoral heatedness, the female could find herself involuntarily subject to a contamination that originated in the body that went beyond excesses in heat, as blood congealed and humours corrupted. While the sexual liberties of masculine adolescence were certainly thought capable of damaging the male body (and male reputation) if such liberties went too far, the threat of disorderly sexual desire, and its associations with promoting premature rottenness, sat at the centre of medical diagnoses that connected properties of the 'heated' female pubescent body more easily with disease. As King observes, 'Western medical tradition constructed female puberty as a problem' (2004: 71). Greensickness threatened physical damage that placed the adolescent female in a particularly precarious situation: she must, as ever, abide by codes of female chastity, but failure to address imbalances according to her pubescent body could also hasten her decline into illness. Inaction as well as action on the adolescent female's part threatened perils related to greensickness.

The early modern humoral body was always underscored by a 'body/mind overlap' (Wynne-Smith, 2008: 463) that meant bodily alterations were bound to identity. However, the particular rootedness of the pubescent female's 'flowerings' and 'contagions' within the body seems to have aided the way that early modern culture framed the 'disorderly' elements of female maturation as being especially beyond the adolescent's own ability to avoid. As my reading of Ophelia's rue suggests, efforts at self-regulation and remedial treatments were imaginable in early modern culture, but 'signs' of illness could also justify the ways in which the 'well' around the greensick female would guide a young woman to safety, and interventions on behalf of a greensick female could include the arrangement of marriages and sexual intercourse as the 'cure' for her sexual malady (see King, 2004; Potter, 2002, 2013). The threatening imagery of abrupt decay that was adopted to characterise greensickness thus made use of age-appropriate imagery in a pointedly gendered way, cultivating a distrust of female sexual desire and the maturing and mature female body. Gonzaga, in Robert Greene's *Mamillia*, for example, anticipates a future maligned by disease or sexual indiscretion for his daughter who is yet unmarried:

> the grasse being ready for the sieth [scythe], would wither if it were not cut; and the apples being rype, for want of plucking would rotte on the tree; that his daughter being at the age of twentie yeeres, would either fall into greensickness for want of a husband, or els if she scaped that disease, incurre a farther inconvenience [in seeking sexual satisfaction outside of marriage]. (1583: 8)

At twenty years old, the young woman who is described would likely still be considered an adolescent in early modern terms, her age being a little younger than the average age at which women married (Ingram, 1987: 129). Yet the father's account contemplates images of over-ripeness and greensickness that already loom for his daughter. Gonzaga's concerns suggest that female sexual maturity, whether emergent or fully achieved, create particular anxieties about an unused fruitfulness that readily conflates images of ripeness with rottenness. Sickness or shame, in seeking sex outside of marriage, are all that Gonzago can envisage for his daughter's future, which hinges not on the daughter's possible self-management in terms of modifying her humoral heat, but on whether a marriage can be arranged to avoid dangerous sexual impulses.

Theseus's threat to Hermia in *A Midsummer Night's Dream*, therefore, takes on an additional urgency that is linked to Hermia's gendered adolescence. It is perhaps not a future where Hermia languishes in lengthy celibate solitude across her lifespan that Theseus describes, but an immediate and impending threat to her adolescent promise and health. By swiftly converting the image of a beautiful rose into a withered flower on a 'virgin thorn', Theseus's observations about Hermia seem to utilise familiar ideas about the 'virgin's disease' of greensickness. Moreover, Theseus's partnering of Hermia with Demetrius can also suggest efforts at remedial action, whereby social and physical redemption for the potentially greensick girl is achieved through a man (of her father and Theseus's choosing) and his reproductive body.

By comparison, the humoral logic that depicted girls as potentially sick due to puberty was applied to male adolescents in a way that allowed room for similar heated, rash behaviour to be interpreted as evidence of promising physical maturation. In adulthood, such behaviour would need to be kept in check to balance virility with expectations of manly self-control (Schoenfeldt, 1999). However, as a phase that was temporary in the adolescent's progression towards adulthood, energetic liberties did not inevitably have to be framed as negative for the pubescent male. Donald Lupton's *Emblems of Rarities*, for example, observed that a care-free outlook should be regarded as appropriate to male adolescence, and that an exaggerated seriousness at this time could have detrimental physical and mental consequences: 'feare and unquietnesse of minde in youth, doth much enervate and weaken the strength of the body, and a sad and heavy spirit dryeth the bones too much so that such a body cannot take his just encrease' (1636: 88). Indeed, here it is imposed restraint upon the adolescent male's spirit that appears harmful, inhibiting development and threatening the drier bodily state of older age. Adolescence, in a sense, should be left to run its course in young men as efforts to check their behaviour could be damaging or deemed futile. For example, one collection of emblems included the motto: 'Nothing can temper yong mens rage, / 'Till they be tamed with old age' (La Perrière, 1614: Bv^r). The process of ageing here shapes and moderates masculinity; intervention and limitations upon the masculine self, the model concedes, have little point and the male adolescent is permitted personal liberty during his maturation. The humoral excesses associated with the production of reproductive seed that produced concerns about greensickness in adolescent girls, permitted the male adolescent be applauded – or at least treated as medically well – for the signs of impending manhood that his lightness of spirit or even his rage would be thought to demonstrate. In being a male, moreover, the life-cycle trajectory anticipates that the individual will have the chance to assert control over such impulses in adulthood. By contrast, unruliness in girlhood, if articulated as sexual unruliness and diagnosed as greensickness, could not so easily be reversed, redeemed, or celebrated, as scholarship about constructions of femininity has repeatedly shown (Hull, 1982; Newman, 1991; Paster, 1993).

The scope for male adolescents to 'flower' and make redeemable mistakes is notably permitted for some male characters in Shakespearean drama. In *As You Like It*, Oliver, though not the virtuous adolescent like the celebrated Orlando in the play, is forgiven and altered in his movement into adulthood through timely conversion to a loving brother and his forging of a hasty love match. Both brothers become good men by different routes, albeit with Orlando's being the more reassuringly predictable trajectory. In Lodge's 'source-text' for the play, *Rosalynde* (1590), for example, we might note that the older brother's fate is starkly different, and his unrepentant mistreatment of his brother leads to his death as his sibling forcibly reclaims his position in the family. For the adolescent male, however, though the riskier route through adolescent errors did not guarantee a positive transition into adulthood, both models were potentially available and permitted the male adolescent some license to transgress. Tiffany Stern notes how the performance of Oliver's transformed state in *As You Like It* seems to purposely disorientate the audience (2004: 107). Attired in a new costume, the actor playing Oliver returns to the stage. While the audience might recognise the same actor, the common practice of character doubling and the elusive speech that Oliver provides make confirmation of identity difficult. After describing the lion's attack on Orlando from an oddly distanced position, Oliver acknowledges his shift in character 'Twas I: but 'tis not I' (4.3.134). Oliver's transformation from cruel brother into promising young man works within the scope of early modern framings of masculine adolescence and is staged in a way that may remind an audience that such conversions cannot simply be expected. And yet, the existence of both Orlando and Oliver in *As You Like It* testifies to the early modern double standards whereby the errors of masculine adolescence can be excused and not leave permanent marks upon the individual, except, perhaps, valuable self-knowledge.

The leniency upon male adolescents in early modern culture here seems to recall the Bible's forgiveness of the prodigal son. Christian doctrine includes some scope for young women to avoid reproach, as lectures published by George Abbott suggest, including the forgiveness of the 'adulterous harlot' (1600: 489) alongside the prodigal son. However, as Lamb's study of early modern books for children has shown, instructions for children were largely gendered, where the female reader was imagined as passive and strictly bound to ideas of virtue (2018: 151–90). Robert Abbot's *Milk for Babes*, which provided catechisms for children, certainly seems to fashion acceptably wayward behaviour as male-orientated in Christian teachings; the godly father's forgiveness is articulated most clearly through male affective bonds, where 'a prodigall son is a son still' (1646: 187). Though not regarded as straightforward (and narratives of young men whose misdemeanours bring ruin abound),[7] masculine adolescence was contemplated in a way that allowed the adolescent to toy with ruinous behaviour and not incur the horrors of premature rotting, something that seems far less imaginable for female adolescents for whom a diagnosis of greensickness loomed.

While early modern culture used the same agricultural language of adolescence to contemplate male and female, the issue of *where* the 'flowering' subject can be positioned in relation to the pubescent changes taking place in their bodies remains key to the gendering of adolescence in early modern culture. For example, although the gender ambiguity at work in Shakespeare's sonnets is more complex than can be fully addressed here, and the canker-rose subject of *The Sonnets* can be seen to resemble Hermia in the singularity with which physical beauty and reproduction are treated for the adolescent subjects, there are also noteworthy differences in the imagery used for Hermia and the lovely male adolescent. Having chosen to elope with Lysander, an action of her adolescence that is geared to shape the trajectory of her adult life, Hermia's loss of her lover's affections provokes the accusation that Helena is a 'canker blossom' and a 'thief of love' (3.2.282, 283). In *A Midsummer Night's Dream*, Hermia depicts not only the image of a parasite devouring a blossoming love, but also the marring of her own flowering adolescence, and with it the promise of her future, which likewise becomes tainted. Here, an important difference emerges between Hermia and the 'cankered' adolescent who is the subject of *The Sonnets*. The subject of *The Sonnets* seems to be the cause of his own mismanaged adolescence, but Hermia identifies the canker as being imposed wilfully by another and, having so powerfully reclaimed the floral motif of her life cycle in her earlier exchanges with Theseus, finds herself disempowered and, in a sense 'de-flowered', by the actions of others.

Hermia's situation again seems to suggest gendered double standards regarding the limitations of the adolescent's licensed self-assertion. Although Hermia is physically chaste in her interactions with Lysander in the forest, her elopement as adolescent 'sport' seems to threaten to overstep the parameters of the honourable conduct that Celia warns Rosalind about in *As You Like It* (1.2.23). Hermia's virtue, made evident through constancy in affection, can only carry through into adulthood if Lysander is likewise constant in his affections. Hermia's dalliances in adolescence, and the subsequent promise of her future selfhood, end up determined by the actions and affections of a changeable young man (one who is tellingly under the influence of the magic 'flower' used by Oberon and Puck). Hermia's reputation is salvaged because Lysander, who can afford to be changeable in his adolescence, returns to her side by the end of *A Midsummer Night's Dream*. While Hermia finally seems to get her way in a pairing with Lysander, she has to endure a nightmarish night in the forest so that her forthright demonstration of will can be identified as feminine constancy. Avoiding a 'canker' becomes less about Hermia's own actions and intent desires and more about Lysander and an older generation of men changing their minds to allow the match.

By contrast, the adolescent male of *The Sonnets* seems to determine the nature of his own flowering state. Cankered or otherwise, the male subject of these sonnets demonstrates distance from the overtly negotiated self-assertions of feminine adolescence that are capped by ideas about female chastity. The silent subject of *The Sonnets* may be unable to respond in words that Hermia, at times, uses to assert her will, but the subject's immovable stance that is constructed by the speaker also suggests that the adolescent of *The Sonnets* enacts a self-willed, if lamented, self-destruction: 'Making a famine where abundance lies – / Thyself thy foe, to thy sweet self too cruel' ('Sonnet 1': lines 7–8). The young man can determine whether cankers corrupt his adolescence and seems to have the choice that Hermia realistically does not, because he can elect to make a drastic about-turn in his behaviour.

Adolescence, as I will show across the chapters of this book, could afford female adolescents scope to broaden horizons and engage in 'sport' (*As You Like It*: 1.2.23). However, the adolescent female's heated blood was not afforded freedoms equivalent to the heated blood of masculinity if female chastity came under question. An older brother might seek the death of his younger sibling and repent in time for the comic conclusion of *As You Like It*. Lysander and Demetrius might pursue Hermia and Helena interchangeably through the woods as part of their 'may day' exploits in *A Midsummer Night's Dream*. Although Theseus suggests some imagistic scope for ideas about age to push constructions of femininity in this manner, the love plots of *Midsummer Night's Dream* ultimately stress that sexual fidelity is the remit of mortal women across the life cycle, and even fairy queens can find themselves subjected to patriarchal will in such matters. The tempered conclusion of female adolescence, which can include assertions of personal will, usually also depends upon male acquiescence for cankers to be avoided.

In this sense, it is clear that early modern dramas do largely re-inscribe cultural double-standards surrounding male and female adolescence. Oberon's interventions, after all, restore patriarchal order whereby Helena, likened to Ovid's 'Daphne', who no longer 'holds the chase' (2.1.231) in sexual relations. And yet, the generic requirements of *A Midsummer Night's Dream* also leave some space for the maturing female's perspective to warrant attention in a way that subverts the typically privileged position of the male adolescent and his assertions of agency during his maturation.[8] Demetrius is compellingly problematic as an adolescent in *A Midsummer Night's Dream*. While Demetrius demonstrates the stereotypical changeability of male adolescence, in switching his affections from Helena to Hermia, his agency is removed, it seems, as punishment for this inconstancy. As he moves towards an adult marital union with Helena, Demetrius is still under the magical influence of the play's purple flower. The adolescent Demetrius, therefore, somewhat symbolically concludes the play influenced by a flower that is not of his own selection, offering a narrative redemption for the character against his will, while Helena obtains the husband she desires.

Within its generic framework of comedy, it may be that *A Midsummer Night's Dream* needs to uphold feminine virtues and so accommodate its characters' girlhood desires, even at the expense of the adolescent males in the play. Linda Bamber (1982) has, after all, suggested that comedy offers far more scope for in depth and varied explorations of female subjectivity than male-centred tragedy in the Shakespearean corpus. As part of a comedy, Demetrius's subjection to another's will seems necessary for acceptable marital pairings to be made in line with the 'constant' affections of the play's female adolescents. This situation is similar to that of Angelo in *Measure for Measure* and Bertram in *All's Well That Ends Well*, where 'bed tricks' are used to deceive male characters into having sex with women they have rejected, but where the women in question have remained constant in their love. Like Demetrius, Angelo and Bertram are denied assertion of their will, albeit not through the influence of a magical flower, but through disturbing episodes of veiled rape as young women obtain the men they desire (see Aebischer, 2008). The use of a 'bed trick' in Thomas Middleton and William Rowley's tragedy *The Changeling* offers a counterpoint for viewing the comic female's constant, and so validated, assertion of 'chaste' desire. The changeable nature of Beatrice-Joanna's affections, moving from Alonso to

Alsemero at the start of *The Changeling*, seem to rework how the 'unvirtuous' Beatrice-Joanna is positioned, including her physical removal from the bed trick of the play. In arranging the switch between the virginal Diaphanta and herself, this time to consummate her own marriage to Alsemero, Beatrice-Joanna's horrifying predicament suggests how the early modern female is bound to ideas about sexual constancy, as her own body becomes reserved for a man she despises: DeFlores, a man whose name means 'deflower'. Having bargained for Beatrice-Joanna's virginity in the murderous plot to remove Alonso, DeFlores seems to have tied Beatrice-Joanna's body only to him. The female's sexual constancy is again retained in a perverse manner, this time outside Beatrice-Joanna's marriage to Alsemero, and against the young female's own desires, because, it seems, unlike our comic heroines, Beatrice-Joanna's desires have tellingly been shown to be changeable.

In Shakespearean romantic comedies, male agency is, in fact, regularly compromised and this seems to be a consequence of the restrictive model of female chastity that, in a comedy, makes accommodating the desires of Helena (*A Midsummer Night's Dream*), Mariana (*Measure for Measure*), and Helen (*All's Well That Ends Well*) a necessity. For all to end 'happily', the strict bounds upon sexual behaviour during female puberty ends up superseding the more typical framing of male adolescence as a time when young men can be changeable in their affections and progress to an acceptable model of adulthood. Therefore, in the fictional generic bounds of comedy, female flowering appears somewhat protected from suffering permanent contagion if the character's own will abides by a constant affection to a particular man. This is not the same as permitting equal sexual freedoms to adolescent male and female characters, clearly disallowing anything beyond monogamous, heteronormative unions and where characters like Isabella in *Measure for Measure* cannot be happily accommodated. Isabella's intended celibacy is, as we saw with Hermia in *A Midsummer Night's Dream*, hard for Shakespeare's powerful male characters to imagine, and the result is a narrative in which male characters attempt to coerce Isabella into sex and marriage (Aebischer, 2008). However, the female adolescent of comedy can, sometimes, obtain her sexual desires without these being framed as unruly. So, while Shakespeare reminds us that Romeo *is* allowed to drop his attachment to Rosaline in *Romeo and Juliet*, and such actions remain unthinkable for any 'virtuous' female character, comic love plots can also, somewhat unexpectedly, place value upon the female's self-assertion as part of the imagined transitions between 'flowering' adolescence and adulthood. Such outspoken adolescent girl characters are, we will see, actually quite common in Shakespearean plays, which, in turn, contributed to wider cultural constructions of female adolescence that kept girls sexually 'modest' but also recognised settings for their celebrated assertiveness.

By the end of *A Midsummer Night's Dream*, Hermia circumnavigates the image of the withered and cankered bloom, it seems, largely because her adolescent will can be articulated as sexual fidelity and accommodated within the comic mould. This theatrical formula suggests space in the early modern cultural imagination to consider, and root for, adolescent females in ways that move beyond the untrusting stance expressed towards the assertive 'green girl' (*Hamlet* 1.3.100). As I will show across the subsequent chapters of this book, the female adolescent character who is wilful and chaste, especially if she is the proponent for her own chastity, provides a recognisable means by which girls could assert control over cultural responses to their 'heated' bodies and receive recognition for being commendably outspoken.

Notes

1 David Crystal and Ben Crystal's definitions of 'hourly' also suggest scope for further wordplay, where the word's pronunciation also suggests the secondary meaning of 'like a whore' (2002: 'hourly').
2 See, for example, Sharp's description of reproduction (usually called 'generation'), where 'the yard [penis] is as it were the Plow' and 'Woman is the Patient or Ground to be tilled, who brings Seed also as well as the Man to sow the ground with' (Hobby, 1999: 32).
3 In Vivian Thomas and Nicki Faircloth's *Dictionary of Shakespeare's Plants and Gardens* (2016) the uses of roses are particularly noted for describing a 'woman of great beauty'. It should be noted, however, that Thomas and Faircloth do not limit their record to this usage. The same flower is also said to indicate 'health or vitality'.
4 Some readings suggest the nonsensical nature of Ophelia's floral props, which seems to underplay the pertinent symbolism of the scene's botanic aspects. See Bushnell (2003: 138).
5 The age disparity between Othello and Desdemona fashions Desdemona as an adolescent. Desdemona, who is of marriageable age, has rejected her initial suitors and disobeyed her father in secretly marrying Othello. Brabanzio fears that Othello has 'Abused her delicate youth' (1.2.74) in enthralling his daughter.
6 Stephen Booth observes the 'notoriously creative scholarship' (1977: 546) involved in attempting to identify the addressee for *The Sonnets* in his analytical notes for his edition of the poems.
7 John Ford's *The Broken Heart*, for example, presents an interesting formulation of adolescent mistakes: Ithocles's treatment of his sister and her beloved Orgilus sets in motion a plot wherein rash adolescents disrupt each other's progression to adulthood. Ithocles, who disregards the pre-contracted bond between Penthea and Orgilus, weds Penthea to the much older Bassanes before

the play begins. Ithocles becomes a problematic villain, however, in that he shows regret for what has taken place and blames the impulsiveness of his adolescence (2008: 2.2.44–9).
8 Ben-Amos's study of work opportunities for adolescents notes that, while adolescence granted young women some scope for autonomy and power, such opportunities were more varied and more easily available to young men (1994: 28–89, 50–1).

2

Beards and blushes: fertile complexions in Shakespeare's plays

> The colour of the Humours, unlesse they retire into the most inward parts of the Body, appeares evidently in the skinne: but chiefly in the Face, because that the skinne of that part is more thin and fine, then of any other part; and therefore the more apt to receive the tincture of the Putrified Humours. (Jacques Ferrand, 1640: 123–4)

As we have seen, in early modern culture it was understood that puberty involved important bodily changes for the adolescent male and female.[1] Excess heat and moisture was emitted from developing 'seed' and this manifested as physical developments across the body, which were identified as appropriate to the sex of the maturing individual. For example, humidity emitting from the seed of the male was thought to be subject to greater heat than in the female, rising higher in the body to significantly alter vocal chords, while humidity in the female was commonly associated with swelling breasts (Elam, 1996; Read, 2013: 47–8). Similarly, the faces of adolescent boys and girls were noted for the way that their humoral dispositions could be registered. The production and development of 'hot' generative seed that sat at the centre of early modern ideas about puberty was a process that remained largely concealed within the body itself. However, as Ferrand's observations from *Erotomania* demonstrate, this did not mean that the humoral qualities of this seed were considered inaccessible to those who could recognise and understand the signs that such development left elsewhere upon the body.

The face was especially thought to offer a site where humoral change 'appears evidently in the skinne'. As Ferrand articulates, faces 'receive[d] the tincture' of the humoral changes at work in the more hidden recesses of the body, explaining the dual meaning of 'complexion' in early modern culture, where an individual's complexion could mean their humoral disposition, more broadly, as well as the particular and connected meaning of the appearance of the skin upon someone's face. While this ability to read humours through the evidence of faces was something that might be used in relation to any age or gender (and we might, moreover, consider how often facial complexion is used in the diagnosis of sickness or the description of extreme emotion), the humoral excesses of heat and moisture that were associated with puberty lead to especial attention being paid to facial signs that offered evidence of sexual maturation taking place. Facial complexions could be studied for signs of emergent sexual maturity.

In this chapter, I explore how the facial adornments of beards and blushes were interpreted in relation to puberty. I discuss how early modern medical writings recognised symmetry and difference in female and male bodies, tracing how the movement of humoral heat and moisture appropriate to adolescence were made manifest through facial complexions. The evidence of maturation could be evaluated as providing a sign of deficiency and 'lack' in a discernibly non-adult body; however, such signs were also included in representations of promising growth and the age-appropriate development of the individual. As I demonstrate in this chapter, a variety of Shakespeare's plays drew upon the cultural and medical fashioning of pubescent 'heated' faces in its styling of beards and blushes in relation to adolescent characters.

Heated faces of adolescence: beards and blushes

Looking to an early modern adolescent's face enabled evaluation of their sexual maturation. This was especially the case for adolescent males, whose growth of facial hair was understood as being directly connected to the humoral qualities of their generative seed. Body hair, and particularly facial hair, was considered the humoral outgrowth of the maturing body; hair was a product of excess heat and moisture that abounded once generative seed was produced. Thomas Hill's *Contemplation of Mankinde* observes the connection between the man's development of a beard and his seed: 'The bearde in man (after the agreement of the aunctient writers) beginneth to appear in the neather jawe [...] through the heate and moisture, caried unto the same, from the forepart of the heade, drawne from the genitours' (1571: 145$^\text{r}$–6$^\text{v}$). For an adolescent male, the growth of facial hair was regarded as a promising sign of developing manliness. As Will Greenwood observed in his description of apparently alluring traits in matters of love: 'Hairinesse, saith *Aristotle*, is a signe of abundance of excrements' (1657: 87). The fuller the beard, the greater the indication of a man's reproductive strength. In medical writings, the absence of a beard was commonly associated with male infertility. In *The Womans Doctour*, for example, Nicholas Fonteyne noted that 'Barren men are commonly beardless' (1652: 131) and the surgeon John Tanner observed, in *The Hidden Treasures of the Art of*

Physick, that one sign of infertility in a man was 'if he hath no Beard' (1659: 346). The reproductive potential of a man was indicated by his ability to grow facial hair, which was itself a product of superfluous heat and moisture radiating from his appropriately masculine 'hot' seed.

An amusing anecdote from *Galenteo Espagnos*, a pamphlet from 1640, helps demonstrate both the importance that the beard might hold in confirming masculinity and the beard's association with genital condition in early modern culture:

> a smooth faced youth, without a Beard, being with his Wife, in his Chamber, a messenger came in thither, to looke for him, that had a message to deliver to him: and being there, and seeing them both so trimmed up, and one as well as the other, without a Beard, hee asked, which of their Worships was the Gentleman to whom hee was sent to, that hee might not bee mistaken in his message? then the Husband put off his Nightgeere, and resolved, no more to put it on, till hee should have a Beard. (Gracián, 1640: 206)

The show of manhood here comically requires exposure of the young man's genitals in the absence of his beard. Husband and wife cannot otherwise be distinguished, being 'trimmed up' in the same fashion, a description that suggests both clothing in the couple's non-gendered night-gear and the fashion of a beard's cut. Here the beard is completely absent for both parties. A clear reciprocal relationship between the beard and genitals is established; the beard and male genitals act as substitutes for each other when the other is not visible. The presence of a beard would, the scenario suggests, remove the husband's need to demonstrate his sex by revealing his penis.

The wit of the episode, however, does not only reside in the messenger's confusion; the biggest laugh is achieved through the husband's reaction. In rejecting his 'nightgere', the husband may assert his refusal to be mistaken for a woman, but restoring clarity requires the husband suffer the humiliation of continuing in a naked state. The exposed penis may, in a sense, confirm maleness, but the overblown response that centres upon the penis being a sign of manhood also paradoxically renders the male additionally emasculated. The presence of the penis seems to be only part of the signification process needed to denote manliness; the penis must be present (as the young man's reaction naively demonstrates), but that presence should be accessible through other bodily signs that make the actual exposure of the penis unnecessary. Revealing his genitals makes the young man appear absurd. Consequently, the husband acknowledges that the effectiveness of the penis as a sign of manhood depends upon a responsive relationship between body parts, and social constructions of masculinity, because he admits that while his face lacks hair his genital condition will be in question.

The setting for the episode, in being the marital bedchamber, seems important too. That the wife is addressed by the messenger as being as much a gentleman as her husband presents an unclear differentiation in sex but also gender, because the husband's expected authority and, here, sexual mastery over his wife in the bedchamber might well be questioned. The young man's reaction, after all, appears motivated by a need to distinguish man from woman, but, more particularly, husband from wife. By exposing his penis, the husband seems to intend to affirm (perhaps less convincingly than he might hope) that he has what is required of him as a husband in marriage. The anecdote serves, therefore, to highlight just how important a man's beard might be in gendering the relations between marital partners. What can and cannot usually be publicly viewed, both the man's penis and what goes on in the bedchamber between husband and wife, would, it seems, be implied if this young man simply had a beard.

The anecdote's suggestive exploration of the relationship between beards and genitals in the context of marriage accords with early modern medical discourses, which likewise placed emphasis upon the beard as a bodily distinction between man and woman and observed connections between the man's reproductive function and his growth of facial hair. However, some care needs to be taken in using the anecdote as evidence that a beardless male is easily conflated with a woman. As Will Fisher's work has shown, beards were particularly central to early modern constructions of adult masculinity (2001, 2002). This fashioning of adult masculinity is largely set in opposition to adult womanhood due to the way in which a woman's maturation actively dissociated her from the humoral logic behind the growth of manly beards. Sexual maturation in women was understood to explain *why* women remained relatively hair-free, most notably on the face. As one medical text, *The Problemes of Aristotle*, put it, 'the matter and cause of the hayre of the bodies is expelled with their monthly tearmes, the which superfluitie remaineth in men' (1595: A7^r). Menstruation ('monthly tearmes') not only demonstrated the generative potential of the pubescent and sexually maturing female but also removed excess moisture from the body that produced beards in men. In Daniel Sennert's seventeenth-century medical text, what initially appears as a rather blunt categorisation where 'men have beards, Women have none' (1661: 2612), becomes more clearly tied to humorally specific notions about beard growth in sexually mature men and women. In the man excess heat and moisture from his seed rises to the face and produces a beard; the cooler (but still heated) heaviness of the humoral excess in the woman, by comparison, is evidenced and then largely expelled through menstruation. Beardlessness is deemed a 'womanly' quality in large part because of this association with the maturation of a reproductive body.

The humoral logic, however, importantly distinguishes the pubescent male's beardlessness from that of the woman: her beardlessness can signal fully achieved female maturation while the male's suggests awaited change and the retention of humoral 'superfluitie' that the woman's body has expelled. So, while smooth faces are both womanish and boyish (and this can be taken advantage of by adolescents performing female parts in the theatre or in witty confusions in anecdotes), the elision of these kinds of beardlessness should be treated with caution. The 'beardless' woman and the beardless boy were still often conceptually separated in terms of what the hairless face might signify in terms of sexual development and age.

Often, the hairless face is pointedly that of a boy. In Ben Jonson's *Epicœne* (c. 1609), the final scene infamously includes the revelation that Morose's young bride is in fact a boy, with the theatrical revelation being accompanied by the removal of the player's wig. The boy behind the woman, here in a children's playing company, is exposed simply because he no longer wears a wig. Albeit more subtle than the young man's exposure of his genitals to the messenger in the pamphlet from 1640, the wig's removal in *Epicœne* functions in a similar way: exposure of the body demands that onlookers attend to signs of sex that are revealed beneath what are now characterised as misleading aspects of external, gendered costume. While the scenario in *Epicœne*, and all early modern theatrical fiction, hinges upon the fact that a boy *could* be fashioned as a woman, such staged revelations also play with when and how a distinction between a boy and a woman can also be made.

What is not often noted in responses to the revelation of Epicœne's boyhood in Jonson's play is that it is followed by another similar revelation: the disguised characters of Otter and Cutbeard (who is a barber, no less) remove their false beards.[2] Although it is possible that each character had a second false beard, it seems more likely that the bare-headed actor playing Epicœne, revealed as a boy who has been acting as young woman, is joined by the bare-faced boys who had been playing the parts of adult men. The joke against Morose and the audience is not only that they have taken boys for women, but that boys have performed all the roles in the play and have been taken for men. The bare-face of the boy actor here becomes demonstrably recognisable as that of a boy, and not simply 'blank' (Dusinberre, 1998: 2). Signs of both gender and age have been manipulated in the performance, and the flexible coding of theatrical signs (such as cosmetics, beards, or wigs) utilises the ways facial complexion contributes to an understanding of age and gender.

In literally revealing that there are boys behind the hair-orientated properties in the finale to *Epicœne*, Jonson draws attention to the boys' bodies beneath their fictive roles. The scene centres upon highlighting actors' bodies that are now distanced from the adult male and female states they have seemed to perform in the play. While the adult male's beard can be removed through an appointment with a barber and the act of shaving, an adolescent's beardless face seems showcased in a different way, here through removing a whole, prosthetic beard in one theatrical gesture. As Eleanor Rycroft has observed, an age-specific emphasis is suggested in the way that the possible meanings of 'trimming' can be selectively understood in relation to male bodies (2019: 32). While 'trimming' might suggest the actions of a barber, gradually removing hair from an adult man, the idea of 'trimming' a young body that is perceived as somehow 'still bare' is more easily associated with the word's meaning of embellishment (Rycroft, 2019: 32). The boy actor's wearing of a full prosthetic beard is exposed as an artificial adornment that confirms his adolescence; he has not achieved a manly beard and the boy rather than the beard is acted upon in processes of decorative trimming. This act of adorning and then revealing the boy actor's body becomes '[a] facet of his desirability, theatrically, if not sexually' with 'the different sort of "trimness" that he presents onstage compared to the barbered male' (Rycroft, 2019: 32). Confronted as neither female nor as an adult male (although theatrical adornments can give the illusion of both), the beardless adolescent actor's body in *Epicœne* appears to be treated with fascination because it is recognised as being in a state of transition. The nature of that transition anticipates full manhood ('he is almost of years' (*Epicœne* 5.4.244)), but the still-changing mobility of the boy's 'journey' towards becoming a man becomes susceptible to fetishisation and positions the adolescent male body as one that is to be acted upon by others in processes of adornment.

Fisher's examination of the ways adult men could shave to perform younger roles, or where boys might don prosthetic beards to assume adult guises, highlights that performances of beardless/bearded ages could, however, also be manipulated in ways that recognised connections between adult and adolescent males (2002, 2006).[3] Young and older male faces could be understood in the context of the same gender framework, and an age-specific masculinity could be made recognisable through the management of facial hair. Fisher's conclusion that boys were ultimately treated as a different gender to men, however, plays down this connection between male faces, illuminating instead the distinctions that were drawn between male adolescent and adulthood. Yet bare chins could be understood to anticipate hair growth appropriate to adulthood, where masculine identities and gradual beard growth were mapped along a trajectory of age (Fisher, 2002: 236).[4] A beardless face was not always framed as being at a far remove from a bearded one.

Although lacking a beard was associated with men who were 'commonly cold and impotent' (Greenwood, 1657: 87), such ideas are only selectively applicable to adolescent males who might be insulted as lacking adequate signs of masculinity in this manner. In *Henry IV, Part 2*, for example, Falstaff insults Prince Hal, 'whose chin is not fledged' (1.2.13–14) by commenting on his beardlessness. The challenge to Hal's manliness, however, works by stressing that the beardless adolescent will remain so: 'I will sooner have a beard in / the palm of my hand than he shall get one on his / cheek' (1.2.14–16). Falstaff claims that, even once Hal has reached full maturity, 'a barber shall never earn sixpence' from the prince (1.2.19). Falstaff takes advantage of the bare chin of the adolescent prince to infer its significance for indicating an individual's anticipated adult masculinity. Hal's beard growth is framed as already belated and so unpromising in terms of the way adolescent masculinity offered signs of the man that the adolescent might become. Cleopatra similarly shows derision for Octavius Caesar by insulting him as 'the scarce-bearded Caesar' (1.1.22). The insult makes Octavius boyish rather than manly, contrasted to the Caesar Cleopatra has already known and to whom the adolescent is implicitly compared. By selectively framing Octavius as incomplete in his development, Cleopatra sets up a comparison of achieved and as-yet unachieved masculine prime in order to suggest comparable lack instead of emergent promise.

By contrast, Coriolanus is described as already exhibiting unmatched masculinity in an anecdote about when he was sixteen and beardless: 'with his Amazonian chin he drove / The bristled lips before him' (2.2.87–8). For Fisher, who reads this description as being about the adult Coriolanus rather than a reference to his adolescence, Coriolanus is the exception to the rule regarding the early modern beard's connotations of adult manliness. Fisher suggests that the 'beardless' Coriolanus reveals himself to be a man, and an adult, through other means (2001: 155). But the adult Coriolanus is not clearly beardless in the main action of Shakespeare's play. It seems likely that in recalling how promising he was at sixteen, when Coriolanus *was* beardless (but with hair growth encouragingly in process, as the idea of a bare chin but 'bristled lips' suggests), Cominius asks the audience to marvel at the man, fully formed, and probably bearded, before them. This man's masculine strength has always been palpable. As a story about Coriolanus's adolescence, recalled by his supporter Cominius, Coriolanus's exploits at sixteen with 'his Amazonian chin' seem fittingly designed to stress that Coriolanus's military potential was already recognisable in adolescence, and this helps construct an image of the man Coriolanus now is. The logical trajectory for masculine development sees this un-bearded adolescent soldier ripen into an even more intimidating adult. As Cominius informs his audience, Coriolanus has succeeded in seventeen other military campaigns since his bare-chinned victory. Tracing Coriolanus's maturation alongside military victory, including the period during which his 'manly' beard would grow, creates an opportunity for Cominius to stress Coriolanus's unmatched strength in adulthood: 'The man I speak of cannot in the world / Be singly counterpoised' (2.2.82–3). Cominius seems, then, to track an exceptionally exaggerated, but otherwise normative, trajectory for Coriolanus's masculine maturation.

Adolescent, beardless men, for whom generative heat was expected to accumulate, could anticipate timely beards that might be framed as part of an adolescent's promising masculine vitality. Lacking a beard, when no beard was yet expected, did not inevitably hamper constructions of masculine selves. The gradual growth of the male's beard offered, moreover, an outwardly traceable sign of an adolescent's developing fertility. I return here to Cuffe's description of male puberty being when 'our cheekes and other more hidden parts begin to be clothed with that mossie excrement of haire' (1607: 118). Cuffe demonstrates how any consideration of beard growth offers a means of mapping the development of 'more hidden parts'. For Cuffe, this 'budding of hair' (1607: 114–15) was not a sudden revision of the adolescent's humoral make-up, but rather an anticipated change that was appropriate to the humoral temperament of a particular individual during a particular life stage. The ageing process recorded 'the variation of our originall constitution' (Cuffe, 1607: 115), where beardless adolescent males were understood in relation to the masculine selves they were expected to become in adulthood. So, while the development of a manly beard might sometimes have been approached with anxiety, most early modern writers assumed that the anticipated trajectory of maturation would be fulfilled by young men for whom 'Tenderness of Age hinders conception only for a time' (Riverius, 1655: 506). Moreover, the humoral rationale that explained the developing qualities of the adolescent male's seed recognised that adolescent males were not, therefore, simply excluded from sexual activity. Seed production and the ability to achieve an erection did not depend on the seed being fully 'ripe'. As acknowledged in Lemnius's comments about the adolescent male's seed being 'to[o] cold and thinne' to produce healthy offspring, adolescent males could still engage in sexual intercourse even if their production of children was considered hampered or unlikely (1576: 43, also see Evans, 2016: 320).

The female's maturation was certainly less outwardly visible than the seed/beard correlation made possible for the pubescent male. In a female, production of generative substance was, after all, demonstrated by the beard she *did not* have on her face. Yet the pubescent female had more in common with the humoral 'complexion' of the beard-growing adolescent than his beardless junior. As Sharp observed, the girl who had begun menstruating recognised symmetry with the maturation of the adolescent male, even though the signs of sexual maturation were distinct for male and female. Sharp, discussing the onset of menstruation in girls around the age of fourteen, notes: 'Men about the same age begin to change their faces and to grow downy with hair' (1671: 69). Though pubescent changes are clearly 'sexed', they also recognise a shared stage of development for male and female according to age. Puberty created excess heat and moisture in both the male and female body and these humoral excesses were expelled from the body one way or another, primarily as menstrual blood in adolescent girls and partially as the 'excrement' of facial hair in adolescent boys.

Moreover, as early modern puns frequently remind us, the female who had reached puberty *did* produce a 'beard', albeit a beard not on the face but on her genitals. The playful linguistic interchange of beards on the face and genitals is a long-standing one. Alison's gleeful tricking of Absolon in Chaucer's 'The Miller's Tale' sees Absolon kiss Alison's bottom as it protrudes from her casement window. The jest depends upon Absolon's confusion when he encounters Alison's pubic beard; that 'a woman hath no beerd' enables Absolon's painful realisation that he has been humiliated (line 551). While neither facial nor pubic beard were anticipated by Absolon in the scenario, only the latter can explain the 'beard' he finds on Alison's body. The seventeenth-century jest, 'A Surprize', similarly puns upon the distinction between womanly and manly 'beards', where the recognition of the womanly beard quickly becomes a prelude to sexual activity: 'A Gentleman being newly trimmed, the Barber left only some hairs on his upper lipp, visiting a Gentelwoman; she innocently said *Sir, you have a beard above and none below; and you* Says he Madam, *have a beard below, and none above,* Say you so, says she, *then put one against t'other*' (1674). A sexual encounter, it seems, logically follows the recognition of sexual maturity in references to each party's 'beard'.

While such bawdy humour plays upon an appreciation for the type of beard that is and is not possessed by a woman, the linguistic connection between facial and genital beards also suggests that such body hair was understood in similar terms. Mark Albert Johnston, who has similarly recognised connections between men's facial beards and women's pubic beards, suggests that the modelling of beards 'above' and 'below' help inscribe the inferiority of early modern women upon their bodies and the beards they produce (2011: 168–71). However, in early modern culture the female's pubic beard was also a sign of sexual maturity, functioning in a manner not unlike the masculine facial beard. Menstrual bleeding may have diverted excess moisture away from the female's face, but the humoral excess that derived from the female's seed was thought to stimulate hair growth around the genitals, and so the female's pubic beard was understood to appear after menstruation had begun. Early modern generative discourses thus observed a connection between the female's growth of pubic hair and the developing reproductive qualities of her body. *The Problemes of Aristotle* relates signs of the female's fecundity to her pubic hair: 'women shew their ripnes by the hayre on their privie part' (1595: A6ʳ). Likewise, Sharp notes how 'hair coming forth shews Virgins to be ready for procreation' (1671: 34). Indeed, as the reproductive seeds of both the pubescent male and female were understood as the source of the heat and moisture that spread throughout the body, both sexes were noted to grow pubic hair. Batman identified this hair as having a key correlation to puberty in both sexes: 'the yere of *Puberte*, that is when yᵉ nether beard haire groweth first in the flesh' (1582: 73). While the man produced two beards, one of which appeared on the face and one that also surrounded his humorally moist genitals, the woman produced a single 'beard' on her genitals that was equally understood to demonstrate her sexual maturity, her 'ripnes'.

The hair growth of a pubic beard, as a sign of sexual maturity, might have been especially associated with adolescent girls whose emergent maturity was distinct from that of older adult women. Fully mature women were generally regarded as having tempered their humoral excesses through the expulsion of humoral heat and moisture through the process of ageing and through its expulsion during sexual activity. After the initial 'ripening' stage of their lives, women seem to have been thought to produce less pubic hair. Sharp suggests this distinction when observing differences between wives and maids: 'In those women that are married [the labia] lye lower and smoother than in maids; when maids are ripe they are full of hair that grows upon them, but they are more curled in women than the hair of maids' (1671: 42). Hair that grows in abundance upon the genitals is constructed as a sign of the emergent 'ripeness' of female adolescence. The recent production of plentiful pubic hair seems to have been imagined in a way that connected ideas of adolescent heated desires with this bodily 'excrement' it was thought to produce. Sharp continues to observe how an individual's sexual appetites might be understood through considering such factors as hair growth upon the genitals and age, where having 'much hair' and being 'very young' suggests a disposition 'much given to venery' (1671: 42).

Clearly, however, while puns and comments about genital beards might allude to a girl's maturation, the physical signs could not be easily viewed on the body or performed onstage. This is probably why Fisher does not consider women's pubic beards in his discussion of materialised signs of gender in early modern culture: this beard can usually only be imagined to have materialised (2006). In all-male theatre companies, commonly noted signs of female puberty such as developing breasts might be suggested through the use of corsetry and even padding, but actual breasts (like the woman's 'beard') could not be viewed in the same manner as the male's facial hair. Puns about women's beards, however, work in a manner that is telling in relation to staging pubescent femininity, because the act of looking at the woman's face (even for what is *not* there in the beard) allows for an imagined access to her genital maturity that corresponds to that available for the male.

As the quotation from Ferrand that opened this chapter highlighted, faces were expected to 'receive the tincture' that made humoral dispositions visible (1640: 124). The connection between facial complexion and the generative heat that saw the maturing male grow a beard, was similarly applied to the pubescent female whose heated seed was discernible in the framing of the pubescent female's blush. A girl's increasing womanliness was often discussed in relation to reddened cheeks, where the heating of generative seed and blood was thought to produce a blush, if not a beard, on a girl's face. As George Sandys observed, the 'resort of blood to the face ... [is] most apparent in those that are young; in regard of their greater heat, and tender complexions' (1632: 361). While people blush for various reasons and at various ages, blushing *at a certain age* was often used to shape an image of the sexual readiness associated with emergent adulthood.[5] The agricultural terminology so often used by early modern writers demonstrates how red cheeks could signify fertility, where, as in *Novembris Monstrum*, 'blushing ripeness' indicates fruitfulness (1641: 100).

It is, moreover, often upon the adolescent's cheek that we find allusion to the 'flowering' stage of life that I examined in the last chapter. While boys have 'budding' beards (Cuffe, 1607: 114–15), girls have rosy cheeks. Isabella, the novice nun of *Measure for Measure*, is, for example, said to possess 'cheek-roses' (1.4.17), and Hermia is asked what it is that afflicts her by Lysander who reads her complexion in terms of her expected adolescent glow in *A Midsummer Night's Dream*: 'How now, my love, why is your cheek so pale? / How chance the roses there do fade so fast?' (1.1.128–9). As the 'rose' of adolescence might be found upon the pubescent female's cheek, so too might the idea of the fading blush be a focus for imagery of premature decline that we saw commonly threaten adolescent promise in chapter one. The plot for faking Juliet's death in *Romeo and Juliet* includes the familiar stark comparison between adolescence and death, focussing attention upon Juliet's cheeks: 'The roses of thy lips and cheeks shall fade / To wanny ashes' (4.1.99–100). Likewise, Robert Herrick's well-known carpe diem poem 'To the Virgins, To Make Much of Time' reminds virgins to 'gather ye rosebuds whilst you may' (1648: line 1) in imagery that is reflective of transient adolescence. In his lesser-known poem, 'To a Gentlewoman, Objecting to Him His Gray Hairs', Herrick provides a similar warning about the temporary nature of adolescence, this time by drawing attention to how the 'decline' of ageing is made manifest upon a woman's face as she loses the 'rose-bud in your cheek' (1648: line 9).

The reddened face of the adolescent female was often seen as particularly enticing, being eroticised because of the way the face seemed to draw attention to unseen parts of the body. The blush, as with the man's beard, was understood as being produced by heated blood that could be traced back to the young woman's seed, which, in turn, signalled her maturation and burgeoning readiness for reproductive sex. The blush is often read as an anticipation of the sexual act in early modern texts. In *The Resoluer*, for example, the 'Vermillion blush' registers young lovers' anticipation of sexual intercourse. Heated passion (itself a symptom of puberty) is recognised in blushing adolescents who 'in hope, or assurance to enjoy their loves […] are red, and have the extremities of their bodies hot, the blood running and spreading over all the parts' (Dupleix, 1635: 20). Juliet, eager for her wedding night with Romeo, is therefore keen for night to come so that her untamed desires, visible through her blushes, can be concealed. Night, for Juliet, promises to 'Hood my unmanned blood, bating in my cheeks' (3.2.14). For Perdita too, in *The Winter's Tale*, interaction with her suitor, Florizel, at the shepherd's feast is enough to excite her blood. Perdita blushes at Florizel's words, which are tantalisingly unheard by those who observe: 'He tells her something / That makes her blood look on't' (4.4.159–60). The sixteen-year-old Perdita who, as we have seen, is associated with flowers and springtime in *The Winter's Tale*, is also interpreted as possessing the promising signs of emergent 'ripeness' that are understood to be inscribed upon her cheek. The emergent blush, like the budding beard, makes the hidden changes of adolescence accessible from an external viewpoint, and, what is more, the signs of puberty become theatrically performable.

Performing male puberty: beards

In the central love plot of *As You Like It*, an awaited beard is used to assess the adolescent Orlando's readiness for romantic coupling with Rosalind. Upon hearing she has an admirer, Rosalind asks: '[is] his chin worth a beard?' (3.2.189). Possession of a manly character and an appropriate physicality for being a suitor includes an evaluation of Orlando's facial hair. In response to Rosalind's question, Celia informs us that Orlando, and so the presumably trimmed Burbage who played him, 'hath but a little beard' (3.2.190). Orlando, by the evidence of his beard, is said to need more time to flourish as a lover, a point that is reiterated when Orlando enters the scene and attention is again drawn to his small beard. Rosalind, in her guise of Ganymede, assesses how far Orlando exhibits the signs of lovesickness, concluding that all signs (including a lean cheek and an unkempt appearance) are absent. Orlando most notably lacks the symptom of a 'beard neglected' (3.2.344), something that Orlando is reminded 'you have not [...] for your having in beard is a younger brother's revenue' (3.2.344–6). Orlando's pubescent state, where maturation has begun but not been fulfilled, is made evident in Rosalind's querying how far Orlando's lovesick desires, themselves indicative of adolescent, heated passion, have registered upon his appearance.

An understanding of Orlando's ongoing maturation becomes attached to an appreciation of his beard that is expected to grow. For Rosalind, the promise of Orlando's 'chin' is enough to encourage her to await his sexual maturation: she will 'stay the growth of his beard' (3.2.192). She has, after all, already deemed this adolescent a promising candidate for fathering her children (1.3.11). As Rosalind sets out to begin tutoring Orlando as her prospective husband, the representation of Orlando's growing beard depicts puberty as an uncomplicated and temporary condition that leads to sexual maturation, simply with the passing of time. Orlando's representation suggests a promising 'pre-adult' masculinity rather than a feminised adolescence. Orlando can, after all, win a wrestling match against the Duke's champion in Act 1, Scene 2, despite having further growing to do. Indeed, the actor's performance of strength in the wrestling scene *as* youthful is bolstered for the audience by the words of other characters who fear for Orlando's safety and relentlessly comment upon his young age. No fewer than sixteen direct references are made about Orlando being young/a youth between his entrance at line 119 and his victorious acceptance of Rosalind's chain at line 214. The exclamations of the stage audience make sure to contextualise the wrestling: Orlando's strength is exceptional and promising for an adolescent and not to be understood as the exertions of full maturity. Likewise, Orlando's beard is in the process of growing, and, while it is unlikely that Burbage would appear in later scenes donning a full beard to signal his achievement of sexual maturity, the promise of Orlando's small beard seems realised (as expected) when other signs of adult masculinity are made evident. Orlando's development from the 'young and tender' (1.1.111) 'boy' (1.1.148) of Act One to the 'man' who – in case we were in any doubt – can fight a lion by Act Five (5.2.106) is traced across a play that reminds its audience 'from hour to hour we ripe and ripe' (2.7.26). Like Coriolanus, considered above, Orlando is identified according to the expected model of masculine maturation, where adolescent promise (and a small beard) helps the audience assess the 'worth' of the man he becomes.

While *As You Like It* accommodates an uncomplicated model of puberty, following an expected trajectory of maturation for its characters, *Twelfth Night* offers a more complex staging of the signs of puberty. *Twelfth Night* seems to delight in the gradual nature of sexual maturation and pointedly defers bodily changes for characters, when such changes were probably being experienced by the adolescent actors playing the roles. Viola's disguise as Cesario centres upon the absence of expected signs of puberty, including facial and pubic 'beards'. In Act 3, Feste mocks Cesario's lack of a beard, to which Cesario responds: 'I am almost sick for one, / though I would not have it grow on my chin' (3.1.41–2). Although traditionally seen to indicate Viola's lovesickness for Duke Orsino (the supposed 'beard' in question), this exchange also highlights Cesario's lack of a beard, both on the face and upon the genitals (the pun, after all, invites us to once again consider beards that do not grow on the chin).[6]

Cesario's beardlessness suggests a physical immaturity that is applicable to the prepubescent male or female figures involved in this scene: Feste believes he is in conversation with a male adolescent who is awaiting the growth of his manly beard, whereas the audience is likely to detect the Viola character in the statement. However, this is not simply recourse back to the idea that beardlessness is equally womanly and boyish. Cesario's comment implies that pubic hair would be preferable to facial hair, highlighting that there are different types of beards. In the context of the play's gender confusions, Cesario's articulation of desire for a single beard, disassociated from the masculine facial beard, seems to privilege Viola, and her anticipation of a single womanly 'beard'. The scene's imagery may delight in the familiar bawdy distinction between manly and womanly beards only to stress the continued *absence* of such beards for Cesario/Viola. *Twelfth Night*, which has regularly been discussed for its references to ambiguously gendered voice and genitalia (Howard, 1988; Jardine, 1989; Stallybrass, 1991; Callaghan, 1993; Orgel, 1996; Elam, 1996), has not generally been considered according to this key point: the theatrical illusion of sameness between male and female adolescent, which underpins the play's narrative, continually defers the signs of emergent 'ripeness'. The gender ambiguity at work in the play should, therefore, be understood with this management of age signifiers in mind, as the framing of bodies in *Twelfth Night* is not a representative model of early modern puberty or its use in early modern drama.

Although Orlando fulfils the masculine promise of his 'chin' by the end of *As You Like It*, in Act Five of *Twelfth Night*, Orsino is still wondering how puberty will alter Cesario: 'What wilt thou be / When time hath sowed a grizzle on thy case?' (5.1.157–8). Thinking that his page has betrayed him by pursuing Olivia, Orsino's observation is initially akin to Rosalind's anticipation of Orlando's beard, which is expected to grow according to the indications of masculine selfhood already in evidence. Orsino considers how what Cesario is capable of in adolescence will be exaggerated in adulthood, when the adolescent has hair upon his 'case' (genitals). However, unlike Orlando's beard, which is already in the process of growing and likely to continue its promising course, Cesario/Viola has no beard (facial or pubic, it seems), just when the marital unions of the comedy are expected. If this were only about facial beards, and, notably, Orsino's comment is again shaped to specify pubic hair, Viola's lack of body hair might easily be absorbed into that familiar model, where a crossdressed sexually mature woman is helpfully, but superficially, interchangeable with a beardless young male. Yet in the 'recognition scene' that concludes *Twelfth Night*, a clear complication to the marriage unions is apparent. The marvelling at 'One face, one voice, one habit' (5.1.206), 'habit' being a term for humoral disposition as well as clothing, in response to the twins pointedly leaves key signs of sexual maturation of both beardless twins undetected.

Indeed, while Viola's twin, Sebastian, is victorious in his duel with the foppish Andrew Aguecheek, his actions and bodily representation do not really tally with Robert Lublin's suggestion that Sebastian should be understood as 'emerging from adolescence and ready to assume adult responsibilities' (2011: 26). Sebastian is, after all, taken by surprise by Olivia's attentions and Aguecheek's challenge, where such actions only loosely resemble the actively pursued activities of 'heated' adolescence. Sebastian, who also volunteers the information that he is sexually inexperienced in this final scene (5.1.256), is a character who appears somewhat prematurely propelled into staging acts of masculine adolescence that his physical framing in the play otherwise undermines. With an opponent called 'Aguecheek', a name that connotes either a flushed or blanched complexion, often associated with fevers rather than 'ruddiness', or, indeed, beardedness, Sebastian's comparative framing is against a male whose complexion is itself without signs of promise.

In the play's final scene, moreover, the age of the twins is suggested in a recent memory of the twins' thirteenth birthday (5.1.238). The inclusion of this numerical age situates the twins in relation to the early developments of adolescence and corresponds with the play's insistence that neither twin's body records signs of 'ripening'. The 'unripe' representation of the twins thus allows for different-sex twins to be mistaken for each other. The twins' shared 'beardless' 'complexion' further undermines the idea of a 'fruitful' marriage between sexually mature adults in the play's conclusion, and facial similarity may even have been signalled using matching degrees of stage make-up on the actors' 'twinned' faces (Karim-Cooper, 2006: 199). Sebastian and Viola may ostensibly be organised into heterosexual adult couplings, but the 'sexed' implications of puberty are resisted through the signs of the twins' persistent sameness.

Therefore, by leaving puberty pending, *Twelfth Night* decentres the normative marital resolution of comedy and draws attention to its theatrical constructions of age and gender. While continued references to Viola's singing voice, in a play where Viola does not sing, may suggest revision of the play to accommodate a player's breaking voice (Stern, 2000: 101), the play also offers a surprisingly spirited acknowledgement of pubescent bodily changes that are awaited but never realised for its characters. This management of the maturing actor's bodily changes goes beyond more typical theatrical strategy, where the crossdressed female's masculine guise allows room for the actor's own acknowledged maturation. Portia's crossdressing as a pubescent male in *The Merchant of Venice* sees the character draw upon 'A thousand raw tricks of these bragging Jacks, / Which I will practice' (3.4.77–8), including adopting a voice 'between the change of man and boy' (3.4.66). Portia's speech recognises that an adolescent female character and an adolescent male theatrical construct are not seamlessly merged, but require acts of performance ('raw tricks') in the manipulation of voice and behaviour that distinguish the two. Here, however, the real adolescent actor emerges in a fascinating but familiar way: his altering body is Portia's theatrical fiction. Portia acknowledges the cultural acceptance of signs associated with the pubescent male and puts them to use in a manner that works both to highlight and then conveniently submerge the pubescent changes of the male adolescent playing Portia.

Allusions to the sexually immature bodies of the twins in *Twelfth Night* also allude to pubescent processes of 'ripening', although such bodily changes are pointedly represented as having barely begun.[7] The play's celebration of its theatrical illusion of the twins' sameness may offer a fantasy of its own: fluid gender identities are constructed that resist the 'sexed', body-focused changes that become connected to gender identities during puberty. That such a fantasy can be performed in *Twelfth Night* is testament to the skills of acting companies to *make* 'blank' the bodies of its actors as they manage the culturally recognised signs of puberty. The theatrical efforts made to manage signifiers of adolescence and gender in *Twelfth Night* (c. 1602) are more complex than those evident in most of Shakespeare's plays, and so should not be used simply as a representative model for cultural ideas about puberty. However, *Twelfth Night*, which offers explorations of adolescent subjectivities that come later than those presented in *As You Like It* (c. 1599), seems to indicate a trajectory of experimentation in Shakespeare's use of adolescence in his plays to realise subversion of cultural norms. In its Viola/Sebastian plot, *Twelfth Night* seems to delight in the symmetry, rather than the 'sexed' difference, of cultural constructions of male and female adolescence. In the play's conclusion, gender identities retain fluidity whereby marital unions, perhaps reimagined rather than deferred, suggest imagistic scope for continuity in the projected futures of the ambiguously gendered twins. In *Twelfth Night*, 'adult' gender identities can, perchance, also begin to be imagined in a way that remains at a distance from 'sexed' bodily signifiers that are bound to insistent notions that adult male and females must be able to demonstrate reproductive 'ripeness'.

Performing female puberty: blushes before beards?

Performances of female puberty by the boy actors in Shakespeare's company included allusions to blushing faces that realise nuances in the relationship between 'real', 'sexed' bodies and the theatrical bodies presented on Shakespeare's stage. Cultural constructions of femininity in relation to newly glowing cheeks offered one means of representing puberty that worked in a similar manner to allusions to beard growth, but where the heated, hair-free cheek could be used to distinguish female from male maturation on stage. In this section, I explore how blushes are used to characterise female adolescence in Shakespeare's plays, and I suggest how cosmetic blushes are contextualised in relation to a character's age. Moreover, in the representation of Ganymede's complexion in *As You Like It*, I suggest how the 'blushing' and pointedly beardless crossdressing character, set in opposition to that of Orlando, can draw into focus the management of the boy actor's own adolescence in Shakespeare's plays.

King's analysis of female puberty (2004) includes some consideration of the blush as a culturally recognised sign of sexual maturation. King notes how writers expressed an eroticised fascination with the ripening body, being 'barely able to resist charms of a pubescent girl, reddened cheeks and plump body signalling fertility' (2004: 90). As King argues, signs of being just 'ripe' upon the female body often rendered the female vulnerable to male attention. In *Measure for Measure*, Isabella's virginity and sexual appeal seem identified through her 'cheek-roses' (1.4.17); her reddened face is eroticised because her body advertises the development of womanly sexuality that male observers might seek to exploit. As Potter observes, Isabella's 'rosy cheeks give her sexual "ripeness" away' (2013: 434).

By associating Isabella with the bodily changes of puberty that signal the beginnings of her womanly distinction from girlishness, *Measure for Measure* stages the heated process of her maturation. In Act Two, Scene Two, Isabella confronts Angelo to plead for her brother's life, and Lucio twice chastises Isabella with the words: 'You are too cold' (2.2.46, 57). For Pascale Aebischer, this suggests that 'Lucio is urging Isabella to be hotter, he is urging her to behave more like a man' (2008: 11). The allusion to heat is understood in terms of the 'masculine' heat stressed in Laqueur's 'one-sex' model (1990). However, it seems more likely that the adolescent Isabella is being encouraged to let her emergent womanly 'heat' show in order to manipulate Angelo in this interaction, while Lucio simultaneously highlights the issue of Isabella's sexual maturation for the audience. The sexual demands Angelo makes of Isabella certainly depend upon his recognition of her maturation towards womanhood, which he assumes comes with sexual appetites: 'Be that you are, / That is, a woman […] as you are well expressed

/ By all external warrants' (2.4.131–4). The audience is invited to recognise signs of emergent womanhood expressed in the physical performance of Isabella's character, her 'external warrants'. These signs include more blushing. Finding resistance to his proposition, Angelo tells Isabella to 'Lay by all nicety and prolixious blushes / That banish what they sue for' (2.4.159–60). Modest blushes do not help, they are superfluous to a virtuous cause, and, because they spur on Angelo's desire rather than his mercy, they 'banish what they sue for', acting as an 'external warrant' of her sexual maturation.

We might recall here the disguised courtiers who observe Perdita's blush in *The Winter's Tale*. In what manner does recognition of the 'external warrants' of Perdita's 'ripeness' invite the attentions of men? At the shepherds' feast, all delight in the beauty of 'the prettiest low-born lass' (4.4.156). If we bear in mind Higginbotham's analysis of the relationship between social status, gender, and age in constructions of girlhood, the representation of a blushing Perdita poses questions about the way characters view her as both physically ripening *and* a lowly shepherd's daughter. Perdita, who the audience know is really a princess, is never called 'wench', the term Higginbotham highlights as merging ideas about pubescent licentious desires and the sexual voraciousness associated with low birth (2013: 20–61). The shepherds' celebrations do, however, certainly include many who are identified as 'wenches' (4.4.310). While observers repeatedly comment upon the adolescent Perdita's exceptional qualities, she is said to be 'Too noble for this place' (4.4.159), the scene presents a provocative framing of Perdita's maturation when she both is and is not viewed in the context of being a low-born pubescent woman.

On the one hand, being perceived as a country wench might mean Perdita has scope to pursue pubescent desires that are fuelled by her heated blood. Like Juliet, Perdita's story of elopement seems to demonstrate that high-born pubescent girls can pursue a path that is forged through desire and gain the audience's sympathy. Unlike Juliet, Perdita's understanding that she is of low birth may additionally allow her freedoms to express her desires without 'wronging the ancientry' (*The Winter's Tale* 3.3.61) to the same degree that proves disastrous for Juliet. On the other hand, it is important to remember how Perdita's reddened face is available for all to see and interpret. The bodily changes of puberty were not necessarily a source of self-assertion; they could be a source of vulnerability, perhaps especially when social rank can be mistaken. That his surrogate daughter's blushing cheeks might appear inappropriate for the feast's public display is suggested in the shepherd's instructions: 'Come, quench your blushes and present yourself' (4.4.67). The staging of puberty as a bodily as well as a social process realises tensions in class-bound constructions of female sexual desire if the nun, the princess, or the country wench is seen to blush in a pubescent manner, because girls' blushes are constructed in a way that anticipates an evaluation of sexual decorum.

Allusions to blushing faces in early modern drama often suggest that a blush of some sort would have been produced on stage, and that audiences were primed and encouraged to interpret its meaning. Henry Jackson's oft-quoted account of a performance of *Othello* in 1610 is suggestive of how an audience's attention could be drawn to an actor's face in interpreting character. In celebration of a particular Desdemona's winning performance, Jackson includes the observation that 'she entreated the pity of the spectators by her very countenance' (cited in Neill, 2006: 9). However, upon the early modern stage, reading a female character's face and, particularly, interpreting the meaning of blushes was quite literally a layered business. Boy actors almost certainly wore cosmetics to signify their femininity (Karim-Cooper, 2006: 144). A combination of whitening make-up, probably with a white lead base, and reddening tints to indicate a blush, likely using mercury-based vermillion, would have provided the material foundation – as it were – for understanding female characters in early modern drama (Karim Cooper, 2006: 44; Stevens, 2013: 54).

The cosmetic nature of all female blushes that were represented on the early modern stage adds complexity to the wider cultural framing of artificial blushes. A natural blush would usually be regarded as something that 'can bee neither put on or restrained' (Sandys, 1632: 361). Part of a blush's usefulness in the processes of interpreting character, especially when interrogating ideas of female virtue, hinged upon the understanding that an authentic blush was an involuntary action. Actors performing male roles in 'bare' face might be applauded for their skills in reproducing the blush that was notoriously hard to fake, as in observations about Burbage who could allegedly 'look Pallid for fear' and then 'Recall his Bloud' (Bancroft, 1658: 44) on cue. However, boy actors who portrayed female characters, and used cosmetics to do so, would not have had this trick available to them, although they might well have had the skill. Allusions to female blushes must, however, have directed audience attention to the actor's painted face.[8]

All theatrical female blushes were, of course, artificial and, as the work of Farah Karim-Cooper and Andrea Ria Stevens has shown, the visual effects of boy players' cosmetics would often have been far from naturalistic (Karim-Cooper, 2006: 178; Stevens, 2013: 3). Making use of such ingredients as crushed shells and (for more expensive recipes) crushed pearl, and with the glossy application of egg glazes, 'cosmetic bases in early modern England were thick and shimmering' (Karim-Cooper, 2006: 178). Although the degree of thickness and effect of the applied make-up would likely differ according to the roles being performed, the early modern theatrical 'blush' would need contextualising efforts to appear 'natural'. In presenting an artificial 'countenance', the boy actor's female impersonation becomes implicated by the anti-cosmetic arguments that circulated in early modern society and warned against deceptive surfaces (Karim-Cooper, 2006: 40). Fears about false faces particularly focused upon the role cosmetics might play in the misrepresentation of female virtue. As Frances Dolan argues, women who used cosmetics came under suspicion for processes of self-creation and the deception that their assumption of masculine agency in their use of 'the Pencil' implied (1993: 224–39). The 'painted lady', as Barnabe Rich lamented, compromised the means by which appearances of feminine virtue might be distinguished from those of vice:

> [Women] are so paynted so be periwigd, so be poudered, so be perfumed, so bee starched, so be laced ... that I cannot tell what mental virtues they may have that they do keepe inwardly to themselves, but I am sure, to the outward show, it is a hard matter in the church it selfe to distinguish between a good woman, and a bad. (1615: 15)

By creating an artificial surface, the 'made up' woman disrupts visual cues that enable the observer, here a decidedly frustrated Rich, from reading signs of her virtue or vice through her facial complexion. The idea that internal humoral states become externalised and made evident through the face, as observed by Ferrand at the start of this chapter, becomes disrupted. Indeed, as Stevens's analysis of court masques (2013) suggests, cosmetics offered a means by which women could avoid unwanted scrutiny of their blushes. In court masques, cosmetic strategies included the use of blackface make-up, where, in being 'blacked up, impregnable to the gaze, and chaste' (Stevens, 2013: 108), women – who would have no doubt have reddened with the exertions of dancing in a masque – could rest assured that onlookers' interpretations of their heated blushes were avoided. However, by engaging with practices of concealment that disable the differentiation 'between a good woman, and a bad', as Rich so clearly desires, women who used cosmetics did more than obfuscate categories; their use of cosmetics threatened to align them with the vice of deception.

Upon the early modern stage, however, adolescent boy players used face paints and set about achieving what Rich deems impossible: to differentiate between virtuous and villainous female characters through cosmetic means. While anti-theatrical writings attest to the fact that theatrical cosmetics were enmeshed in much of the anti-cosmetic sentiment of early modern culture (Gosson, 1579: 32), the handling of these staged complexions in the contexts of certain plays indicates that players and audiences were prepared to respond to cues for re-fashioning the theatrical painted face into a signifier appropriate to a particular character's identity. Jackson is, after all, clear that Desdemona is deserving of his pity as he observes her 'countenance', whether his understanding of her character directly recognises the paintedness of that countenance or not. As Karim-Cooper observes, 'cosmetics on an actor's face signal his staged identity' (2006: 158), and this meant that even if a boy actor were painted, the character he was playing may not have been regarded as such, being associated with 'natural' beauty. The stained cheeks of the boy who portrayed a virtuous adolescent female might then be managed so that the visual significance of the blush becomes indicative of the character's 'rosy' adolescence, which helps navigate associations between painted faces and duplicity.

There are linguistic prompts that help shape audience interpretations of the painted blushes involved in the performed femininities of Shakespeare's plays. For example, the previously mentioned reference to Isabella's 'cheek-roses' (1.4.17) in *Measure for Measure* provides a clear cue to how an audience should read the character's cosmeticised femininity. The description of Isabella's rose-like complexion uses the language of adolescent beauty that I discussed in the previous chapter. Isabella's red cheeks are to be viewed as cheek-roses, a signifier of adolescence. If the audience pauses long enough to acknowledge that the cheeks are painted and artificial, the linguistic framing may also remind the viewer that the materials behind cosmetics can also be associated with the flowers indicative of adolescence, seeing as flowers such as roses were 'very popular ingredients in the cosmetic recipes of the period, providing a link between poetic prescriptions and cosmetic practice' (Karim-Cooper, 2006: 17).

Indeed, much of the appeal of cosmetic beauty was based upon the understanding that products would help produce a youthful complexion. Whether through layering make-up upon the face or by using cosmetic products designed to exfoliate the skin (some having the corrosive effect of something akin to chemical peels), cosmetics were meant to make the skin glow in a way that imitated what early modern culture understood as the appearance of youth (Karim-Cooper, 2006: 26, 53–4, 194). As Kim Hall has shown in *Things of Darkness*, ideas about female beauty were racialised to privilege whiteness in early modern culture (1995: 62–73). Depictions of adolescence, the age that realised the pinnacle of female beauty, also adopted and compounded this racialised model, where the default adolescent complexion that is exalted is reddened cheeks on white skin.

While women who strove to retrieve this complexion of adolescence were often rebuked in early modern satire, an understanding of cosmeticised beauty does not work in quite the same way for the *painted* adolescent. The female adolescent might well aim for the idealised, fashionable (and fictive) version of beauty revered in early modern English culture, but her use of cosmetics is more likely to be seen as a process that accentuates and modifies her own adolescent facial features. Used upon adolescent faces, there is the potential for cosmetic use to be criticised because it is seen as unnecessary rather than solely misleading. In this way, then, the adolescent female character who is represented on Shakespeare's stage would not inevitably become embroiled with anti-cosmetic ideologies, because, within the fiction of the play, the cosmetic signifier of adolescent feminine beauty (the reddened cheek) accords with the beautiful, adolescent character being represented. The cosmetic blush might be utilised in different ways, of course, say where paintedness might be pointedly highlighted in a character's portrayal, evoking ideas about sexual or moral duplicity in a player's performance of a certain theatrical identity.

For Isabella, in *Measure for Measure*, it may well be her blushing face that provides the audience with its final cue for reading her character in the play. As Aebischer notes, silences in the final scene of *Measure for Measure* include 'implicit stage directions' (2008: 5) but no words for the boy playing Isabella. Urged by the Duke to 'Give me your hand, and say you will be mine' (5.1.496), the scene requests spoken lines from the actor that do not exist. Taking into account the cue-script culture and limited rehearsal times of early modern theatre, Aebischer argues that a first performance would likely include the 'actor's visible discomfort' (2008: 5) in performing the novice nun's response to the unexpected advances of the Duke. Such discomfort might well have been accentuated by the implications of the makeup used on the character. The script for *Measure for Measure* confirms that Isabella has rosy cheeks, and Isabella's cheeks may become contextualised by the potential for awkwardness in the boy actor's reaction in this scene. In the first performance of the play's finale, Isabella's reddened cheeks may signal her adolescence but also the discomfort of the reluctant subject who is made the object of male desire. If so, this kind of blushing has been seen before in the play, recalling Isabella's scenes with Angelo discussed above. The Duke also positions the blushing, would-be nun Isabella as the source of erotic desire, and Isabella's value is once again measured against male desires that exist in conflict with her own.

Hero's blushing face, in Act 4, Scene 1 of *Much Ado About Nothing*, is similarly key to the staging of the play's character interactions. Shakespeare again positions an adolescent female character's blush as the focus of male characters' attentions. This time, Hero's blush becomes central 'evidence' in the debates being held by the men onstage regarding the accusation of sexual indiscretion that has been made against her. When Claudio identifies a blush in the scene, 'Behold, how like a maid she blushes' (4.1.33), the observation begins as a comment about appearances of feminine virtue that does not necessarily demand any physical performance from the actor playing Hero. Claudio's words begin to draw attention to the blush that theatrical cosmetics have made visible upon the actor's face. Claudio's accusation of Hero, however, becomes fixed upon this blush, as he progressively scrutinises its implications: 'Comes not that blood as modest evidence' (4.1.36). The audience know Claudio is wrong to change his reading of maidenly modesty for one of sexual shame, where 'She knows the heat of a luxurious bed / Her blush is guiltiness' (4.1.40–1). However, the audience is repeatedly directed to look to Hero's blush and weigh up its meaning. Even if characters debate its implications in this scene, all agree that a blush is there. The Friar says, for example, how he has 'marked / A thousand blushing apparitions / To start into her face' (4.1.156–8). Even a defence of Hero returns to the evidence of her visibly reddened face.

Although cosmetics would have been used to produce a fixed blush for Hero in this scene, the Friar's words suggest an appreciation for an altering redness ('To start into her face') when he describes Hero's complexion. Even though the painted boy actor who performed the role would not have been able to offer any visible impromptu blush of modesty, the Friar's lines seem to act as a cue to the audience to disregard the cosmeticised nature of Hero's stage beauty. The line suggests that the character's face should be understood as 'bare' and capable of spontaneous blushing. The Friar's words recall early modern ideas about natural beauty and its association with signs of feminine modesty. Castiglione's *The Book of the Courtier* includes, for example, these observations: 'how much more attractive than all others is a pretty woman who is quite clearly wearing no make-up on her face, which is neither too pallid nor too red, and whose own colouring is natural and somewhat pale (but occasionally blushes openly from embarrassment or for some other reason)' (1588: 86). Female beauty is associated with skin that flushes and records emotion to present virtuous transparency as well as the traditional mix of 'perfect' pallor and redness. It is this kind of beautiful and virtuous complexion that appears to be being attributed to Hero. Indeed, while characters debate at length the sinful or virtuous meaning of the silent Hero's blush (silence that also accords with early modern notions of feminine virtue), all the commentators accept that Hero's blush is authentic and the effect of blood rushing to her face rather than the result of cosmetics. The actors' words, therefore, insist that the audience recognise the boy player's artificially reddened face as part of the characterisation of an adolescent Hero, and their words work together in denying the cosmetic application of the stage blush.

The inclusion of 'blushing ripeness' in both a play's script and materialised performance helped underpin theatrical constructions of age and gender. Whether staging female or male puberty, it appears that early modern playing companies were well-equipped to manufacture and make use of real pubescent bodies in performance. Beardlessness is a key example of how the same physical characteristic could be used to manufacture the womanly cheek that blushes (through the application of cosmetics), the adolescent male's promising chin or the incarnation of emasculating lack. Early modern drama seems to have deftly drawn upon cultural understandings of puberty in order to selectively highlight, disguise, and re-signify the actor's 'body beneath' the theatrical role (Stallybrass, 1991).

The apparently simple model where the male has a beard and woman does not, could, for instance, be adopted in early modern theatre to stage complex gendering of character. In *As You Like It*, a notable distinction is made between the complexions of Orlando as a male adolescent and Rosalind, who, in the guise of Ganymede, performs the role of another male adolescent in the play. While Orlando has a small and promising beard growing, Ganymede is pointedly beardless in the play. Before the crossdressing narrative begins, Touchstone asks Celia and Rosalind to 'swear by your beards' (1.2.64), to which Celia acquiesces: 'By our beards, if we had them' (1.2.65). The exchange highlights the hair-free faces of the actors playing the girls, perhaps jokingly alluding to the boy players' faces for whom the lack of a beard would be temporary. This may also indicate that the feminising cosmetics typical for female impersonation were retained in the crossdressing aspects of the *As You Like It*.[9] As I discussed in the previous chapter, the adolescent beauty of 'rosy' complexions was often associated with male as well as female adolescents. It is possible that Ganymede still wears the cosmetics used to signify Rosalind's femininity in the opening scenes of the play, where the make-up works to maintain a sign of sex for the audience, but in a way that also allows for the play's gender ambiguity to work. A 'light' application of cosmetics that constructs a character aligned with 'natural' adolescent beauty in Rosalind could also signal beauty attributed to the still-beardless, male adolescent when viewing Ganymede.

Phoebe's observations about Ganymede's face in *As You Like It* seem to draw attention to the play's construction of adolescent fictions. Phoebe praises Ganymede, observing 'He'll make a proper man. The best thing in him / Is his complexion' (3.5.114–15). On the surface, Phoebe's comments work with early modern ideas about promising masculine adolescence: a proper man can be gauged by the promise of his as-yet beardless cheek, and his rose like attributes. However, because the audience are aware of the crossdressing plot and view Ganymede and Rosalind in all that Phoebe praises, the audience is offered a layered response to the character's facial complexion that reveals how the face has been coded in terms of age and gender in the play. Phoebe continues to offer a pleasing blazon of Ganymede, filling out her description of Ganymede's complexion in the following way: 'There was a pretty redness in his lip, / A little riper and more lusty red / Than that mix'd in his cheek; 'twas just the difference / Betwixt the constant red and mingled damask' (3.5.119–22). This moment has been noted in important scholarship about the ambiguity of the play's eroticism, and it is, in part, through the staging of complexion that this ambiguity is achieved (Traub, 2002: 170, 174). While Phoebe's comments about Ganymede's promising facial features can legitimately be applied to a male adolescent, the stress upon the blushing cheek of Ganymede draws female maturation more insistently into the picture, leaving palpable room for the same-sex eroticism of Phoebe's observations to be recognised, and enjoyed, by the audience who were used to this sign of female puberty being used in the theatre.

Phoebe's commentary upon complexion, moreover, reminds modern readers of Shakespeare that Ganymede and Orlando are not set up as equivalent performances of masculine adolescence in *As You Like It*. Beyond more pronounced comparisons between a swooning Ganymede and the lion-fighting Orlando, a physical distinction is made in how the crossdressing of Rosalind was staged in terms of facial complexion, because one performance of male adolescence excludes facial hair and may include 'beautifying' make-up (Ganymede) while the other includes a beard's emergent growth (Orlando). While the ambiguous gendering of Ganymede remains central to the eroticism of characters' exchanges within the play (Howard, 1988; Stallybrass, 1991; Orgel, 1996), the performance never fully collapses the age-gender fashioning of Ganymede in comparison to Orlando. As I will examine further in discussion of height in the book's final chapter, adolescent masculinities in *As You Like It* are not presented as equivalent in terms of age and physicality. Burbage-as-Orlando is distinct from the boy actor-as-Rosalind/Ganymede. In exchanges between Ganymede and Orlando we see male–male eroticism as the interplay between the older and younger 'adolescent', as well as older/younger actor (Digangi, 1995).

In *As You Like It*, being without a beard can be understood as part of a 'proper man's' progression towards adulthood, as Orlando and Phoebe's understanding of Ganymede as an adolescent male suggests. The audience, in being privy to the knowledge that Ganymede is really Rosalind, is also positioned to read the theatrical sign of total beardlessness and glowing complexion as a sign of female puberty throughout the exchanges. As the narrative confusions of *As you Like It* playfully toy with the boundaries between male and female in its love plots, the staging of characters that is implicit in the script regarding comparative complexions also reveal ways in which male and female could also be strategically kept distinct. Management of such physical features as facial hair and cosmetics would allow the audience to follow a play in which the crossdressing boy player performs as a heroine who then also crossdresses, all the while promoting engagement with the gender ambiguities and eroticism available within such a layered performance.

Studies about early modern theatre have commented on the skill of maturing actors at the end of their time playing women, acknowledging the negotiated nature of performances that come under pressure as the result of the bodily changes that accompany puberty (Brown, 2014; McManus, 2015). Such negotiated performances would, however, have been required of the boy actor throughout his career impersonating women. This would have necessitated not only the management of his own pubescent physicality but also the cultivation of a performance that included recognisable signs of age and gender that were appropriate to a character. However, while actors constructed performances of age and gender, early modern theatrical practice does seem to have recognised limitations based on an actor's own maturing physicality that would eventually intrude upon a performance of femininity. In *Twelfth Night*, a play I have already noted for its nuanced engagement with cultural signs of maturation, there is also acknowledgement of the temporary nature of such theatrical fictions. Act 2, Scene 4 of *Twelfth Night* seems to reflect upon the boy-player's flexible but ultimately impermanent representation of gender ambiguity. In the scene, as in the play as a whole, Viola is unable to clarify her sex identity: she dwells upon her position as both the son and daughter of her father's house. Like the adolescent boy actor who plays her, Viola can pass for either gender with the aid of costume and performance tactics. In this scene, however, the audience is also asked to consider the imaginary crossdressing of the older Orsino, who was likely played by Burbage who was in his mid-thirties when *Twelfth Night* was first performed in c. 1602. Unaware that he is the object of Cesario's affections, Orsino assumes that Cesario is describing a woman whom the boy desires. In response to the description that Cesario provides, Orsino rejects the vision of womanhood that incorporates his own age and 'complexion' (2.4.24). As a phrase that implicated humoral disposition, the reference to Orsino's complexion highlights the understanding that an older man, like the older player, cannot convincingly perform the roles of women: his body will more readily betray his adult masculinity and produce a disagreeable vision of womanhood. Play upon the word 'complexion', moreover, draws particular attention to Orsino's face, one which *is* likely to possess a beard. Although this scene highlights a means by which a male actor could extend his time playing the beautiful female's part (beards can be shaved and cosmetics applied to forge the required 'feminine' complexion), the exchange also admits that such an illusion cannot be sustained forever. There came a point in theatrical practice when the early modern male actor became disconnected from the adolescent bodily state that might be *made* to appear feminine, and whereby the physical attributes of an adult masculinity, even in a theatrical context, included being no longer 'semblative a woman's part' (1.4.33). Imagining Burbage-as-Orsino, beard and all, as a woman, might well have promoted laughter for an early modern audience. Yet the melancholic Viola's interactions with the older Orsino in the scene could also have promoted reflection upon the gender fluidity of every actor's adolescent career, including Burbage, who likely began his lengthy acting career with female impersonation (Power, 2003: 220). Realistically, the early modern adolescent actor would have known that he would not be able to play crossdressed and ambiguously gendered characters forever. Act 2, Scene 4, paired with the poignant open-endedness of the final scene in *Twelfth Night*, suggests, however, that imagining that possibility of a gender-fluid adulthood, if not staging it, could be contemplated in early modern theatrical culture, at the margins of its plays.

Notes

1. This chapter is developed out of an existing article (Sparey, 2015). Copyright © Johns Hopkins University Press. This article first appeared in *Shakespeare Bulletin*, Volume 33, Issue 3, Fall, 2015, pages 441–67.
2. Both stage directions, to remove Epicœne's peruke and Otter and Cutbeard's beards, appear in quartos of *The Silent Woman* (1620) and in Jonson's *Works* (1616). Some quartos from 1620 (entitled, *Epiceone, or the Silent Woman*) only have the removal of beards recorded in the stage directions.
3. Fisher also notes how eggshells may have been used to conceal facial hair so that female roles could be performed by young men (2002: 244).
4. Fisher's work has been invaluable to studies of early modern performance and cultural representations of masculinity. However, the influence of Laqueur's 'one-sex' model, discussed in the introduction, remains evident in Fisher's modelling of sexual difference in his study, where sex is 'primarily conceptualized in terms of degree' (2002: 235–6).
5. The dramatised blush could frame a character in terms of older age. Adriana, in *Comedy of Errors*, suggests she is no longer treated by her husband as being in the full bloom of youth: 'homely age the alluring beauty took / From my poor cheek' (2.1.87–8).
6. Mark Johnston is, to my knowledge, one of the few scholars to identify the pun upon Viola's pubic hair in this exchange. For Johnston, Viola's words recognise her 'lower' beard's 'subordination to the primacy of the male beard' in early modern society (2011: 167). My own reading suggests the character's privileging of a pubic beard for its associations with age.
7. Mark Albert Johnston (2017) has examined the erotic framing of the 'infertile' twins in *Twelfth Night*. Johnston observes how adolescent actors, themselves often pubescent, were understood as infertile but capable of sex, and, in being regarded as unthreatening in this manner, could be found sexually appealing to female audience members. The degree of immaturity observed in the characterisation of the play's twins in this chapter heightens the implications of

Johnston's findings, where the eroticism of a pre-adult state can be observed through the fashioning of the 'beardless' Viola and Sebastian.
8 To further understand Burbage's alleged talent for manipulating his complexion, we might look to modern performances for examples of how red faces can be produced to order on stage. For example, The Globe's 2010 production of *Merry Wives of Windsor* (dir. Christopher Luscombe) included Andrew Havill's performance as Master Ford, where his breathless delivery of long speeches was accompanied by a very red face.
9 It is unclear how the whitening make-up and reddened cheeks typical in the representation of femininity in early modern drama would feature in the many plays that include crossdressed characters. Here, the crossdressed character is understood as male by other characters and viewed with a dual consciousness by the audience. I am grateful to Farah Karim-Cooper for the insights she has offered in discussing this issue via Twitter (@ProfFarahKC).

3

Voicing adolescence: the heated words of puberty

[W]ords do well
When he that speaks them pleases those that hear.
It is a pretty youth.
(Shakespeare, *As You Like It* 3.5.110–12)

Shakespeare scholarship has explored, in some depth, how vocal changes that take place during male adolescence carried implications for early modern theatrical practice (Brown, 1990; Dusinberre, 1996; Callaghan, 2000: 49–74; Bloom, 2007). In early modern culture, 'breaking' voices were recognised as an audible cue that signalled a male's impending transition into adulthood. Set in the particular context of early modern theatre, alterations to an adolescent actor's voice also presented a source of disruption within – and imminent end to – his impersonations of femininity onstage. As Hamlet notes when he welcomes a player that he knows for performing female roles, hopes for a good performance depend upon whether the player's voice 'be not cracked within the ring' (2.2.452–3). Gina Bloom's study of 'the aural dimensions of the Elizabethan theater' (2007: 21) has suggested how the vocal changes associated with puberty could be understood as part of a 'fragile condition' (2007: 22) attributed to the adolescent male. Pubescent changes to the voice made manifest the individual's transitional and unstable state between boy and man. As a symptom of an 'unmanageable body' (Bloom, 2007: 17), the wavering vocals of a breaking voice, subjected to the maturing body's increased heat, fits, in many ways, with cultural ideas about unruly adolescence.

In this chapter, however, I examine more expansive meanings that were attached to adolescent voices in early modern culture. The humoral heat thought to inform how adolescents spoke, in terms of the tonal and stylistic qualities of the sounds made, was also thought to promote mental agility that meant adolescence was associated with a witty and engaging nature, which made anticipating what an adolescent might say an especially pleasing experience. In this chapter I consider what made an adolescent voice recognisable as such, and performable on the early modern stage. As we have seen, plenty of Shakespearean characters are adolescents, and so qualities of the adolescent voice were not roundly avoided in theatrical presentations that included stylised speech as part of those performances. Across the sections of this chapter, I investigate how the 'heated' attributes of adolescent voices were not always fashioned as vocal vulnerability. Indeed, I suggest that the 'heated' articulations of adolescence were often represented as a source of delight and celebration in early modern theatrical cultures.

Positioning childhood in relation to adulthood becomes especially important when commenting on young voices in the early modern period. Much criticism has discussed how far children could be active agents when adults were so prominent in shaping, receiving, and interpreting the words that they spoke. For example, Greteman's work on John Milton's writings, which includes discussion of other writers, such as Ben Jonson, William Prynne, and Thomas Hobbes, has shown how early modern ideas about childish voices were complex (2013). Realising qualities of mimesis, while also offering freedoms and licence, and with aspects of obligation, children could assert politicised agency or be distanced from the words that they spoke. Lamb's findings in *Reading Children* (2018), and Seth Lerer's (2012) analyses of children's marginalia in medieval texts, moreover, have illuminated the ways in which 'children were never wholly passive or innocent readers' (Lamb, 2018: 17). Moreover, Jennifer Richards has observed 'the interaction between voices and books' (2019: 238) in her exploration of the performative nature of the 'oral reading' (2019: 2) at work in early modern education practices. Speech, here evidently connected to such interactive reading models, was likewise a contested area of childhood expression, where assertions of agency involved negotiating the child's position in relation to the authority of adults.

In the context of childhood studies, we have seen that the adolescent speaker inhabited a transitional state between child and adult. This heightened stage of mutability, fuelled by humoral heat, provided the adolescent speaker with a particularly complicated position from which to assert agency. In the theatrical cultures of early modern England, moreover, power relations existed between company members, where adult and child would exist in hierarchical working relationships that may have either inhibited or enabled adolescent actors' contributions to theatrical productions. In this chapter, I examine the adult/child relationships particular to early modern theatrical contexts, where exploitation of children certainly took place, but where I suggest that there is also scope to perceive relationships that realised more positive formulations, and where the cultural value attached to the words that an adolescent might utter is particularly demonstrated. While an esteemed character onstage does not translate into well-treated individuals behind the role, reassessing the cultural importance of adolescent voices and subjectivities does implicitly revise assumptions about boy players being 'fairly low on everyone's list of priorities' (Belsey, 2005: 53) in theatre companies *because* of their age.

Across the sections of this chapter, my analysis of compelling adolescent characters in Shakespeare's plays attends to their voices. After all, though Egeus sees his daughter's words as evidence of 'stubborn harshness' (1.1.38), the action of *A Midsummer Night's Dream* and other Shakespearean comedies, in particular, place value on what adolescent characters say or do, giving them space to positively shape their futures. Vibrant adolescent speakers, as actors and fictive characters, were undeniably a large part of what the audience paid to hear and observe across the action of early modern plays. In the first section of the chapter, I analyse the features attributed to the adolescent's 'heated' speech in early modern culture. I use contemporary medical writings to consider how the movement of humoral heat was understood to realise age-specific changes to the minds and voices of adolescents as they underwent the changes of puberty. While attention to pitch ultimately realised a distinction between male and female vocal maturation, I demonstrate how there was room for both the adolescent male and female to be regularly attributed similar cognitive and vocal skills that their humorally hot life stage promoted. In the second section of the chapter, however, I tease out when and why 'words do well' (*As You Like It* 3.5.110), or not, for Shakespeare's female adolescents to suggest how gendered navigations are at work in constructions of adolescent voices. I explore when, how, and why familiar gendered restrictions on female voices, more rigidly applied through early modern ideas about womanhood, intrude upon girlhood vocality and compare such moments with Shakespearean girl characters who appear to find means to navigate these limitations and assert agency through their adolescent voices. Here, I particularly draw upon Bicks's (2021) recent work on girls' cognition in early modern culture. I develop Bicks's observations about girlhood 'brainwork' to suggest how cultural attitudes towards adolescent voices offered a related means of constructing adolescent femininities in early modern drama. I examine a range of Shakespearean characters to suggest where girls' voices could take advantage of accolades associated with early modern adolescence. Shakespeare offers striking contrasts between his girl characters' speech, and comparisons, for example, between Rosalind's extolled multiplicity and Phoebe's castigated duplicity in *As You Like It* particularly help unpack constructions of adolescent voices. Fashioning favourable adolescent subjectivities, I suggest, depends on the adolescent speaker's management of listeners as well as the delivery of their own 'heated' words.

In the final section of the chapter, I return to the potential vocal volatility that has so often been attributed to boy players (Dusinberre, 1996; Bloom, 2007). I reconsider how meta-theatrical allusions to unwieldy vocals and 'squeaking' (5.2.218) boys in *Antony and Cleopatra* may intersect with more positive depictions of adolescent voices. The actor playing the 'wide-ranging' role of Cleopatra (McMillin, 2004: 257), I argue, alludes to wobbly and pitchy voices to offer stark comparison with esteemed qualities of 'boyish' voices in early modern culture. The boy player's management of character could see the actor advantageously placed to show off his voice as 'crafted air' (Bloom, 2007: 2), and actively work in opposition to images of vocal vulnerability through the actor's celebration of his own performance and energised eloquence. Moreover, I suggest the implications of understanding Cleopatra's representation *as* the 'boyish' accomplishment of the white, male actor who is applauded in moments of metatheatre. Complexities in the construction of Cleopatra's racial and gender identity become pointedly undercut by the insistent presence of the talented, adolescent white boy who is recognised as the point of origin for the Egyptian Queen's admired representation.

Across this chapter, changeable pitch might well loom as a destabilising quality of the adolescent's voice. However, I will show how the 'heated' voice, that 'pleases those that hear' (*As You Like It* 3.5.111) was also commonly attributed to the adolescent who demonstrated commanding and commended vocal mutability. By attending to the handling of adolescent voices in early modern culture and a variety of Shakespeare's plays, moreover, I consider what we may learn about the negotiations at work that determine who speaks and how, who gets heard, and who gets silenced.

The rising heat of adolescence: body, mind, and voice

The humoral properties associated with age influenced the characteristics attributed to, and expected of, an individual's voice in the early modern period. For example, in Bacon's discussion of voices in *Sylvia Sylvanum* (1626), a broad differentiation between children and adult males is made that also allows Bacon to group together all bodies that he perceives as possessing less humoral heat (and, consequently, narrower vocal passages) than adult men. In Bacon's evaluation of vocal properties, we find the mature male – the normative model for which assumes fertility – set in opposition to children, women, and eunuchs:[1]

> *Children, Women, Eunuchs* haue more small and shrill *Voices*, than *Men*. The Reason is, not for that *Men* haue greater Heat, which may make the

> *Voice* stronger (for the strength of a *Voice* or *Sound,* doth make a difference in the *Loudnesse* or *Softnesse,* but not in the *Tone;*) But from the Dilatation of the Organ; which (it is true) is likewise caused by Heat. But the Cause of *Changing* the *Voice,* at the yeares of Puberty, is more obscure. It seemeth to be, for that when much of the Moisture of the Body, which did before irrigate the Parts, is drawne downe to the Spermaticall vessels; it leaueth the Body more hot than it was; whence commeth the Dilatation of the Pipes: For we see plainly, all Effects of Heat, doe then come on; As Pilosity, more Roughnesse of the Skinne, Hardnesse of the Flesh, &c. (Francis Bacon, 1626: 180)

Bacon's grouping of women, children and eunuchs together because of their lack of 'manly' heat here clearly rests largely upon an assessment of humoral heat in relation to vocal pitch. Settled and deepened tones become features by which the adult male voice is commendably distinguished from the 'shrill Voices' of '*Children, Women, Eunuchs*' (Bacon, 1626: 180). Viewed from this perspective, fully 'broken', adult voices can be seen to offer a reassuring end point to the instability experienced by the adolescent male during his maturation.

However, there are evident tensions in Bacon's modelling of voices, which only works while it continues to focus upon the influence of heat upon degrees of dilation for pipes rather than on how voices relate to entire bodies and selves. While early modern theatrical production took advantage of surface similarities that were perceived in the vocal pitches of the voices of adolescent males, women and eunuchs, the conflation of humoral dispositions that might merge physical states identified as male and female, child and adult, are more nuanced than Bacon's comments initially suggest. Qualities of 'heated' or less heated voices extended beyond disruptions to vocal tone. As I have shown in previous chapters, similarities regarding humoral heat or coolness were often accompanied by physical manifestations that were understood to distinguish male from female, and these distinguishing attributes hinged upon contextualising ideas about heat in relation to an understanding of age and reproductive 'ripenness'. Bacon's comparison of heated/less-heated voices serves its purpose in privileging a certain male voice with its dilated vocal pipes, deeper tone, and greater volume, but early modern humoral thinking identified significant differences in the cultural framing of the bodies and voices of women, children, and eunuchs that went beyond sharing the characteristic of a 'shrill' voice. These differences, in turn, help illuminate the position of adolescent voices that responded to humoral heat in ways that exceeded the simple threat of the voice 'breaking'.

Eunuchs, for example, are typically framed as emasculated males in early modern writings, being regularly described as humorally cooler and 'womanish' (Crooke, 1615: 242) when compared to other men. However, the reasoning behind observations about a eunuch's humoral disposition hinged upon an understanding of 'the alteration of the temper, habit and manners' (Crooke, 1615: 243) that responded to the absence of hot, reproductive seed. Helkiah Crooke notes the implications of heated seed in his discussion of eunuchs: 'For *Hippocrates* saith, that seede is of Nature fiery and aery; by the aery part it distendeth the whole frame of Nature, and by the fiery setteth it on worke, or a gog as we say, transporting not the body onely, but the minde' (1615: 242). Regarded as lacking the heat required to radiate through the body and shape the mind, the eunuch was associated with the humoral coolness of femininity, because female bodies were also often set in opposition to a normative 'hot' body that was male and implicitly adult. However, the eunuch also realises clear tensions in the binaries that such comparisons use (male/female, hot/cold) because the eunuch's position in the reproductive framing of 'heated' bodies is different to that of the sexually mature female. As we have seen, a woman was understood to produce 'heated' generative seed of her own. To be likened to a woman, for the eunuch, registers his difference from a model of masculinity that hinges upon fertility (Evans, 2016: 312), but, in being marginalised in this way, the eunuch is also set in contrast to the way women's bodies were also bound to reproductive features in early modern culture. Adult female identities were, somewhat emphatically, understood in relation to biological properties that centred upon reproduction, as a wealth of research into the cultural framing of menstruation and pregnancy has suggested (Paster, 1993; Gowing, 2003: Read, 2013).

The alignment of women and eunuchs realises inadequacies in categorising sex through binary, reproduction-focused associations. By attributing 'imperfection' to the eunuch's body, the eunuch-as-woman analogy falls back upon misogynistic models that understand maleness as superior to femaleness, and which associates such manhood with the generative efficacy of genitals. Moreover, while prepubescent and pubescent males might not be considered fertile, I have shown in previous chapters how the adolescent male could be viewed as anticipating such manhood in his 'ripening' promise, and this was not imaginable for castrated males whose infertility was permanent. The eunuch is perhaps most commonly described as womanish rather than boyish, then, because a perceived 'lack' is more easily associated with femininity in the context of early modern patriarchy.

Further instability is realised in eunuchs being attributed vocal traits similar to women, because female voices were also understood in relation to constructions of the early modern life cycle. A woman's voice could logically be understood as differing from a 'girlish' voice, as the maturing female body underwent alterations in humoral heat across the life cycle that had implications for her speech as it did for the male. The adult female's 'womanly' voice was implicitly bound to notions of sexual maturity. As critics and historians have repeatedly shown, women's words and silence – or, what they did with their 'shrill' voices – would be interpreted in relation to ideas about sexual activity (Hull, 1982; Newman, 1989; Paster, 1993). Speaking or writing as a sexually mature woman entailed navigating concepts of female virtue and chastity, which meant women and eunuchs were not substantively aligned in early modern thinking about the way women used their voices (Hobby, 1988; Larson, 2011). The eunuch, whose voice and body are presented as neither fully mannish nor womanish in light of early modern models of the life cycle, persists as an important indication that a 'neat' male/female distinction based on assumptions about genital and reproductive states is historically an unstable concept.

For adult women, sexual immodesty could easily be assumed using the evidence of 'excessive verbal fluency' (Paster, 1993: 25), but these limitations may not have worked in the same manner for the adolescent girl whose voice and reproductive body were still maturing. Although the alterations that take place for male adolescent voices during puberty have received much scholarly attention, the reasoning that Bacon notes about vocal changes resulting from the increased heat that 'leaueth the Body more hot than it was' (Bacon, 1626: 180) includes the adolescent female, as the previous chapters have shown. While Bacon's male-centred modelling of voice selectively prioritises a male adult subject, set in opposition to women, children, and eunuchs, this age-specific development once again attests to symmetry in male and female maturation. Indeed, as Aristotle observes in *Historia animalium*, 'In girls, too, about this time the voice changes to a deeper note' (Aristotle, 1910: 851b). Not only does this suggest symmetry across the male and female life cycle, but, as Aristotle notes, it also indicates distinction in gendered categories: 'while in general the woman's voice is higher than the man, so also the voices of girls are pitched in a higher key than the elder women's' (Aristotle, 1910: 581b). Matters of voice become less clearly about gendered binaries and involve greater discussion of age-appropriate bodily developments.

Indeed, as Bacon's description continues, the more nuanced role of heat in early modern understandings of maturing reproductive bodies and voices becomes apparent. Puberty disrupts a simplistic dualistic modelling of voice (as being either an achieved 'heated' adult masculine voice or the lack thereof), because Bacon acknowledges that the heat of puberty produces an especially complex change to the voice that is rooted in changes across the whole body. During puberty, Bacon observes that 'all Effects of Heat, doe then come on' as 'the Moisture of the Body, which did before irrigate the Parts, is drawne downe to the Spermaticall vessels' (1626: 180). Bacon repeats the familiar framing of early modern adolescence, where puberty involves change that 'leaueth the Body more hot than it was'. As such, 'Changing the voice' is recognised as part of the broader physiological responses that take place during puberty (Bacon, 1626: 180). Bacon's gestures towards altered 'flesh', 'pilosity' (hairiness), and 'skin' in *Sylvia Sylvanum* (1626: 180) suggest how the heat that dilated vocal passages during puberty was symptomatic of a whole body that was undergoing transformation. The vocal mechanics of heated and dilated pipes, which had the propensity to see voices 'break' or 'crack' in ways largely used to distinguish between male and female (Bloom, 2007: 25), offer only partial insight into how adolescent voices were understood in relation to the maturing individuals whose voices were subject to more extensive humoral change.

In particular, the rising heat of puberty that produced physical alteration, such as dilated pipes and the blushes and beards of the previous chapter, also influenced the workings of the adolescent minds. Set in relation to cognitive development, we begin to see how aspects of voice offer not only a symptom of puberty but also a means by which the thoughts and 'heated' experiences that were associated with adolescence might be made especially comprehensible. Approached as such, the adolescent's voice, the quality of which shall be shown to have involved more than efforts to control pitch in the successful delivery of speech both on and off the early modern stage, offered a unique means by which adolescent subjectivities could be articulated.

As I outlined in the introduction to this book, an adolescent's 'heated' thoughts have often been characterised as taking the form of lusty imaginings and lascivious intent in early modern cultural representations, whereby thoughts could spill over into the manner of speech and actions of 'unruly' adolescence. Portia, in *The Merchant of Venice*, includes familiar stereotypes about volatile adolescence when she decides to disguise herself as an adolescent male, including consideration of how her speech might be convincingly altered. Portia contemplates assuming the characteristics of 'bragging Jacks' (3.4.77) who 'speak of frays' (3.4.68) and 'tell quaint lies' (3.4.69). The adolescent male, according to Portia, will talk in an exaggerated and misleading manner that describe acts of violence and sexual conquest.

A similar version of Portia's imagined model of aggressive adolescent masculinity is apparent in *Romeo and Juliet*. As has been discussed at length by Kahn, Shakespeare's play 'links sexual intercourse with aggression and violence towards women' (1978: 6) as adolescents seek to demonstrate manhood, where 'those fighting the feud are defined as men' (1978: 6). On the streets of Verona, masculine adolescence is often voiced in line with this 'phallic competitiveness' (Kahn, 1978: 7) as with Samson and Gregory's misogynistic and sexually violent threats towards the maids of the Montague household (1.1.12–25). A more nuanced version of articulating masculine adolescence in this hostile vein is evident in Mercutio's fantasies that involve the 'hag' (1.4.90), Queen Mab. Mercutio speaks of his distrust of love, which is described as the supernatural mischief of a fairy who sways 'lovers' brains' (1.4.69). As Kahn observes, Mercutio's 'speech is as aggressive as his fighting' (1978: 9) as love is rejected and a self-destructive model of masculine adolescence is presented in line with this verbal and physical violence.

The bravado of the ill-fated, male adolescents in *Romeo and Juliet* begins to recognise how verbal elements are included in early modern cultural models of 'unruly' adolescence. In Castiglione's *The Courtier*, for example, adolescent males are similarly chastised for 'bragginge and vnshamefull praising himself' (1588: D1^r). Yet such immoderate speech is not imagined as the inevitable or only formulation of adolescent voices. In *The Courtier*, aggressive speech and behaviour is counterbalanced with behaviour that is deemed appropriate for promising young gentlemen. A 'bragging' adolescent's speech is criticised as unimpressive in its failure to convince an audience of the individual's worth or virtue: 'for therewith a man always purchaseth himself the hatred and yll will of the hearers' (1588: D1^{r-v}). By contrast, Castiglione's figure of the Count praises the Cardinal of Ferrara, who is 'but young', for his skills in conversation and public display. This adolescent is described in *The Courtier* as a noteworthy example, who is worthy of imitation, because he possesses the ability to enthral an audience: 'he hath in him certaine sweetnes, and so comely demeanours, that who so speaketh with him, or yet beholdeth him, must needs beare him an affection forever' (1588: C1^{r-v}). Adolescents can, therefore, be characterised as effective speakers in early modern representations, and *The Courtier*, offering conduct advice to young gentlemen, anticipates adolescent readers who will want to aspire to this model whereby their words will enchant listeners.

The Courtier records room for adolescent modes of speech that have pleasing qualities, and which extend beyond the brawling and bragging stereotype. With some notable tragic exceptions, including, for example, the particularly vicious fashioning of adolescent bravado of Chiron and Demetrius in *Titus Andronicus* (Knowles, 2013: 63–89), Shakespeare's adolescent male and female characters are not usually set upon heat-driven triviality or devastating recklessness. Typically, Shakespeare's adolescents do not simply appear to be acting upon self-destructive thoughts that emanate from those 'boiled brains' that Shakespeare's fatherly Shepherd imagine (*The Winter's Tale* 3.3.62). It is, as we will see, the 'gentlemanly' decorum models, outlined in advice and education texts, against which Shakespeare's adolescents seem to primarily be evaluated. Social factors and aspirations, therefore, additionally influence how Shakespeare represents adolescent mental and vocal skills, although this chapter also attends to the 'lowly' actors and girl characters that Shakespeare deems capable of displays of enthralling eloquence, suggesting how humoral, age-based features of voice make social, as well as gendered, constraints on voice less fixed. Portia certainly discards the vision of the brawling and bragging adolescent that she imagines in *The Merchant of Venice*, electing to disguise herself as a young barrister whose speech is measured and orientates around ideas of reason, law, and Christian 'mercy' (4.1.182–203). Such characters, here clearly played by an adolescent actor, held the stage and managed audience engagement. Portia's displays of eloquence in the guise of Balthazar include, therefore, her selection of a performance of male adolescence that uses the 'heat' attributed to this age to support a positive construction of character and voice. Indeed, as I address in the next section, Portia's self-conscious and controlled performance *as* Balthazar also implicates her own mental and vocal agility appropriate to female adolescence.

Bacon, in his essay 'Of Youth and Age', observes the kinds of voice deemed appropriate to age when he notes that 'a fluent and Luxuriant Speech [...] becomes *Youth* well, but not *Age*' (1625: 250). An abundance in words is attributed to adolescence, which is framed by Bacon as pleasing during this life stage, if not during old age. Adolescent voices, being subject to change, heat, and activity, could be identified as enriched and invigorated, where the over-spilling of pubescent heat takes the form of words (as it had for, say, beards and blushes). In the early modern cultural imagination, as Bicks's important interventions about the fashioning of female puberty have begun to highlight, adolescence could be positively understood as a time of increased humoral heat that enabled a 'cognitively agile period' (2021: 28) in the life cycle. The heated and, to use one of Bicks's terms, 'incited minds' (2016: 187) of female as well as male adolescents could result in admirable activity of the mind, voice, and body.

In early modern writings, differentiating between commendable articulations of 'heated' agency and those that are perceived as unruly seems to have involved evaluating age-specific humoral temperaments alongside ideas about the ability to apply reason. In the context of humoral theory, moisture was understood to dampen rationality in having sluggish properties, and, while excess heat fuelled activity verging on unpredictability, coldness threatened to produce inactive minds. Medical writer, Lemnius, observes in *Touchstone of Complexions* that children of fifteen years and under, who were thought to possess a hot and moist complexion, would think, act, and speak without reason or control; they are 'vnmodest, malapert, saucie, proude, wythoute wit' (1576: 67^r). According to Lemnius, all children up until this threshold of puberty (which, at fifteen, may have begun but would not have been completed) are associated with a lightness of spirit and an impulsive changeability that is understood in relation to a mind afflicted by a humoral excess appropriate to age.

Carefree play, for Lemnius, is also evidence of children's disorderly mental, physical, and vocal characteristics: 'clapping of hands, light songes, vayne ioyfulnes, where there is no cause, immoderate myrth [...] vncertayne motion & gate: all which do signify a shuttle waueryng nature, & a mynde subiect to great mutability and vnco[n]stancy, procedyng and caused of the boyling of theyr bloude wythin them, which boyleth vp' (1576: 67ʳ). Such untamed heat and moisture, with its manifestations across the body and mind, could be seen to carry over into Shakespearean images of untamed adolescence and its 'boiled-brains' (*The Winter's Tale* 3.3.62–3). However, the 'heated' lack of control that Lemnius observes in early childhood was also thought to be reshaped in adolescence, where a sense of purpose and positive aspects of 'great mutability' might be achieved. With the 'sluggish' implications of moisture being decreased during puberty, a heated adolescent constitution could produce exalted verbal activity, as the dulling influence of excess moisture was expelled in the production of beards and menstrual blood to create conditions for the adolescent speaker to achieve conversational dexterity. Lemnius, for example, commends a hot disposition in individuals who are 'liuely, lusty and applyable: of tongue, trowling, perfect, & perswasiue: delyuering their words distinctly, plainlye and pleasauntlye' (1576: 45ᵛ). Strikingly, Lemnius moves from the heated vibrancy of character and body to skills in speaking. In his description of the voices of men with cold complexions, Lemnius is comparatively damning: 'Such persons haue foltering tongues, and nothing ready in vtterau[n]ce' (1576: 65ᵛ).

Although vocal pitch must still be navigated in Lemnius's ideas about the ideal voice 'not squekinge and slender, but streynable, comely and audible', Lemnius observes that promising qualities of voice involve more than 'the wydenes of the breast and vocall Artery', which helps to make 'the voice bigge' (1576: 45ᵛ). Heat that widens passages and alters pitch is also associated with the way speech can move and convince those who listen. Such voices are said to depend upon 'internall heate, from whence proceedeth the earnest affections, vehemente motions, and feruent desyers of the mynde' (Lemnius, 1576: 45ᵛ). Persuasive and pleasing voices depend on heated minds.

Adolescence, affiliated as it was with a particularly heated humoral condition, presented a time when the minds and voices of individuals were considered especially noteworthy. According to the physician Thomas Willis in his *Essay of the Pathology of the Brain*, adolescence is a stage during which the individual is primed to exercise a keenness of mind:

> About the time of ripe age, as the Blood pours forth something before destinated for the brain, through the Spermatic Arteries, to the genitals, so also it receives as a recompense, a certain ferment from those parts, through the

veins: to wit, certain particles imbued with a seminal tincture, are caryed back into the bloody mass, which makes it vigorous, and inspire into it a new and lively virtue, wherefore at that time, the gifts both of the Body and minde, chiefly shew themselves; Hairs break out, the voyce becomes greater, the courses of women flow, and other accidents happen, whereby it is plain, that both the blood and nervous Juce, are impregnated with a certain fresh ferment. (1681: 18)

The thoughts of adolescence are imagined as taking on a 'seminal tincture' from the seed via the blood, and Willis notably adds 'gifts both of the body and minde' to the list of alterations associated with puberty. Pubescent bodies and minds are accorded positive and exciting attributes, as vigour inspires 'lively virtue', and thoughts and actions become influenced by 'a certain fresh ferment'. Willis's language indicates the influence and rise of chemical medicine across the seventeenth century, where processes of fermentation merged with ideas more commonly expressed in terms of humoral heat. However, Willis's reasoning testifies to persistent overlaps between coexisting medical doctrines in the early modern period, where qualities of 'ferment', like the heat of humoral theory, travelled upwards through the pubescent body from genitals to minds.[2] Broadly speaking, medical writers indicate complementary ideas about puberty, sharing deep-rooted assumptions about adolescent abilities to articulate thoughts and engage enigmatically with mental stimuli.

Adolescent minds are frequently accredited with this capacity for mental agility in early modern writings. For Will Greenwood, however, this adolescent condition still warranted caution. In *Description of the Passion of Love*, Greenwood warns that during the '*vehemency of Adolescency*' individuals 'have greatest need of a bridle' in order to control their thoughts. To 'let loose the raines' otherwise incurs 'subjection of this passion' (Greenwood, 1657: 82). To ensure that adolescent 'gifts' (Willis, 1681: 18) are showcased, rather than unleashed as disorderly passions, early modern writers regularly recommend how behaviour and speech should be managed in order to demonstrate the adolescent speaker's controlled and reasoned stance, as well as their 'lively virtue'. Contrary to negative stereotypes of hot-headed adolescents being unheeding of advice, which is perhaps implicit in the more forceful 'bridle' imagery used by Greenwood, a more positive version of heated, suppleness was readily available in early modern constructions of applauded adolescent activity and education. Early modern educational texts explicitly acknowledge how the qualities of voice in adolescents were thought to respond positively to a heated disposition, and where the mutability of the adolescent's heated state also made the individual receptive to instruction. Mulcaster, for example, understands his young students as possessing bodies, minds, and voices that are 'pliable to the traine' (1581: 36). Exercises in vocal control and agility are mainstays of early modern education writings. Richards's descriptions of educational scenarios for boys model similarly dynamic but controlled interactions between the adolescent, the textual base of his lesson, and his acts of speaking aloud; combining cognitive and vocal talents, which typically included the use of memory, understanding, pronunciation, gesture and style, the activities of boyhood education regularly relied upon the assumption that the adolescent's 'voice could be used to breathe life into written words' (2019: 24). As Lerer has similarly shown in his discussion of *Hamlet*, educational practices for boys included 'arts of argument and the structures of interrogation that controlled instruction in verbal performance' (2017: 17). In this sense, such speech acts made young men recognisable as adolescents, because of the age-focused associations of these educational practices and uses of conversational rhetoric. For example, in his exchanges with his university friends, Rosencrantz and Guildenstern, Hamlet primarily seems to not only contextualise his relationship to his 'schoolfellows' by calling them such (3.4.203), but the group – as Lerer points out – also rehearse the kind of conversational exchanges that characterise them as adolescents who are trying out their skills in rhetoric (2017: 17).

A model of esteemed adolescent expression emerges in early modern cultural discourses that value a combination of lively vigour and the speaker's clear command over words, behaviour, and reception. Control in a speech's delivery could, for example, be demonstrated through delivery and timing. In *Youths Behaviour*, a text that describes in detail how young men should engage in conversation, adolescents are advised to 'speake with measure, and in due time' (Hawkins, 1646: 38). Adolescent trainees were considered pliable but responsive, receiving direction while asserting control over their minds, bodies, and voices through their application of their learning. Greteman has observed how aspects of play and performance, for students at schools and universities as well as those in playing companies, 'were supposed to create self-disciplined subjects' (2013: 15–16). Adults might authorise and instruct, but skills in self-control were identified as qualities possessed by an engaged adolescent subject. 'Heated' adolescents were, therefore, regularly imagined as possessing enlivened minds that should be encouraged to flourish in thought, being given some scope to practise their skills in speaking their minds, as long as it was done in a demonstrably controlled manner. Such eloquent adolescents, moreover, were regarded as especially compelling individuals, as with the Cardinal of Ferrara in Castiglione's *The Courtier* (1588: C1^v).

The adolescent who is busy sharpening the mind thus appears to be differentiated from early modern ideas about childish speech as 'wavering, uncertain, repetitive, unreasoning and imitative – the product of a fundamental lack of self-control' (Munro, 2017: 84). Lucy Munro's helpful list of 'a set of stock structures and vocabulary' (2017: 88) used in performances of childhood, which make use of 'monosyllables, simple sentence structure, deference to adult authority, and an impression of naïveté' (2017: 89), seems most fitting for representations of prepubescent childhood. Indeed, Munro's examples mostly relate to characters who are judged to be around eight or nine years old. Such characters would have been associated with high proportions of moisture and heat, which, as Lemnius's disparaging remarks about younger children demonstrate, were presented as an obstacle to reasoned thought and speech. Early modern legal rights reflect the greater degree of responsibility and reason attributed to older children (Ben-Amos, 1994: 30). At fourteen, boys had the right to dispose of goods and consent to marry, although they were likely to be considered 'unripe' in body for consummation. At fourteen it was also a legal requirement that boys and girls attend morning and evening prayer, even if this was difficult to enforce (Ben-Amos, 1994: 189–90). Adolescents, regarded as still maturing but possessing reasoning powers that were considered emergent rather than fully attained, were also seen as able to assume degrees of social responsibility that younger children could not. Teenage characters, who Munro sees as able to occasionally 'transcend their childish incapacity' (Munro, 2017: 96) through wordplay, begin to indicate ways by which the vocal styling of adolescents could have been discernibly different to performances of younger childhood in early modern theatre.

The idea that adolescent voices possessed recognisable qualities is suggested in *As You Like It*, where speech is presented as a fundamental cue to identifying any age in the life cycle and also its theatrical representation. As Majorie Garber notes, the meta-theatrical description of the 'seven ages of man' (2.7.139–66) in *As You Like It* ties life stages to linguistic properties (1997: 1–3). For example, the infant exists at one end of the life cycle, making incomprehensible cries ('mewling') that indicate a lack of language and reason. The trajectory for life follows a progression through 'whining' and making 'oaths', until the loss of a 'big manly voice' is tracked to a soundless and sightless 'mere oblivion' at life's end (2.7.139–66). The adolescent is imagined in this framework as an impassioned lover, whose audible characteristics include the expulsion of wordless, but notably 'heated', sighs. The audible features of adolescence are represented as 'sighing like a furnace' and reciting 'ballad[s]' (2.7.145–65). Here, the 'heated' adolescent's 'feruent desyers of the mynde' (Lemnius, 1576: 45^v) are yoked to romantic desire to form a culturally recognisable model of adolescent speech.

Ferrand offers the following description of the sighing infatuations of an adolescent in love:

> Sighing is caused in Melancholy Lovers, by reason that they many times forget to draw their breath, being wholy taken up with the strong Imaginations that they have, either in beholding the beauty of their Loves, or else, in their Absence, contemplating on their rare perfections, and contriving the meanes how to compasse their Desires. So that at length recollecting themselves, Nature is constrained to draw as much Aire at once. (1640: 132)

Sighing, as most modern viewers would expect, indicates unfulfilled desire. These frustrated desires, however, are not simply described as a source of sadness here. Desires correspond to an intensity of thoughts, or 'strong Imaginations', that become all-consuming so that the enthralled lover forgets to draw breath. In this image of the adolescent in love, voice is not solely shaped by pitch or language, but the sudden intake and dramatic expulsion of air, which demonstrates strength of emotion.

As well as furnace-like sighing, the lovesick adolescent of Jaques's 'seven ages' speech is granted the ability to order language into poetry. This combination of vocal styling is evident through Orlando's characterisation in *As You Like It*. In addition to the performance strategies that were discussed in the previous two chapters in constructing Burbage's Orlando as an adolescent, *As You Like It* allocates the character a romantically enthralled mind and hampered speech in his early encounters with Rosalind. Orlando muses at his inability to speak to Rosalind in Act 1, Scene 2: 'What passion hangs these weights upon my tongue? / I cannot speak to her, yet she urged conference' (226–7). As has long been noted in analysis of the play, under Rosalind's tutelage, Orlando's development as a suitor is tracked across the action of *As You Like It* (Brooks, 1960; Jenson, 1972). Linguistic development, however, not only works in the realms of love and literature, however; Orlando's improvements in speech also work in the context of the vocal training of early modern adolescents. Orlando moves from love-struck silence to the besotted lover who produces 'lame' (3.2.154) poetry: 'Run, run, Orlando – carve on every tree / The fair, the chaste and unexpressive she' (3.2.9–10). He then demonstrates the development of his use of language through the controlled eloquence that is at work in the scenes that he shares with Ganymede.

Only in being schooled in the arts of conversation by Rosalind/Ganymede's 'good counsel' (3.2.334) can Orlando hone his oratory skills and take advantage of the 'pliable' (Mulcaster, 1581: 36) quality attributed to his adolescent age. As Courtney Bailey has suggested, Ganymede's lessons replicate and teach behaviours outlined in Castiglione's *The Courtier* (2020: 27–51). By rehearsing the 'implements for conversation' that Thomas Hoby commended in his introduction to his translation of *The Courtier*, young gentlemen could expect to 'garnish their minds with morall vertues' (1588:

C2ᵛ). Ganymede/Rosalind's choice of instructive mode, therefore, also helps fashion Orlando's age, because the schooling he receives, largely in how to speak and how to behave in conversation, is appropriate for an adolescent who is training to be a gentleman. Rosalind/Ganymede's tutelage of Orlando, therefore, also fills the educational void that Orlando laments being denied by his elder brother in his opening lines of the play (1.1.1–21). Within his 'lessons' with Rosalind, Orlando is advised to demonstrate restraint around heated action, and he is encouraged to direct his fervour into thoughtful speech in the courtship scenarios that are rehearsed. When Orlando states that he had rather 'kiss before I spoke' (4.1.63), Ganymede pointedly suggests that kissing fills gaps in intelligent conversation and serves to suggest the individual's 'lack of matter' (4.1.65). Speaking well is an opportunity for an adolescent to direct a heated disposition into words rather than action, and, in so doing, exhibit promising qualities that will win over listeners (and the courted lover).

Indeed, in humoral terms, speech could serve as a therapeutic means for expelling heat, which itself helped moderate the humoral excesses of puberty that might prove unruly. While the speech of 'bragging Jacks' serves as a symptom of a heated disposition that was not within the individual's control, talking could itself help remove excess humours. As Mulcaster observes, speaking carries implications for the health of the individual: 'talking hath great meane either to make or marre' (1581: 63). Mulcaster notes, for example, how the spitting that accompanies talking can help to expel phlegm, while the regular expulsion of hot breath offers a means of cooling the body. According to Mulcaster, a person's breath 'is always exceeding warme, when one exerciseth the voice, it is so thronged and crushed with taking in and letting out' (1581: 56). Speaking becomes, therefore, not only a manifestation of someone's humoral characteristics, but also an exertion of the humoral body. By speaking well, and avoiding overuse or straining of their voices, the adolescent can demonstrate control over their whole body in a way that might additionally be seen to aid the removal of humoral superfluities. Vocal dexterity that was also presented as self-management indicated the adolescent's commanding position in shaping the condition of body and voice, which were made 'pure, fine, and strong, whereby the partes being sound and cleare more strength growth on to healthward, and lesse to disease' (Mulcaster, 1581: 56).[3] Aristotle goes further than writers like Mulcaster, suggesting that efforts to exert control over an adolescent male's voice could even delay its tonal change, presumably through a similar tempering of humours: 'For if a lad strive diligently to hinder his voice from breaking, as some do of those who devote themselves to music, the voice lasts a long while unbroken' (Aristotle, 1910: 581a). Exercises in speech, therefore, offered a potentially self-affirming activity for the eloquent adolescent who, in demonstrating his oratory skills, showed his command over his humorally charged body.

What is more, the male adolescent's eloquent and moderated speech could be thought to reveal Christian virtue. Samuel Crossman, in *The Young Man's Monitor*, muses on the intoxicating qualities of the adolescent's virtuous words:

> The care that he bestows upon his speech is plainly this. That it may be truly accented with *Discretion*, uttered with *Modesty*, seasoned with *Grace*, continually shedding and sending forth a sweet odour wherever he becomes. He easily perswades himself, That Tongue would scarce be fit to praise God in heaven, which hath been used to filthy and light words here on earth. (1665: 99–100)

The virtuous adolescent handles his words carefully, having, it seems, the power to infiltrate the senses of others with the 'sweet odour' he can produce. By contrast, 'filthy and light words' indicate sinfulness and only persuade the speaker of his own worth. Crossman condemns unmannered speech, but he also presents an image of pleasing adolescence, where an adolescent's mode of speech become evidence of self-control that is valued. Crossman's formulation of the adolescent voice, akin to that presented in *The Courtier*, recognises words of a pleasing nature and a community of listeners who are predisposed to favour the utterances of the compelling adolescent speaker.

While early modern adolescent voices are clearly subjected to adult-centred regulations that assess what is and is not pleasing, constructions of adolescent speakers also actively anticipate valued contributions from the adolescent who speaks. As the opening poem to the instructive text, *Youths Behaviour*, concludes, 'nor think't unfit / A Child should teach the world more wit' (Hawkins, 1646: n.p.). Despite the prescriptive tenets for appearing virtuous and in control of their adolescent fervour, the early modern adolescent was permitted scope to formulate how their 'wit' was presented. A space for creativity and self-assertion appears to have been written into models of 'acceptable' adolescent behaviour and speech, which early modern culture was then also predisposed to applaud and not only condemn.

Navigating gendered liberties: girls speaking their minds

Thus far, early modern texts appear most willing to afford adolescent male voices eloquence that is praised. But what of Rosalind in the 'gentlemanly' exchanges between the adolescent Ganymede and Orlando in *As You Like It*? In this section, I explore more fully the theatrical and cultural space that was available, and its limitations, for articulating a vibrant experience of female adolescent selfhood. A degree of cultural acceptance and interest in 'active' and 'witty' female adolescents is tangible in early modern texts. As Higginbotham's analysis of girlhood identities have begun to suggest, adolescence offered girls 'a time of relative freedom compared to womanhood' (2013: 63). Research into the lives of real young women, moreover, has demonstrated that girls could be revered as speakers, writers, and even performers (Chedgzoy, 2013; Williams, 2017: Lamb, 2018). For example, the Mildmay-Fane family has been discussed Chedgzoy for its emphasis upon a 'female intellectual lineage' (2013: 264). Although such educational models were only available during girlhood in elite families, the contexts that enable such valuing of girls' voices help us identify processes for navigating patriarchy that were available to female adolescents, and broader school/education contexts notably feature in the readings of Shakespeare's plays that I offer here.

As important studies have demonstrated, cultural associations existed between the observance of female chastity and silence, which acted to restrict women's words in early modern society. Women's words were especially easy to characterise as unruly and immodest (Hull, 1982; Newman, 1989; Paster, 1993). As Katherine Larson observes in her discussion of female conversation, 'Nearly every conduct manual of the period emphasizes this correspondence between one's language and one's body' (2011: 21). How a woman used her words was scrutinised for how she might also use her body. Yet despite early modern perspectives on voice being gendered, research into women's lives, writings, and communities has also shown the varied ways by which women could be 'Dancing in the net' of the patriarchal society in which they lived (Wall, 1993: 279). Elaine Hobby's survey of around 200 women's writings in *Virtue of Necessity* (1988), for example, highlighted over three decades ago how the voices of early modern female speakers could possess authority and recognised value, often achieving nuanced modes of speech in seventeenth-century culture. Numerous, ever-expanding studies continue to identify fascinating female figures who had much to say: from the spiritual advice offered by the adolescent Sarah Wight to the politicised spiritualism of Anna Trapnel to the domineering combination of Puritan and maternal authority presented by Dorothy Leigh, outspoken females played a significant part of early modern literary production (Hobby, 1988; Wall, 1993; Sylvia Brown, 1999; French, 2015; Chegdzoy, 2019). Many female speakers found ways to navigate the gendered constraints upon their voices.

Here, I examine how the life stage of adolescence could enable such 'negotiated action' (Larson, 2011: 34) that not only enabled girls to speak but also presented opportunities for girls to demonstrate a flair for speaking.

Adolescence and the heat of puberty was not, as discussions of the female affliction of greensickness have highlighted (King, 2004; Potter, 2013), a source of simple freedoms for adolescent girls. Outspokenness, we have seen, could more easily be construed as a symptom of a forthright, and so 'disordered', body. As Larson notes, 'A woman engaging authoritatively in conversation risked censure' (2011: 31), and pubescent girls clearly could not afford to entirely dismiss the trajectory of the life cycle that connected girlhood and womanhood.

Adolescence did, however, grant girls certain liberties in the way they could speak and engage with others. Robert Codrington, who wrote a treatise in response to Hawkins's *Youths Behaviour*, directed his attention to issues of decency in the conversation of adolescent girls. Codrington observes potential for female students to learn in a way that observes 'pliable' minds that are similar to those imagined in Mulcaster's educational writings: 'Youth as it is more tender, so it is more tractable and more apt to receive, and to retain Instructions' (1664: 'Letter to Mrs Ellinor Pargiter', n.p.). Additional restrictions upon female learners and speakers become immediately clear, however. Codrington continues, 'the female Sex being of a more delicate Constitution than the Masculine, is exposed to greater Dangers of Temptation' (1664: 'Letter to Mrs Ellinor Pargiter', n.p.). While Hawkins's parallel work for adolescent males begins with a poem that highlights what the child can teach the world, Codrington begins his book for girls with a Biblical quotation from Proverbs 12:4: 'A vertuous Woman is the Crown of her Husband' (1664: n.p.). Girls should aspire to become good wives. However, room to appreciate loquacious adolescent girls is acknowledged as part of the narrow purpose Codrington imagines. Codrington hopes to instruct girls to become proficient speakers so that rich conversations can continue into adulthood: 'I should not do well to go about to frame a Conversation of dumb persons, but to make a powerfull warre against all Noise and Clamour' (1664: 30). The silent woman as wife is not presented as an ideal, and cultivating informed and controlled speech that avoids being 'Noise' is, in several ways, like the controlled speech that was encouraged in boys.

Codrington recasts female silence as measured pauses *within* speech, where 'Silence gives I know not what grace to Speech it self, and there is nothing truer, than as *Rests* in Musick, so pauses in Discourse being well used, do make that more plainly appear, which is the best of all and the sweetest in it' (1664: 30). As such, Codrington recognises that girls who apply themselves to learning become women who 'are capable as well as men' (1664: 61). Codrington shows resistance towards the gender-bias shown in contemporary attitudes towards female voices, noting how double standards have inhibited access to women's words in print: 'it is much to be lamented, that the tyranny of Custome hath hindered many of them [women] from publishing their Works' (1664: 62). Therefore, although he acknowledges cultural pressures and gender biases that discourage female speech, Codrington also insists upon logic that is grounded in the expectation that his adolescent female readers can achieve skills in conversation, where vitality is valued in girls, which could be cultivated through qualities of voice.

Mulcaster also, somewhat begrudgingly, affords female students skills in thought and speech. Mulcaster, unlike Codrington, makes it clear that such talents in girls should be regarded as temporary: 'girles seeme commonly to haue a quicker ripening in witte, then boyes haue, for all that seeming, yet it is not so. Their naturall weaknesse which cannot holde long, deliuers very soone' (1581: 176). Granted a limited window for demonstrating verbal flair, girls are noted to 'commonly' outshine their male counterparts in educational settings. This temporary outspokenness that Mulcaster attributes to girls suggests that aspects of 'witte', and not only unruly articulations, could be identified in adolescent female speakers, and this verbal assertiveness was not deemed in need of immediate remediation. Mulcaster's praise of women 'so excellently well trained, and so rarely qua|lified, either for the toungues themselues, or for the matter in the toungues' (1581: 186) suggests, moreover, that some retention of learning is evident as girls become women, although a male-centred narrative is apparent when the purpose of such training is once again framed as providing men with companions 'to garnish our alonenesse' (1581: 169). During the process of training adolescent female voices and bodies for somewhat limited social futures, however, Mulcaster notably recommends 'the same freedom in cases of libertie, when they commodiously may, being reserued to parentes in their daughters, which I allowed them in their sonnes' (Mulcaster, 1581: 175–6). In certain contexts, especially educational ones that were clearly geared towards the end point of marriage, early modern writers observed that vocal dexterity was an accepted and even valued attribute of female adolescence.

The different ways in which adolescent female voices are fashioned in Shakespeare's drama offer further insights into conditions that enabled girls' voices to be either celebrated or silenced. Before I turn to Rosalind's complex representation as a skilled orator in *As You Like It*, an examination of Katherine's linguistic refashioning across the plot of *The Taming of the Shrew* offers a useful starting point and stark reminder for considering the circumstances that Shakespeare presents as incurring limitations upon girls' speech. Katherine's numerical age is unclear in *The Taming of the Shrew*. We know she is an older sister, but still a young woman who is likely within the protracted age-range of early modern adolescence. Katherine is 'young and beauteous' (1.2.84) and described as a 'girl' (3.2.27, 46). Although

Higginbotham highlights that 'definitions of girlhood as female childhood co-existed with definitions of girlhood as unruly femininity' (2013: 73–4), both daughters (one shrewish, one relatively obedient) in *The Taming of the Shrew* are called 'girl' (1.1.77, 152; 2.1.24). Comparable models of female adolescence appear to be explored as both girls navigate the process of maturation towards adulthood and marriage.

The words that Katherine uses convey humoral qualities that are strikingly appropriate to an adolescent character, whose 'heated' temperament is made evident in her talkative 'shrewish' behaviour:

> Why, sir, I trust I may have leave to speak,
> And speak I will. I am no child, no babe.
> Your betters have endured me say my mind,
> And if you cannot, best you stop your ears.
> My tongue will tell the anger of my heart,
> Or else my heart, concealing it, will break,
> And rather than it shall, I will be free,
> Even to the uttermost as I please in words. (4.3.74–81)

Emotion and activity in Katherine's heart and mind are directly connected to activity in words. Katherine's description of the connection between her feelings and words are reminiscent of Lemnius's account of the 'internall heate' that can drive speech (1576: 45^v). Katherine asserts her maturity beyond the age of a child and claims a freedom to speak and be heard in a model of unstoppable verbal over-spilling, where she may 'utter' 'most'. But, while Katherine differentiates between her state and that of a child, where her words have purpose and must be expressed, those around her do not recognise self-control in the management of her words. As Katherine notes, she does not seek to please her audience, who 'best stop your ears'. Katherine does not acquiesce to the recommendations of early modern educators in presenting her words 'with measure, and in due time' (Hawkins, 1646: 38).

After all, interpretations of voices involve negotiations between speaker and listener. As Bloom's work on speech and its reception has shown, early modern understandings of how sound travelled, as and through air, and from one individual to be heard by another, uses of voice involved aspects of self-assertion and dissolution (2007: 69, 66–110). The voice might manipulate others by infiltrating minds but speaking also inevitably involved relinquishing control of sounds that had to leave the body and enter that of another (possibly many others) for communication to take place. While an early modern audience may have been predisposed to be enthralled by adolescent speech, knowing when and to whom speech can be uttered, and especially judging when a girl might 'speak what they think', carried heightened significance as girls who could less afford to displease those who were listening (Larson, 2011). Therefore, a girl's experimentations with words needed to be sure that the reception of those words would not be hostile.

What might, in another context, be the celebrated over-spilling of the vehement emotion of heated adolescence, is, for Katherine in *The Taming of the Shrew*, deemed threatening and presumptuous agency, as Katherine resists the will – and ignores the ears – of the men around her. This kind of speech in a girl character is not celebrated for its energetic delivery or impassioned framing of mind. Moreover, adolescent self-assertion becomes linguistically marred, with the speaker of unacceptable agency being labelled 'Kate the curst' (2.1.186). Katherine's vocal character becomes categorised in terms of an affliction that is an external imposition, suggesting the subject's lack of control. By being identified as cursed, where power in words belong to the person cursing Katherine and not the girl herself, Katherine is classified as a subject whose speech acts register disorder and unwanted humoral excess. External intervention, as seen with the 'greensick' girl, is, moreover, once again imagined in the form of the remedial influence of a husband: Petruchio.

Katherine's heated, adolescent temperament is suggested throughout the play's overarching 'taming' narrative, which seeks to adjust Katherine's condition so that she becomes Petruchio's vision of her: 'not hot, but temperate as the morn' (2.I.292). Paster, for example, sees Katherine as a disorderly woman (rather than a girl) whose humoral behaviour is forcibly 'cooled in order to be socialized as a wife' (2004: 29). As we have seen, female speech placed female bodies under scrutiny: 'the talkative woman is frequently imagined as synonymous with the sexually available woman, her open mouth the signifier for invited entrance elsewhere' (Boose, 1991: 196). Even though she never expresses explicit sexual desire, and certainly no particular desire for Petruchio, Katherine's wordy adolescence incurs the same corrective actions imagined for greensick girls with their uncontainable desires. Katherine speaks what she feels, and, though her feelings do not initially seem to include uncontrolled sexual desire, her 'excessive verbal fluency' (Paster, 1993: 25) does not register required aspects of moderation or control. Fervent speech from a female speaker that shows no concern for exerting care in achieving this approval is enough to anticipate bodily 'leakiness' and the threat of sexual indiscretion (Paster, 1993: 25).

Petruchio's treatment of Katherine equates to an extreme form of humoral tempering whereby her engagement with the natural world through eating and sleeping, two of the 'non-naturals' that informed day-to-day humoral management, are modified.[4] In Act 4, Scene 1, Petruchio pointedly deprives Katherine of food that will exacerbate her perceived heatedness, with both 'over-roasted flesh' (4.1.157) and mustard that is 'too hot' (4.3.25) being rejected. Although Galenic medicine would normally pursue remedial action whereby any humoral excess would be 'reduced by contraries' (Elyot, 1539: 42), Petruchio imposes abstinence upon Katherine in a pseudo-medical response to her characterisation as overheated.[5] Treatment of the body, moreover, takes the form of a 'speaking cure' in the play, and, as Nathaniel B. Smith (2014) has observed, excesses in humoral heat are indicated through Katherine's words. Smith's evaluation of Katherine's infamous final speech sets the assessment in terms of humoral theory, although age does not feature significantly in Smith's reading: 'What is the "temperature," after all, of Kate's final speech: obediently cold or aggressively hot?' (2014: 207). Quantity in words in a long speech is not necessarily as heated as short 'waspish' (2.1.210) exchanges, and performative self-control is evident in how the speech is presented to onstage listeners. For Katherine, growing up into married adulthood appears to mean learning to use her words so that they please others, primarily men, more than herself. Bicks identifies a shrinking narrative at work in Katherine's cognitive redaction that is forcibly encouraged across the play. Katherine, who reflects upon a time when 'My mind hath been as big as yours' (5.2.170), exhibits a 'shrunken mind' that has been 'beaten down to size' (Bicks, 2021: 19), as her mental powers become directed solely towards the wifely duties that she has not herself sought in defining her girlhood. *The Taming of the Shrew*, therefore, seems to present a coming of age narrative that registers how modes of female speech map onto a trajectory of maturation for a character, which contributes to an 'uninspiring legacy when it comes to the study of female minds' (Bicks, 2016: 180). The men who are assembled for the final scene of *The Taming of the Shrew* notably applaud Katherine's modified speech, which no longer offends their ears.

As we have seen, cognitive and linguistic flair could be observed in girls, but, while eloquent boys unquestionably become eloquent men in early modern thinking, the situation was less clear-cut for girls. Indeed, as we saw with Mulcaster, commentators could pointedly describe adolescent wit as a temporary part of a girl's development, rather than a continuous trend in the life-cycle trajectory. Character traits specific to girlhood thus become understood through a comparison with requirements of adulthood, which infringe upon how value is attributed to girlish accomplishments. Crooke's anatomical writings state as commonplace the assumption that adult women have little mental capacity, expressing concern that weighty concerns will 'drive a woman as wee say out of her little wits' (1615: 274). Therefore, girls' demonstrations of proficiency in thinking and speaking could be contemplated in light of this oppressive model ascribed to adult female bodies and minds. The transitory nature of adolescence that may enable flexibility in behavioural models is also used to play down the significance of a girl's talent. Mulcaster, for example, saw the degree to which girls' brains were activated by maturation as incomparable to the development of boys' brains in the following terms: 'their braines be not so much charged, neither with weight nor with multitude of matters, as boyes heades be' (1581: 176). Early modern gender biases are evident in Mulcaster's predisposition to dismiss the value of the words that girls utter; such words, he says, stem from unretentive minds, which 'like empty caske they make the greater noise' (1581: 176). Although girls' words might be entertaining, being 'very quicke witted by some sudden pretie aunswere, or some sharp replie' (Mulcaster, 1581: 176), a girl's mutability that is identified as fluency in boys is not represented as such by Mulcaster.

Indeed, girls' witty words quickly become hampered by culturally restrictive models of women's words for Mulcaster and he describes a 'natural' and desired 'dulling' of girls' wits, which he actively encourages as they reach maturation (1581: 176). Mulcaster contextualises his ideas about intellectual retention in girls by returning to an understanding of 'sexed' bodies. The mind, he notes, will be hampered by a 'feminine' corporeality: 'As for bodies the *maidens* be more weake, most commonly euen by nature, as of a moonish influence' (1581: 176). Maturation that heats pliable minds also, as we have seen, realises 'sexed' restrictions because female puberty centred upon the humoral logic that explained invigorated minds *and* menstruation. The pubescent female's compelling dexterity in speech and wit had the additional hurdle of more negative discourses about changeability that were associated with the 'inconstant moon' (*Romeo and Juliet* 2.2.151), which presided as the natural force associated with menstruation. Therefore, the boy who spoke well could demonstrate heated promise in different terms to that of a girl; the adolescent male's expulsion of words moderates and emboldens an admired strength of mind that patriarchal structures wanted him to retain to some degree into adulthood. The girl, however, must additionally set her words in line with some of the demands placed upon female adulthood because the changes to her pubescent body were centred upon bodily alterations that were more emphatically scrutinised for evidence of instability and inconstancy. The talkative Katherine's fate of imposed marriage in *The Taming of the Shrew* is, therefore, perhaps unsurprisingly reminiscent of the 'remedial' actions taken on the behalf of the greensick girl.

However, although *The Taming of the Shrew* ascribes to cultural forces that limited female speech, the play's framing of Katherine's 'unruly' voice *as* adolescent may explain why Katherine is not *yet* regarded as sexually licentious *because* she talks. Lack of verbal restraint in this character does not immediately equate to a lack of chastity, as is often the case for women in early modern drama (Newman, 1989: 503–18). For example, Elizabeth Cary records more familiar correlations between female behaviour and speech when the titular character of *The Tragedy of Mariam* is judged according to her aural, oral, and sexual availability: 'she's unchaste; / Her mouth will open to every stranger's ear' (4.7. 77–8). Likewise, Morose in Jonson's *Epicœne* exclaims, 'O immodesty! A manifest woman' (3.4.37) upon discovering that his new wife is not silent as he had hoped. Katherine's independent thought-speech formulation is deemed devastatingly in need of forcible revision in *The Taming of the Shrew* but could, albeit as a small mercy, suggest how the temporary life stage of adolescence provided a context in which girls could articulate their own self-revisions in ways that were not yet fully bound to the word/sexualised body alignment of womanhood. Outspoken girls might avoid complete reputational ruin, if not the pressures that could be asserted if achieving an acceptable adult persona was thought to be in doubt. The mutability of Katherine's girlhood that is so harshly subjected to Petruchio's domineering influence in *The Taming of the Shrew* can, therefore, be 'successfully' redirected towards a marital future, with Katherine being presented as a girl whose speech acts initially resist contemplating that projected outcome.

That girls could shape, revise, and test out their own voices in order to influence the form a future marriage may take is, however, suggested in Bianca's strategic movements in *The Taming of the Shrew*. The younger sister's elected moments of quiet and self-assertion manage to retain her qualities of feminine 'virtue' in a self-representation that is received in terms of the 'Maid's mild behaviour and sobriety' (1.1.71). As Patricia Parker puts it: 'Bianca becomes the master of both of her potential masters [...] and finally emerges as anything but a tamed wife by the play's post-marital end' (2007: 193). For Parker, Bianca's control is subtle but powerfully rooted in her management of her would-be tutors' lessons, whereby Bianca reworks her masters' words in order to assert control over courtship negotiations. Courtship, in the guise of tuition, places Bianca in the position of a student, an identity that Bianca can legitimately perform with some outspokenness. The precociousness commonly attributed to students (Parker, 2007; Bicks, 2021: 105–26), which is also suggested in Mulcaster's 'witty' female students and Codrington's capable learners, offers a means by which Bianca can interact with her tutors/suitors and shape her selection of a marital partner using terms that recognise her mental capabilities.

Bianca is not, then, the silent opposite to her talkative sister who speaks her husband's mind by the end of the play; Bianca is another adolescent character who speaks her thoughts in ways that navigate the restrictions and liberties that her age and gender allow. Articulations of 'chaste' self-control, as Larson's (2011) investigation into female conversation through letters has also suggested, could be more expansive than female silence and overtly pronounced expressions of obedience, as is more overtly seen in Katherine's final speech from *The Taming of the Shrew*. Bianca's negotiated agency is, moreover, neither exceptional nor the most pronounced in Shakespeare's representation of adolescent female characters. *The Taming of the Shrew* is an early play in Shakespeare's repertoire (c. 1590–4),[6] and it is possible, likely even, based on findings that I develop across this book, that Shakespeare and his company were in the early stages of their development of adolescent roles when Katherine and Bianca were first represented. Shakespeare's plays from across the 1590s–1610s explore ways by which the voices of adolescent girl characters can shape their own futures and, indeed, the futures of other characters in the fictive worlds they inhabit. What is more, it is by speaking *as* adolescent characters that these characters appear to achieve liberty in ways strikingly dissimilar to Katherine.

An example of an expansive adolescent subjectivity is found in *The Merchant of Venice* (c. 1596–8), a play that was performed at least a few years after *The Taming of The Shrew*. Portia, bound by the casket test of her father in the selection of a husband, initially observes her predicament in humoral terms that allude to cultural constructions of adolescence and frustrated passions. Notably, however, Portia's self-assessment of humoral excesses is presented in a way that indicates self-awareness and calculated self-control: 'The brain may devise laws for the blood, but a hot temper / leaps o'er a cold decree: such a hare is madness, the youth, / to skip o'er the meshes of good counsel, the cripple' (1.2.16–18). Shakespeare rarely states the numeric ages of his characters, and this is the case for Portia, whose role as 'head' of household assigns her some 'adult' responsibilities that may distract the modern reader from signs of her likely adolescence (Pollock, 2001: 191–20). Portia's styling in the language of the play as 'fair' (1.1.162) and comely suggest that she is regarded as adolescent in early modern terms. Her pairing with the clearly adolescent, though less cautious, 'young Venetian' (2.9.86) Bassanio, who is 'something too prodigal' (1.1.129) and likened to April/Spring that 'never came too sweet (2.9.91) also appears to be a match of adolescent lovers on the brink of adulthood. Portia's bind to her father's will, as 'a living daughter / curbed by the will of a dead father' (1.2.21–2), moreover, suggests an action of intergenerational guidance put in place to direct the young.

While Portia is likely older than, say, the thirteen-year-old Juliet, her carefully managed creativity in voice, and competence, which, as we have seen, might more willingly be attributed to a female adolescent rather than a woman of 'little wits' (Crooke, 1615: 274), aligns Portia with adolescence. In her speech, Portia shows awareness of the necessity for 'good counsel', and she makes efforts to use reason to quell the heated impulses that she associates with youth. Portia is alert to the way that such impulses might 'skip o'er' rational thought and, in outlining her internal struggles with her father's casket scheme, she demonstrates command over these emotions. Her conclusion is to assert daughterly obedience: 'I will die as chaste as / Diana unless I be obtained by the manner of my father's will' (1.2.91–2).

Portia's powers of speech in this early part of the play become, therefore, evidence of, and not a challenge to, her assured self-control and chastity.

Once her union with Bassanio is assured, Portia presents herself as 'girlish' by describing herself as mutable in ways reminiscent of Mulcaster's 'pliable' (36) students:

> an unlessoned girl, unschooled, unpractised;
> Happy in this, she is not yet so old
> But she may learn; happier than this,
> She is not bred so dull but she can learn;
> Happiest of all is that her gentle spirit
> Commits itself to yours to be directed,
> As from her lord, her governor, her king. (3.2.159–65)

Identifying her ability to learn and be directed by her husband, and articulated in a way that suggests she is an older girl who has already been educated in arts of conversation and decorum, Portia's maturation from girl to woman is presented in a manner that shares features of Katherine's final speech about husbands being 'thy lord [...] / Thy head, thy sovereign' from *The Taming of the Shrew* (5.2.138–9). Portia also anticipates the direction of 'her lord, her governor, her king' (3.2.165) that so famously indicate Katherine's obedience to Petruchio. However, Portia's demonstrations of control in the face of her 'heated' thoughts, which precede her union with Bassanio, lay the foundations for the adolescent female's exploration of virtues of a mould that is more expansive than those used in Shakespeare's earlier play. Performing traits of the willingly good daughter and submissive bride, Portia realises a vision of adolescence that shows the individual as also being in command of her humoral temper and capable of applying reason. Such reason can then be further demonstrated in the character's performance as the crossdressed-heroine-barrister who is free to exhibit knowledge of the law, and able to outspokenly advocate the Christian 'mercy' (4.1.182–203) that allows her to outwit Shylock and demonstrate an early modern form of Christian virtue.[7] Portia's courtroom display of commanding speech see her interpret the terms of Shylock's 'bond' in intelligent and assertive ways, steering the legal contract from having apparently fixed meaning, 'There is no power in Venice / Can alter a decree established' (4.1.216–17), to opening up what 'The words expressly are' (4.1.305) according to her presentation of its meaning.

With the exception of Shylock, who must submit to Portia's authority ('I am content', 4.1.392), those assembled to witness Portia's compelling wordplay recognise their own indebtedness to the performance. Bassanio acknowledges how 'I and my friend / have by your wisdom been this day acquitted' (4.1.406–7), and Portia is roundly applauded as a thinker and speaker in the scene. For the play's audience, moreover, Portia's skills extend beyond her manipulation of legal and religious discourses, and include recognition of her 'witty' masquerade in performing as Balthazar. Although Portia's activities are broadly contextualised as unthreatening to patriarchal norms in facilitating her marital union, Portia suggests ways by which girls could take advantage of attributes of vitality and creativity associated with their age to voice more expansive subjectivities. What is more, in so doing, Portia seems, like Bianca, to establish her own authoritative position within her marriage by negotiating terms that see her husband and group of friends acknowledge their dependence on her. In managing Bassanio's pledge of obligation, Portia seems to resituate his relationship through their marital vows, constructing another 'bond' of obligation in the additional 'witty' episode that sees Portia/Balthasar oversee the conditions for Bassanio to give her (back) her ring (Wilder, 2008: 377–94).

As suggested in Portia's management of rings in *The Merchant of Venice*, expressions of wit and mirth offered a way by which the female adolescent could be granted greater liberty than she might achieve in adulthood. The ring episode, loaded with innuendo about marital sex (Wilder, 2008: 377–94), makes use of levity in framing Portia's linguistic efforts. The audience is clearly meant to be amused by the husbands' treatment when they return to Belmont without their wives' rings (Wilder, 2008: 377–94). As Lamb notes, wit and merriment is often attributed to youthful discourse, observing that young readers were understood to 'engage with the book in particular ways: reading for wit, mirth, sport and pleasure' (2018: 89). Ezekiah Woodward notes in *A Childe's Patrimony* that childhood and adolescence 'are ages of fancy' (1640: 97) when imaginative faculties are active. Woodward suggests utilising this propensity for imaginative engagement in teaching methods: a father or tutor 'must make great use of the childes senses, for they have the best agreement with its fancy' (1640: 98). A propensity for adolescent 'fancy' can, therefore, be valued and enable teaching opportunities that make mirth manageable and desired rather than problematic. That it may be possible for the adolescent female to teach others through merriment also seems available in Shakespeare's constructions of girl characters who, especially in comedy, can use games to influence their would-be husbands (themselves usually still mutable adolescents in comic plots) to shape the foundation of marital futures.

Rosalind's 'sport' (1.2.22) of falling in love in *As You Like It* (c. 1599), for example, is framed as an entertaining pastime that is a worthy – and prompt – response to Celia's call for mirth and a merrier disposition in a scene that begins with Rosalind reflecting in a subdued manner upon her banished father. Likewise, the Duke's expulsion of Rosalind from his court, upon threat of death, is quickly converted by the pair into a source of amusement.

Whereas the situation could promote despair at imagined dangers, as in the play's source narrative *Rosalynde* (Lodge, 1590), Shakespeare's Rosalind and Celia delight in the fun of, rather than the need for, disguise. Perils familiar to precarious adolescence are reworked into a game in the play's plot, and threats of being harmed in the forest are rendered the source of excitement and mirthful creativity in the safe setting of comedy: 'To liberty and not to banishment' (1.3.134).

As such, Rosalind's erotic 'sport' in *As You Like It* can avoid the implications that the references to 'sport' incur in Leontes's use of the word as an adulterous slur on his wife's reputation in *The Winter's Tale*. Leontes scathingly imagines how Hermione will 'sport herself / With that she's big with' (*The Winter's Tale* 2.1.60–1), even though Hermione hopes that her husband's accusations are a kind of jest: 'What is this? Sport?' (2.1.58). While 'sport' can turn from merriment to threats of peril in Shakespeare's plays – Shylock first describes the nature of his bond with Antonio as 'merry sport' (1.3.138) – 'sport' that is framed as *adolescent* mirth seems more easily presented as harmless. Celia's awareness of restrictions on behaviour serve to situate the characters' 'sport' as appropriately modest: 'no further in sport neither than / with safety of a pure blush thou mayst in honour come off / again' (1.2.23–5). Notably, Celia codes the adolescent blushes of the girl characters as 'pure', navigating the more licentious meanings of blushes that I examined in the previous chapter. Calculated in such terms, where Orlando also accepts that 'he in sport doth call his Rosalind' (4.3.155), the adolescent characters show vivaciousness without recklessness, and the mirth of adolescence offers a context for Rosalind's girlhood mutability and self-assertion to be received as inoffensive to early modern sensibilities.

Indeed, Celia and Rosalind's design to fall in love seems to sit well within the parameters of 'girlish' behaviour. Higginbotham observes that 'material and erotic pursuits are unwomanly, and yet the construction of them as "girl-like" implies that they are inherently feminine' (2013: 73). Expressions of desire in such pursuits, however, require management in a performance that is controlled by boy player and character alike. In *As You Like It*, unlike *The Taming of the Shrew*, the adolescent female's command over her mutable identity is conveyed. The gender ambiguity at play in *As You Like It* is multifaceted but never chaotic; the witty and eroticised interplay of characters in the forest is situated as components of Rosalind's 'sport'. Verbal exchanges between Ganymede and Orlando are vibrant and often eroticised, as much scholarship has attested (Howard, 1988; Jardine, 1989; Stallybrass, 1991; Orgel, 1996). However, the 'heated' exchanges of words are more than symptoms of desire; they are also indicative of each adolescent's intellectual sharpness, especially for Ganymede/Rosalind who controls the exchanges. Rosalind is both an adolescent in command of her self-presentation in her plot to 'play the knave with him' (3.2.275), and an image of male adolescence in the portrayal of Ganymede, mimicking whilst demonstrating the 'nimble wit' (1.1.143) that is also attributed to Orlando (3.2.106–9). The courtship scenes that include the performance of multiple 'Rosalinds' (4.1) in *As You Like It* establish that Rosalind, and the actor performing the part, has an excellent command over words in a performance that enables a layered representation of feminine and masculine adolescence in Rosalind/Ganymede.

Across *As You Like It*, Rosalind is characterised as possessing enviable communicative skills. For example, Duke Frederick's hostile response to Rosalind is geared towards her esteemed self-presentation, which the Duke notes depend upon selective silence and a controlled fashioning of self: 'Her very silence and her patience, / Speak to the people, and they pity her' (1.3.74–5). Rather than being self-effacing, silence is here regarded as a considered, and effective, means of 'speaking' to the people, an example perhaps of 'pauses in Discourse being well used' (Codrington, 1664: 30). Primarily, however, it is through her articulations *in conversation* that Rosalind demonstrates the vibrant management of her voice. Though she is subject to involuntary action associated with female 'frailty' and adolescent impulsiveness, for example, in swooning at the sight of blood (4.3.155), Rosalind is most commonly associated with commanding speech that is celebrated in the play. Celia cherishes Rosalind's words and pleads with her friend to be forthcoming in her speech: 'thy words are too precious to be cast away upon / curs. Throw some of them at me' (1.3.4–5). Linguistic versatility, and command over the performative and imaginative components of public speaking are pronounced in Rosalind's girlhood eloquence.

Being in each other's 'good' company additionally informs the positive framing of Celia and Rosalind's adolescent exchanges. The space in which a young woman's words were expressed, and the audience – usually friends and family – who received them, could ensure the security and well-judged nature of the early modern female's words (Larson, 2011: 40). The female adolescent's thoughts can even spill over into words and 'uttermost' in a manner less disorderly than Katherine's speaking of 'my mind' to unhearing men, if the female tongue is granted *timely* liberty in conversations with friends (4.3.81, 76). The idea of 'good counsel' recurs across Shakespeare's plays, suggesting that skills in conversation, demonstrating an ability to talk, listen, and respond, were key in demonstrations of skilful speech, and the representation of a controlled adolescence. Orlando receives his 'good counsel' (3.2.334) willingly from Ganymede in *As You Like It*. Portia, in conversation with Nerissa, provides her own 'good counsel' (1.2.18) in *The Merchant of Venice*. In *As You Like It*, Rosalind's words run free only in conversation with the trusted Celia; she judges her audience well. Celia and

Rosalind can confess rash feelings in 'private' conversation, partly, perhaps, because the conversation itself offers a means of moderating 'heated' feelings (Mulcaster, 1581: 56). The humoral excesses of adolescent passions can be acknowledged and demonstrably subjected to the reasoned evaluation of heated minds. Rosalind, in conversation with Celia, like Portia in conversation with Nerissa, suggests the moderating effect of speaking and thinking upon the 'hot temper' (*The Merchant of Venice* 1.2.16) of adolescence, and alleviating the impulses to act rashly.

Adolescence as a time of self-assertion, we have seen, is often set alongside an expectation that adolescents will be primed to receive instruction and engage in conversation that offers self-reflection and improvement. Pliable young minds and words are valued in the context of supportive communities that offer help as well as expressing admiration for witty adolescents. The voices of adolescent are not, then, typically celebrated in full isolation, because much of their value emerges through the interplay of their voice with the voices around them. In *Romeo and Juliet*, part of the tragedy seems bound to the way in which the adolescent lovers become isolated from 'good counsel' (1.1.137). Messages go undelivered, relationships with confidantes become compromised, and 'heated' adolescents react with a violent immediacy of passion, often without fully understanding to situations to which they respond (Kahn, 1978). Indeed, the play's action repeatedly suggests that reasoned conversation has the power to abate impassioned reactions. We might remember, for example, that Romeo seems set upon despair over Rosalind before receiving 'good counsel' from Benvolio (1.1.137), and Romeo determines to kill himself following his banishment until the Friar intervenes with words to quell his 'unreasonable fury' (3.3.111).

Moreover, though often regarded (and performed) as the famous romantic centre to *Romeo and Juliet*, Romeo's overhearing of Juliet's private thoughts from her window can be seen as setting the fatal pace of their romance. As words that articulate heated passions and that are uttered without the restraints of conversational decorum, Juliet acknowledges her concern about how her feelings have been conveyed: 'I should have been more strange, I must confess / But that thou overheards't ere I was ware, / My true-love passion' (2.1.144–6). Romeo, 'bescreened in night' (2.1.94), overhears the thirteen-year-old Juliet's words of love, and she makes clear that these words would not have been intentionally said to his face. In this sense, the scene is about the impassioned realisation of mutual love and an untimely relinquishing of Juliet's control over her voice, which is elsewhere demonstrably within her control, as she converses with Romeo to collaborate in creating a sonnet (1.4.208–21). The liminality of speech observed by Bloom, where agency in speaking and listening allows the 'transfer of speech from speaker to listener' (Bloom, 2007: 13), carries heightened implications for the female speaker here. Romeo stakes his claim to Juliet: 'I take thee at thy word' (2.1.91), for she has consented to give herself to Romeo ('Take all myself', 2.1.91), and Romeo completes the iambic pentameter but this time without Juliet meaning for him to hear her.

The heated articulations of adolescence can, therefore, be judged as evidence of positive self-command or disruptive assertions of desire, depending on who is listening. Juliet, in the quiet of night and in her walled garden, utters feelings not intended to be the stuff of conversation; her words are eloquent and compelling for us and Romeo ('She speaks', 2.1.56). What we hear is contextualised as an honest expression of adolescent feeling that is unmediated by reason or an awareness of its self-display. Where, we might ask, is Juliet's sensible young confidante, her Nerissa or Celia, to whom she can talk of such feelings? While the play encourages sympathy for the rose-like Romeo and Juliet in the play, for Juliet to be 'taken at [her] word' in circumstances where words have not been knowingly shared, appears ominous for an adolescent female character who is not speaking from a clear position of reason, mirth, or self-control. Luxuriant in their honesty and feeling, the exchanges between Romeo and Juliet move beyond the more orderly wordplay of their first meeting (1.4.204–21). From this point of hearing Juliet's private thoughts, the interactions between the couple escalate so that the heat and immediacy of passionate responses start to override reasoned evaluations in the play. As the play's tragedy unfolds, we see reason applied in various hurried and responsive stratagems, and Romeo and Juliet's untimely voicing of passionate feelings across the threshold of a window at night could well set the tone for subsequent mistimed communications that poignantly miscarry in the play. Friar Lawrence, in the next scene, warns Romeo, 'They stumble that run fast' (2.2.94), as images of hasty action replace those of timely waiting that are initially recommended in relation to Juliet's maturation: 'Let two more summers wither in their pride / Ere we may think her ripe to be a bride' (1.2.10–11). The renowned exchanges at Juliet's window, when we hear Romeo infamously identified as a 'rose' and Juliet's reticence about the untimely nature of the exchange between the lovers, seems to invite contemporary concerns about unregulated adolescent speech. Moreover, the premature and unmediated nature of the adolescents' communications connect the scene with early modern ideas about disorderly adolescence, immodest talk, and familiar tropes of adolescent promise being paired with decline and death that were discussed in this book's first chapter. Juliet's poetic, oxymoronic language, itself articulating intellect as well as discord, recognises the lovers' farewell as 'sweet sorrow', and allusions to grief and death strikingly accompany the adolescents' moment of parting. Juliet offers an odd analogy for her love of Romeo that concludes their meeting when she describes a tethered bird that is loved with a possessive force. Juliet poignantly observes how she must allow Romeo to leave in order to avoid the bird's fate, but the image presents the concerning and familiar binary of adolescent fervour and death that the pair must navigate: 'I should kill thee with much cherishing' (2.1.225). Ideas of 'dying' were often eroticised in early modern culture (Charney, 2002: 89), the medical reasoning being because an orgasm was understood to expel vital spirit – through seed – and so literally shorten the individual's life. Spoken in relation to adolescent desire, however, the idea of dying as the result of excesses in emotion carries especial urgency in tapping into concerns about the perilous actions that an early modern audience would likely expect to follow any unmoderated feelings and words that were expressed by adolescents.

Juliet's situation swiftly moves beyond her control, most notably once she has married Romeo, the only 'chaste' outcome available to her after her private declarations of love are overheard. Efforts to navigate the dangers of her age prove fruitless for Juliet, despite her display of impressive, independent 'brainwork' across the play (Bicks, 2021: 3). The 'negotiated action' (Larson, 2011: 34) of the adolescent female who can live and thrive appears to rest not only upon the individual's ability to command their own heated thoughts but also in their ability to use their voice to positively engage others in the collaborative nature of communication. Care over conversational context, as we have seen, was especially required for early modern girls who had to be cautious in public. An adolescent male could afford to mismatch words and deeds, as Celia's account of Orlando attests: he 'writes brave verses, speaks / brave words, swears brave oaths, and breaks them bravely' (3.4.35–6). Celia's concerns, here regarding Orlando's character when he is late in meeting with Rosalind, note a gendered double standard in the way that boys do not as keenly appreciate the need for verbal moderation as girls. In a culture where bravado is noted as a familiar model of masculine expression (we need only recall Portia's evaluation of male guises she could adopt), a young man's zealous words are not expected to be so rigidly tied to his actions.

The additional efforts demanded of girls in demonstrating their linguistic prowess during adolescence supports Bicks's conclusions about early modern female adolescence often being attributed *greater* cognitive skills than are typically observed in adolescent males. According to Bicks, girls are represented as especially 'capable of prospection – of projecting themselves into imagined future situations' (2021: 16), demonstrating a concern for the future implications that current actions would have, in 'brainwork' that uses more complex cognitive faculties than boys. By contrast, 'boys were more unstable and vulnerable to their wanton imaginations than girls' (Bicks, 2021: 166), perhaps because boys were granted permissible freedoms that girls were denied. Therefore, girls and boys were understood in the same humoral terms that related to their age, and these humours underpinned the cognition and vocal changes observed, yet constructions of gender identities meant that girls had to do more than boys to impress and actively demonstrate their bodily control through their voices to avoid shame. Beyond the context of early modern theatre, where I will suggest that male adolescent players did face particularly complex vocal demands, girls had greater 'negotiated action' (Larson, 2011: 34) to achieve. Girls' voices, in this sense, had higher standards to meet than the voices of boys to achieve acclaim.

In *As You Like It* (c. 1599), for example, we see how adolescent female articulations can be both complex and applauded, in the representation of Rosalind, and castigated, in the representation of Phoebe. The unsympathetic reception of Phoebe's words serves to indicate how a girl's linguistic negotiations could be deemed inappropriate by others, and realises persistent limitations in Shakespeare's constructions of girlhood, as Phoebe's fate recalls that of Katherine in *The Taming of the Shrew*. While Rosalind seems safeguarded by her disguise as Ganymede, and scenes that establish her mirth and sense of conversational decorum, Phoebe's adolescent voice is repeatedly challenged for its presumptive and misguided qualities. Upon first observing Phoebe in conversation with Silvius, Ganymede chastises Phoebe for her confused vocality: 'you insult, exult, and all at once' (3.5.36). By contrast, Phoebe's attraction to Ganymede includes an appreciation for pleasing speech: 'he talks well' (3.5.109). Indeed, Phoebe indicates her own understanding that the power of words depends on what is said and how those words are heard and interpreted: 'words do well / When he that speaks them pleases those that hear/ It is a pretty youth' (3.5.110–12). Yet Phoebe's own response to Ganymede's words proves problematic when she fails to cause similar pleasure for those who hear her. Although Phoebe's rejection of Silvius and preference for Ganymede are connected to Phoebe's appreciation of the physical and linguistic appeal of the 'pretty youth', Phoebe's desire to 'hear you chide than this man woo' (3.5.65) offers a de-regularising response to words in conversation. The female listener becomes a jarring contributor to conversation as she resists the intentions behind each 'male' speaker's words, disrupting their own displays of eloquence. Phoebe's mismatched response of love to chiding is represented as a misjudgement of the wordplay at work between all parties involved in the conversation, and, while the play uses this mismatching of meaning as a source of humour, it is Phoebe who is characterised as the individual whose voice requires alteration.

Although Rosalind/Ganymede asserts control over conversations with Orlando, the wordplay between Orlando and Ganymede never appears to undermine Orlando's desires in the ways that Phoebe's resist those of Silvius and Ganymede. After all, Orlando agrees to – and appears to enjoy – the unorthodox terms of Ganymede's tutelage. As Larson observes, 'conversational dexterity could be recast in literary texts as evidence of virtuous self-control' (2011: 9), and this seems to be the case for Rosalind, who steers her suitor towards a heteronormative marital conclusion to their courtship, even if the courtship itself explores more expansive possibilities. As Ganymede, Rosalind's words achieve liberty by being contextualised as a kind of well-meaning sport, with which most characters (and the audience) are complicit.

Phoebe, like Rosalind, seems to attempt a managed performance of self in sending the 'taunting letter' (3.5.133) to Ganymede. Telling Silvius that her written word expresses anger, Phoebe seeks a covert means by which she can articulate feelings of love. As scholars have shown, letter writing could open intellectual and spiritual communities to early modern women (Harris, 2011: 108–21; Larson, 2011). However, in articulating unwanted affection, Phoebe's letter is received by Rosalind not as evidence of playful adolescence, but as a record of Phoebe's duplicitous voice. By misjudging her audience, and failing to please 'those that hear', Phoebe communicates passion that makes her vulnerable to criticism. As Alan Stewart's analysis of *Shakespeare's Letters* has shown, love letters 'could be taken extremely seriously – or that could be taken extremely lightly. The key factor here is precisely how they are *taken*' (2008: 239). What is more, the female voice, materialised as a letter, can be handled and judged by all who encounter it. Phoebe's unwanted letter becomes characterised as unruly speech, being attributed a 'boisterous and cruel style' (4.3.31) by Rosalind/Ganymede, who reads the articulations of love as 'railing' (4.3.43) and chiding (4.3.64). Although this interpretation is rendered comic by the disbelief of Silvius who sees no hostility in Phoebe's words, Ganymede demonstrates how the meaning of words, especially women's words, are not always under the individual's control. Ganymede replicates and inverts Phoebe's own conversion of words of chiding into love (3.5.65), but where Rosalind instead plays the male's part in the scenario, and Rosalind's 'liberty' comes at the expense of Phoebe's voice as Ganymede casts a scathing judgement. Words, especially as written letters, 'mean what the recipients let them mean' (Stewart, 2008: 239), and while Phoebe somewhat fairly accuses Ganymede of ungentlemanly indiscretion, 'you have done me much ungentleness / To show the letter that I writ to you' (5.2.68–9), she has also failed to observe conversational decorum in making her words so available to censure. Rosalind as Ganymede may, moreover, rehearse an acceptable response for a woman who receives unwanted attention. Women were expected to demonstrably reject and usually return any unwanted love tokens or letters that had been given (Stewart, 2008: 253–4). The female as writer and recipient of letters was subject to social scrutiny, and Rosalind beneath the guise of Ganymede may need to confirm her rejection of Phoebe's declarations of love as part of her own navigations of models of 'virtuous' femininity, and these would then notably be more pressing than concerns about Ganymede appearing ungentlemanly (Gowing, 1996: 161).

In *As You Like It*, the Rosalind/Ganymede character that enables exploration of gender ambiguity and homoerotic desires as adolescent 'sport' also acts to re-inscribe cultural limitations on another girl's voice and desires. Phoebe's failure to play by the terms of Rosalind's games result in Rosalind asserting control over the interactions, in what might have seemed like skilful reordering of confusions to an early modern audience but appears as Phoebe's forced heteronormative compliance to a modern one. What is more, Phoebe's words are criticised by Rosalind in racialised and religious terms, whereby the 'cruel style' is described as 'Ethiop's words, blacker in their effect / Than in their countenance' (4.3.31, 35–6). In order to articulate her own position of authority, Rosalind (and Shakespeare) uses the racist prejudices of early modern culture to frame Phoebe's attempts at adolescent 'sport' as a 'sinful' lack of decorum and intelligence associated with blackness. Phoebe's self-expression is fashioned as immodesty and likened to irreligious practice, as Rosalind's racist slurs also include likening Phoebe's words to the 'defiance' of 'Turk to Christian' (4.3.32–3). As Karim-Cooper observes, 'Phoebe is racialised based on her social status here, and mocked for her presumption in writing such a letter' (2023: 269, 270). Although Phoebe is not explicitly identified as black in Shakespeare's play, Rosalind's castigation of the low born Phoebe's behaviour uses racial metaphors that also seem linked to early modern assumptions about girls of colour being 'so forward' during adolescence (Burton, 1621: 541).

The problematic terms of Phoebe's condemned duplicity should not be neglected in discussions of Rosalind's commended and controlled adolescent multiplicity in *As You Like It*. Phoebe's assertions of passion not only lead to her advances being rebuffed but – as with Katherine in *The Taming of the Shrew* – incur the fate of being matched with a man she has explicitly rejected in the early stages of the play. Tricked, notably through linguistic play, into consenting to Rosalind's conditions regarding her romantic future ('So is the bargain', 5.4.15), Phoebe concedes to a less-pronounced, but similarly devastating, process of 'taming', as she, like Katherine, subdues her voice in accordance with the play's marital conclusions. In my tracking of a trajectory for Shakespeare's 'development' of adolescent characters, where expansions and intricacies will especially be noted in the next chapter, it is, therefore, important to also record the retention of this misogynistic trope, and the racist language used in its deployment, that sees a female adolescent's own desires disregarded through a prescribed heteronormative marriage.

Across a selection of the adolescent female characters in Shakespeare's plays, we see examples of nuanced demonstrations of will, reason, wit, and mirth that navigate gendered concepts of virtue. Rosalind, Portia, Bianca, and – for a time – Juliet, suggest scope for the 'cognitive gifts' (Bicks, 2021: 182) of adolescent female minds to be voiced and enjoyed in early modern theatrical culture. The girl who achieved recognition for her fluent and 'luxuriant' voice during adolescence (Bacon, 1625: 250), however, performed additional cultural negotiations in order to be heard and applauded. Girls clearly risked more in speaking 'their minds' and judging the disposition of listeners remained imperative to navigating patriarchy. Interpretations of girls' words could become influenced by ideas about female frailty, whether through a diagnosis of greensickness or in a dismissive approach to unretentive minds. Efforts to disregard the words of girls, however, were not absolute in early modern culture. Girls could find spaces to speak of their own experiences and to the experiences of other girls. Despite the limited number of real life examples we might use, strategies of negotiating agency are tantalisingly palpable in the documents that are available and continue to emerge (Larson, 2011; Chedgzoy, 2013, 2019). Moreover, the characters in Shakespeare's plays provide cultural perceptions of adolescence where commanding fictive female characters sit alongside more restrictive representations. While we cannot know how many girls responded to theatrical representations of adolescent femininities, audience members and readers of printed plays had such depictions of adolescence available to them. Some girls, moreover, clearly did navigate patriarchal discourses into adulthood, carrying forward and reworking their means so that they could converse, write, and speak assertively as women (Hobby, 1988: Wall, 1993; Larson, 2011). Despite being told by many that their way with words was a temporary aspect of their adolescence (Mulcaster, 1581: 176; Crooke, 1615: 274), some girls thankfully resisted such lessons and continued to use their influential voices into adulthood.

More than a squeaking boy: eloquent adolescents and controlled versatility in early modern theatrical practice

While we have seen how Shakespearean girl characters could engage with early modern formulations of vibrant adolescent speech, I now turn to the boys performing those roles. Adolescent players were not simply understood as speakers whose high voices were equivalent to the fictitious females they portrayed. As the previous section has suggested, the adolescent male's own agency was subject to fewer restrictions related to gender than the characters he played, although negotiations according to age would, as we will see, still have been at work in the environment of early modern theatre. However, recognising the gender imbalances at work in valuing commendable features of adolescent voices as they mature offers a useful backdrop for returning to the contested issue of the boy actor's voice on the early modern stage. More than the vocal vulnerability of breaking voices clearly contextualised how actors' adolescent voices were likely received by audience members. Indeed, if Kathman's calculations about sixteen or seventeen being the median age at which boys performed female roles is right (2005: 220), then the 'breaking', and even broken, quality of the actors' voices would be something that acting companies must have been somewhat used to accommodating in theatrical practices (changes in pitch vary by degree for individuals, after all), so that vibrant female roles could continue being performed. Bodily changes that accompanied puberty and altered the pitch of a male adolescent's voice hinged upon the movement of heat, moisture and air in the body, and these components also enlivened the mind, energised the body, and added a compelling quality to speech. Theatregoers, theatre companies, and the boy actors themselves, would also have understood adolescent voices in this light.

Adolescent actors were also pointedly guided to speak in ways that utilised linguistic dexterity. Early modern theatrical culture often positioned boys as capable speakers who drew in paying crowds. Henry Killigrew's *Pallantus and Eudora*, which was played by the King's Company in 1635, for example, includes a telling rebuttal to criticism that the play received for its first performance in its 'From the Publisher to the Reader'. The publisher recounts how the single objection received about the play was about the 'indecorum' of the character Cleander 'who being represented a Person of seventeen yeares of age, is made to speak words, that would better sute with the age of thirty' (1653: n.p.). The response that the publisher provides dismisses the complaint as ill-informed, gesturing to the scope of adolescent talent involved in theatrical contexts: 'Sir, 'tis not altogether so Monsterous and Impossible, for One of Seventeen yeares to speake at such a Rate, when He that made him speake in that manner, and writ the whole Play, was Himself no Older' (1653: n.p.). Perhaps more than anywhere, with its adolescent actors and writers, early modern theatrical cultures provided a space within which the qualities of adolescent voices could be regularly showcased.

Theatrical contexts that situate boy actors-as-speakers are, however, subject to complicating factors that need evaluation. The issue of agency in speech acts remains particularly unclear for children in acting companies. For Charlotte Scott, the child is always at a disadvantage in hierarchical structures that involve adults because 'the concept of childhood is always animated by adults' (2017: 59). Child actors worked under the authority of adults, and, while adolescents were understood as being in a state of transition between child and adult, the outspokenness that it is conceptualised for adolescents is still understood in relation to an adult-centred model of the life cycle. While the adolescent could impress or disappoint through verbosity, the adult is culturally framed as the one who is able to judge, value, or condemn such speech.

The circumstances particular to theatre, which could vary from company to company, included additional factors that shaped the ways that boy actors used their voices as a means of self-presentation. Early modern theatre recognises circumstances where the individual's control over their voice is exceptionally mediated, as the lines and performance that are delivered (where the boy may well be highly visible) could also be subject to the directing influence of adult playwrights, master actors, and adult members of the audience who received, consumed and judged the performance. For all boy actors, their performances onstage were shaped by theatrical environments that certainly included the presence and influence of adults.

However, theatrical environments were also more complex than is suggested by a template that places boys simply onstage and being objectified by viewing adults. As Ben-Amos's examination of early modern adolescence has suggested, there was a degree of 'youth culture' available in the entertainments and communities of apprentices, which included theatregoing (1994: 183–207). Likewise, theatrical traditions in the Inns of Court saw law students, many of whom were under twenty-five, participate in theatrical productions by attending and putting on their own plays (Archer et al, 2011; Winston, 2018). Adolescents participated in and formed a significant part of early modern theatrical culture, being key members of audiences as well as acting troupes.

Critics debate the degree to which there was space for autonomy for the adolescent subject in the verbal and visual encounter that took place on the early modern stage. Boy companies would not have had such a disparity between adult and non-adult, at least amongst the actors in the company. The modern-day acting company of Edward's Boys helps suggest how grouping actors together by age and gender can inform working relationships. Harry McCarthy's detailed commentary on Edward's Boys has observed camaraderie and a sense of community between the adolescent male players (2020b). In this modern set up, young actors are granted autonomy in many performance decisions, working with their director Perry Mills. While social hierarchies exist, with Mills still being the boys' teacher/responsible adult/director, the relationship includes aspects of collaboration, and efforts to enable the boys' development as confident performers. Indeed, McCarthy's interviews with players from Edward's Boys suggest that a supportive and collective approach as a company, rather than competing individuals who are alert to power structures, exists as a key part of theatrical practices. McCarthy notes how the actors in Edward's Boys have organically (and sometimes unknowingly to some members) created an informal training process whereby more experienced actors offer newer members support and guidance (McCarthy, 2020b: Chapter 5). Although McCarthy is careful not to collapse differences in terms of the socio-economic status of boys in Edward's Boys who can 'afford (in all senses of the word) to participate in the elite pastime of early modern dramatic performance' (2020b, Chapter 5), a fuller appreciation of how theatrical practice is shaped by interpersonal relationships 'can help us better to understand the performance of early modern drama less as a predominantly text-based exercise and more as a system of behaviours and shared experiences' (McCarthy, 2020b: Chapter 5 n.p.). In her analysis of early modern performance practice, Tribble has, after all, likewise suggested 'the crucial role of the social embodiment and embeddedness of agents within a complex system' (2011: 113). If we are interested in the history of how theatrical culture was experienced by boy actors, and audiences viewing boy actors' performances, we need to attend to how boys were situated in these environments.

In this section, I use social and cultural constructions of adolescence to help illuminate the position of boy actors in Shakespeare's theatre company and plays. This endeavour is not straightforward. McCarthy's work with Edward's Boys reminds us that enabling and affective bonds can be at play in social structures that include relational power, but all-boy acting troupes from early modern children's companies must also be seen as existing at significant remove from modern examples. The careers of boy actors in early modern children's companies, once contextualised within 'the disturbing reality of impressment' (van Es, 2017: 5), particularly signal a very different basis for understanding forms of agency in comparison to modern theatre practice where socio-economic distinctions cannot be disregarded. Van Es also makes this distinction between boy players in early modern adult and children's companies, observing that 'in the world of children's theatre [...] there is little true liberty to be found' (2017: 110). Greteman similarly points out how kidnapped boys were 'essentially chattell' (2013: 34–5) and that a boy's value in this context should be understood in relation to the desires of others: 'his part provides pleasures that are not his own' (2013: 36). Van Es suggests that the adult companies in early modern society 'where child actors were apprenticed to lead players and thus voluntarily pursuing a trade' (van Es, 2017: 105) may have been more readily geared towards recognising the will of the boy involved. Ben-Amos's discussion of apprenticeships has, moreover, documented a system where adolescents, who were still technically children, were repeatedly placed in situations that made their abilities recognisable in ways that could achieve acknowledged levels of respect (1994). While apprentices could hold reputations for disorderly 'adolescent' behaviour that recalls familiar stereotypes of 'heated' excesses, the apprentices in early modern communities were also understood to be capable individuals who contributed to early modern communities as they acquired skills, managed responsibilities in their work, and sought to sustain families through the craft they learnt. Subject to a range of treatments, which could include instances of abuse as well supportive care – with many masters taking their role of loco parentis seriously – the system of apprenticeship could offer a potentially empowering rite of passage for boys, and this was likely the case in many theatrical contexts too.

The diary of Philip Henslowe, which is often regarded as 'the most valuable and important source for information about the working arrangements of the Elizabethan public theatres' (Foakes, 2002: vii) has been interpreted in differing ways for what it shows us about interpersonal relationships in an adult theatre company. Henslowe's financial arrangements with his players have been used to suggest both a system of exploitation and mercenary control (Greg, 1904: xxxv; Gurr, 1992: 94–7), as well as a supportive structure that records personal and professional connections between manager and players (Foakes, 2002: viii–x; Rutter, 1999: 5–9). Foakes suggests, for example, that the repeated financial arrangements and monetary loss Henslowe often suffered for the sake of his players can be seen to record 'dealings for players with whom he had a warm relationship' (2002: ix). Contractual bonds might also be implicitly emotive as well as financial when money and 'as good & faythfull a harte' (Foakes, 2002: 279) are involved in Henslowe's transactions.

Henslowe's documents at least give us some thought-provoking glimpses into the relationships at work in an adult theatre company that included boy players. For example, Henslowe's diary and documents often mention boy actors. In Henslowe's accounts there are entries that concern ensuring 'my boyes Jeames wages' (Foakes, 2002: 164, 118), where Henslowe lends money to the master actor Antony Jeffes so that he can pay his apprentice James Bristo. Thomas Parsons, an actor apprenticed to Thomas Downton, is also recorded as being sent on errands 'to bye dyvers thinges for the playe' (Foakes, 2002: 107). While it is perhaps sensible to identify all parties by name in monetary exchanges that involve lending or entrusting money to someone, Henslowe's inconsistency in naming boys, where the master–apprentice relationship is also used (Parson is also referred to as 'Thomas downton boye' (107)), seems to ultimately suggest that Henslowe is familiar with individuals, and some more than others, in his theatrical dealings. His records suggest not only relationships based on hierarchies of power but also entrusted duties and interactions. The naming of boys is not essential to a bond or exchange where adult masters are accountable and perhaps suggests more than a purely cold and calculating model for necessary exchanges in the business of theatre.

That Henslowe names boy players in inventory entries is perhaps the most suggestive of how theatrical practice kept a sense of an actor's individuality in mind. Inventory entries are sometimes recorded by role, as in the 'hatte for Robin Hoode' (Foakes, 2002: 318) or 'Tamberlane's breches of crimson vellvet' (Foakes, 2002: 322), or simply by item, whether gloves, other items of costume, or 'dragons' (Foakes, 2002: 320). No greater degree of specificity is essential to the nature of this documentation of theatrical expenditure and assets. For children's items, some entries are simply recorded by description of the object, including its implicated size, as with a 'lyttell dublet for boye' (Foakes, 2002: 317). Purchases clearly could be made without any indication of the article's intended user in the record. Such listings do not necessarily suggest coldness on Henslowe's part as items were likely sometimes bought simply in response to an item being available at a good price. Some purchases seem to have taken place without a particular role or actor being in considered, especially since acquiring clothing formed a large part of Henslowe's pawn transactions (Stallybrass, 2000). However, Henslowe's inventory entries also include specificity in naming certain items' users, which includes boy actors. For example, Dobe, who Foakes identifies as probably a boy actor called 'Dab' (Foakes, 2002: 331), has a coat 'of cloth of sylver' (Foakes, 2002: 322) and 'Fierdrackes sewtes' (Foakes, 2002: 317) purchased for his use. The boy actor John Pig has numerous items recorded for his use, including a 'red sewt of cloth for pyge' (Foakes, 2002: 318) and a 'littell [j]acket for Pygge' (Foakes, 2002: 323), as well as several taffeta suits and a damask gown (Foakes, 2002: 321). The particular prominence of John Pig in Henslowe's listed purchases seems likely to correspond to Pig's master's own standing and – by implication – his own in the playhouse hierarchy. John Pig was apprenticed to Edward Alleyn, Henslowe's son-in-law and lead actor (Foakes, 2002: 331). Alleyn unsurprisingly features heavily in Henslowe's diary entries, although he is not always named in the theatre inventory, despite being the known wearer of Tamburlaine's crimson breeches (Foakes, 2002: 322). Although more negative readings of Henslowe's character might still emphasise commercial motives for Henslowe's embellishing the boy actor, himself perhaps also an asset, the record also indicates that Henslowe's thinking individuates boy actors in the purchases that are documented.

While the evidence remains scant and uncertain, it is likely that boy actors would have known certain members of the company better than others and that the nature of those relationships would themselves have been varied. In early modern theatrical worlds where kidnapping, abuse, and exploitation of young boys were common, there is also evidence of care and affection towards boy players. For example, Ben Jonson's commemorative poem for the thirteen-year-old actor Salathiel/Solomon Pavy invites readers to 'Weep with me' (1603: line 1) in honouring a child who is presented as 'The stage's jewel' (1603: line 12). Salathiel, who was a member of the acting troupe the Children of Elizabeth's Chapel, is remembered by Jonson for his 'grace' (1603: line 6) and dazzling acting skill.

Documents that record Alleyn's relationship with his apprentice John Pig may also indicate a playful attachment between master and apprentice. In a letter written to his wife (Foakes, 2002: 'Article 15', 282), Alleyn pretends to be his apprentice. The jesting letter indicates Pig's immersion within the Alleyn-Henslowe household, offering 'humbell comenda[tions] to you and to my goode master hinsley and mystiris and to my mrs sister bess' (Foakes, 2002: 'Article 15', 282). The letter appears to be a combination of mimicry, mockery, and affection that culminates in the use of excessive alliteration as 'Pig' concludes his missive: 'yo[u]r petty pretty pratlyng parlyng pyg' (283). In Alleyn's impersonation of his apprentice, we glimpse human interactions at work beyond records of financial exchange, and, while we do not hear Pig's voice in Alleyn's joke, the letter suggests that the boy actor was not considered 'essentially chattell' (Greteman, 2013: 34–5) but a personality worthy of parody in the Henslowe-Alleyn household. While this letter could be seen as evidence of cruelty in the treatment of Pig, who is clearly being mocked, the tone of the letter seems to be affectionate and places Pig as familiar with family members who probably share in the joke to collectively recognise Pig's excessive use of pleasantries.

The experiences of individual adolescent actors will have differed according to the circumstances that contributed to their involvement in early modern theatre, which would have included the particular adults they encountered. In this sense, the experience of childhood clearly still remains determined by the authority of adults who could enable or disempower the young through their actions. For some boy actors, apparent flair and performances of autonomy might be features encouraged by others in power: 'Even when they pretend to respond spontaneously to the audience, their actions are predetermined' (Greteman, 2013: 37). Who possesses power over the words written, spoken, and received in early modern theatrical settings is complicated by negotiations that could see the boy actor in a position of disempowerment and subject to exploitation.

Yet there was also fame and acclaim for boys who could play an active part in carving out successful careers in the theatre, as the interesting example of Nathan Field suggests (Lamb, 2009: 118–75; McCarthy, 2018). Field, a boy player who was impressed into acting in 1600 and so subject to exploitation, was also actively engaged in his self-presentation in theatrical contexts that informed the rest of his life. Lamb describes Field as someone who 'self-consciously advanced his own career as a player and playwright through constructing his reputation in contemporary culture' (2009: 126). Field's theatrical skill was acknowledged in early modern culture, and he seems to have achieved a celebrity status akin to that of Burbage (Lamb, 2009: 135). Moreover, Field began his successful acting career with the Children of the Queen's Revels in 1600, and he continued acting with the company when it merged with Lady Elizabeth's Men in 1613, finally moving to the King's Men in 1616. Actors from boys' companies could join adult companies. As actors could also be loaned out between companies (McCarthy, 2020a), the distinction between companies, and the power relations within them, is less clear than the adult/child categories for companies initially suggests.

Boys who grew up in a theatrical setting would often become one of the adults who were involved in theatre. For example, theatre musician Ambrose Beeland remained a violinist for the King's Men for fifteen years after he finished apprenticeship (Kathman, 2004: 19). As John Astington notes, Burbage's acting career allegedly began when he was fifteen, meaning that Shakespeare's 'star' actor likely followed the normative training model and began by playing female roles as part of an apprenticeship (2012: 116). Moreover, Kathman's work on theatrical apprenticeships in the Lord Chamberlain's/King's Men has revealed how many apprentices, including Alexander Cooke, musician John Wilson, and William Trigge, went on to take on their own apprentices once they were freemen (2004: 8–11). As Astington suggests, these repeated cycles of apprenticeships indicate room for empathetic and supportive structures for boy players, seeing as boys may have had masters who, having been trained through the same system, would have 'some sympathetic insight when they came to be master actors training their own apprentice' (2012: 116). In adulthood, actors often behaved in ways that suggest an affective bond between master and apprentice, for example, with masters leaving bequests to their old apprentices in wills and apprentices naming children after their old masters (Astington, 2012: 118).

Amid these intersecting social and personal factors that shaped and complicated the circumstances of a boy actor's position in the theatre, the adolescent had a voice that was needed for performances to take place. The actor's own involvement in producing the 'crafted air' (Bloom, 2007: 2) of speech meant adding his voice, to some degree, to the words of the playwright. We might recall Richards's observations about boyhood education practices in early modern England as applicable to reading (and performing) plays, where it was accepted that the speaker would 'breathe life into written words' (2019: 24). Making sounds that could be recognised as commanding speech involved, as instructors like Mulcaster (1581) and Codrington (1664) remind us, the concerted efforts of the individual.

Admired for their theatrical talent, adolescent actors performed demonstrable moments of vocal control and personal agency. Claire Busse sets the relationship between actor and the playwright's words in the following terms: 'Rather than an empty vessel speaking others' words, the child here acquires a power unavailable to the playwright – indeed a particular power over the playwright. For the playwright relies on the child to convey his intentions without distorting or undermining them' (2006: 80). Playwrights must have understood a level of interdependence at work in writing speeches to be actively delivered by adolescent actors. Depictions of boy actors as being devoid of agency when delivering performances tend to use early modern ideas about early childhood, as with Michael Witmore's discussion of early performances in boy companies (2007). Witmore identifies the 'cognitive simplicity of children' in performances by boy companies from the 1590s, when the actors involved were generally prepubescent, being between the ages of ten and fourteen, with some being as young as six (2007: 29). As I demonstrated in the first section of this chapter, in early modern culture the 'heated' adolescent mind was understood to possess entirely different qualities to the minds of younger children. While all boys could certainly be vulnerable members of acting companies, adolescent actors were understood as active participants in the process of putting on plays. Although some playwrights, like Jonson, 'depict child actors as independent and potentially disruptive forces' (Busse, 2006: 80), a level of collaboration and mutuality is also imaginable as playwrights often wrote parts with particular adolescent actors in mind. This would mean that the adolescent actor might be thought to 'add' more to a role than is suggested in a threat of disorderly disruption or, indeed, vocal instability.

Many crossdressing narratives in Shakespeare's plays draw attention to and celebrate the adolescent actor's presence. The 'wide-ranging' (2004: 257) female roles that Scott McMillin has observed in Shakespeare's plays suggest that the skill levels of talented and experienced boy actors were utilised in female-centred plots. Criticism of Shakespeare's plays that include crossdressing have illuminated the fluidity of gender identities at work within the players' interactions, but the boy player's professional credentials are rarely considered as being on display. Indeed, the 'vocal vulnerability' of adolescent male voices is often used to suggest that crossdressing is mainly a theatrical strategy for accommodating the boy's precarious voice. Bloom suggests, for example, that crossdressing plots cultivated a way to use a male's changing voice, where 'many plays attempt to convert the liability of boy actors' voices into a resource' (Bloom, 2007: 40). Tiffany Stern similarly suggests that, 'No doubt one reason why girls are so frequently dressed as boys in Shakespearean dramas is that it is easier for a boy to play a boy than a girl' (2004: 105–6). While accommodating vocal changes would be a beneficial part of the crossdressing involved in Shakespeare's plays, the crossdressed roles also seem to act as a means by which the versatility and vocal skill of particular boy actors could be showcased. These crossdressed roles seem less about making a part 'easier' and more about revelling in the performative complexity that an accomplished adolescent actor could achieve.

With both the vibrancy and potential vulnerability of male adolescent voices in mind, it seems pertinent to turn to the infamous speech from Shakespeare's Cleopatra that highlights the adolescents behind early modern theatrical constructions of femininity, and the character's own performed status in particular. In contemplating Octavius's victory and her own assured downfall, Cleopatra considers how dramatic works will document her life: 'I shall see / Some squeaking Cleopatra boy my greatness' (5.2.217–18). This moment has drawn scholarly attention, because the character of Cleopatra pointedly reminds the audience that female parts are performed by boys (Rackin, 1972; Hammersmith, 1982; Shapiro, 1982; Hill, 1986; Steve Brown, 1990; Dusinberre, 1996). According to Steve Brown, the meta-theatrical moment somewhat undercuts the grandiose performance of queenly strength by highlighting the actor's own performance as 'vile parody' (1990: 243). For Brown, the self-consciousness of the performance destabilises the characterisation of the Egyptian Queen as the boy player's presence somewhat intrudes upon the play's storytelling. Hammersmith (1982) similarly sets the moment in terms of Cleopatra's character and the concern for her reputational legacy, and the inclusion (rather than intrusion) of the boy's presence is understood to play more broadly into the play's fiction and Cleopatra's reflections. Phyllis Rackin sees the scene differently, however, suggesting that metatheatre sets Cleopatra as the comparative showman who exceeds any evidence of squeaking boys, whereby the representation presents an empowered vision of womanhood: 'once she repudiates that performance, she can invoke a fully-theatrical world where she can put on her royalty with its emblem' (1972: 209). For Rackin, the final scene belongs to the character of Cleopatra and not the boy performing the role.

As Sara Munson Deats notes, the response to Cleopatra has produced '350 years of vehemently conflicting interpretations' (2005: 1). However, although critics disagree on its implications, interpretations of the play's gesture to 'squeaking' boy players do share two key components: discussion of the impact of the boy player's visibility, and consideration of how the moment informs the characterisation of Cleopatra. Michael Shapiro sees the two aspects of the play's performance as complementary, arguing that, while 'For a moment the illusion of Cleopatra's character is punctured', the meta-theatrical nod is designed to encourage an audience to 'respond more favourably to Cleopatra's histrionic behaviour' (1982: 13). For Shapiro, the self-reflective moment offers an acceptable model of theatricality that helps situate Cleopatra's changeability as appropriate to the character who is, ultimately, deserving of sympathy. As such, Shapiro reads the boy player's inclusion in the representation as a presence that somewhat serves its purpose in offering reassurance to viewers that all is fiction, only to fade into the representation of the Queen. Shapiro's image of a brief but swiftly remedied 'puncturing' of theatrical illusion is similar to Alison Findlay's account of the purpose of Cleopatra's meta-theatrical gesture: 'The boy actor is carefully subsumed by the female character at such a poised tragic moment' (2010: 52).

Yet, the adolescent player may be more prominent in the complex characterisation of Cleopatra than readings of this as a provocative 'moment' of theatrical self-awareness in the play allows. Cleopatra, while changeable in character in the play's fiction, is a skilled dramatic role that may have consistently pointed towards the versatile adolescent actor throughout his commanding performance. As Dusinberre observes, in its revelling in spectacle and self-conscious performativity, *Antony and Cleopatra* is a play that 'constantly comments on its own status as theatrical performance' (1996: 46). Indeed, references to Cleopatra as a 'gypsy' (1.1.10) in the opening scene of the play that contribute to constructions of Cleopatra's racial identity, 'coincid[ing] with a heightened interest in Egyptian ecology' (de Sousa, 1999: 129), may also point towards the performativity of the role, and so the boy playing the part. Geraldo U. de Sousa observes that the terms 'gypsy' and 'Egyptian' were largely 'interchangeable' (1999: 142) in early modern usage, revealing racist attitudes that conflated foreignness with ideas of duplicitousness. The figure of the 'gypsy' was understood to con others, notably through a counterfeiting performance of identity, whereby 'English gypsies impersonate true gypsies' (1999: 143) to sell goods. Philo's opening speech, therefore, presents a derogatory image of the lust-filled 'gypsy' queen that is racist and misogynist (fitting with the coloniser's patriarchal agenda to subdue an unruly and feminising other), but it also promotes the idea that Cleopatra *as* gypsy is a counterfeit. Mercutio uses this notion of falsified 'Egyptian' performances from gypsies in *Romeo and Juliet* when he criticises Romeo's distorted vision due to love. Mercutio observes how the besotted Romeo might mistake Cleopatra for a gypsy: 'Laura to his lady was but a kitchen / wench [...] Dido / a dowdy, Cleopatra a gypsy' (2.4.37–9). For Mercutio's criticism of his friend to make sense, an audience is expected to recognise associations between Egyptians and gypsies, but the audience should also understand the ridiculousness of the idea that Cleopatra be mistaken for a gypsy. Philo's description of Cleopatra is, therefore, potentially layered in its hostility, not only identifying the queen as socially lower than her regal status, but, as a lusty gypsy, conflating her with the placeless vagabond. In making such a comparison, Philo even questions her being Egyptian at all. Philo's insults conclude by highlighting the idea that the Cleopatra we await is a 'counterfeit Egyptian', where performance and illusion, and quite possibly the presence of the boy player himself, is already included in one of the key speeches that introduce the arrival of Cleopatra onstage.

A brilliant boy performer could feasibly impress, in a way utterly appropriate to cultural constructions of adolescent cognitive agility, in a performance that ranges from presenting 'a dazzling Venus and often [...] a menacing Medusa' (Deats, 2005: 2). The 'ambiguity' (Deats, 2005: 10) so commonly attached to characterisations of Cleopatra start to make a lot of sense when the presence of an esteemed adolescent performer is granted greater visibility in the role. McCarthy's in-depth reading of the character (2022: 147–53) upholds the idea that the writing of plays and particular parts was 'aided and augmented' by the presence of talented boy actors (2022: 153). Being first performed in c. 1607, *Antony and Cleopatra* was devised after Shakespeare had written many complex female roles for his adolescent players (Juliet: 1597; Rosalind: 1599; Lady Macbeth: 1605/6), suggesting that Shakespeare understood what trained and talented boy actors were capable of performing. James L. Hill seems to have poignantly registered how the construction of Shakespeare's Cleopatra encourages an accolade for the actor performing the role: '[Shakespeare's] boy Cleopatra must have been superb' (1986: 251). McMillin's work suggests that Cleopatra is perhaps the pinnacle of Shakespeare's 'wide-ranging' (2004: 257) female roles in terms of the number of lines that it requires and the number of actors from whom the adolescent actor would have received his cues. The actor would have displayed a responsive vocal dexterity, skills in memory, and a commanding stage presence. All of these qualities resonate with the positive attributes of adolescent voices, rather than 'squeaking' fragility.

Indeed, although Bloom (2007) examines adolescent male voices as unmanaged and fragile, her work also highlights a cultural distinction that was made between 'squeaking' and speaking in terms of eloquence. Voices that are interrupted by wavering tones might 'squeak' in the inclusion of high-pitched sounds, but the 'squeaking' voice was also more generally understood as one that lacked fluency: 'Squeaking is not just a signature of difference, but of inferiority' (Bloom, 2007: 25). Herrick, therefore, observed poor acting from adult actors after the lamentable loss of Jonson's instruction in the following terms: 'men did squeake. / Looke red, and blow, and bluster, but not speake' (cited in Stern, 2000: 75). The men who 'squeake' are castigated for poor performance skill as they fail to speak and express meaning through action well. To squeak or not to squeak did not simplistically divide men from boys; ineloquent 'squeaking' was more broadly a 'sign of deficiency' (Bloom, 2007: 25). The adolescent Cleopatra actor may not yet be a man, but he need not then inevitably be thought to squeak if his performance has been commandingly eloquent.

By fully appreciating that the role of Cleopatra in Shakespeare's play is undoubtedly a skilled one, assumptions about hierarchical systems in theatrical companies come under pressure. While McMillin's diligent analysis of boys' roles has helped differentiate between more and less skilled parts, McMillin's calculations (2004: 237, 240), as McCarthy highlights, seem to rest upon the assumption that it was always the boys who *required* cues from masters: 'in isolating this cue-based statistic McMillin implicitly situates the performer as the recipient of extensive support from others, rather than being himself a supporter of his fellow actors (McMillin elides, for instance, the fact that Antony receives more cues from Cleopatra than she does from him)' (2022: 171). The Cleopatra actor himself offers support to his fellow actors, including the 'master' actor, Burbage, as Antony. While Dusinberre may also be right to observe that 'Shakespeare offered the boy playing Cleopatra maximum support not only from the other apprentices who play the parts of Iras and Charmian, but from adult players – Enorbarbus, Alexas, the Soothsayer, the messengers' (1996: 54), the framework she imagines seems to similarly situate the adolescent actor as dependent on others, rather than as the lynchpin that holds the play together.

For such a skilled actor as the one performing as Cleopatra, I would suggest that an allusion to inadequate representations of Cleopatra's 'greatness' stresses, with some confidence, the performance's dissimilarity from the poor theatrical representation that is imagined. Cleopatra, and the accomplished actor playing her, pauses to attend to how others might poorly represent the Egyptian Queen's greatness to most likely uphold rather than undercut the actor's display of verbal and performative proficiency. Ann Blake describes how metatheatre works: 'forc[ing] the audience to contemplate the reality behind the theatrical illusion and, the next moment, to set that aside and accept the illusion with, as it were, a strengthened trust' (cited in Bly, 2009: 481). Meta-theatricality here indicates a moment of staged self-congratulation rather than self-ridicule or parody, and this prepares the audience for what the talented Cleopatra-actor will do next: die in spectacular fashion.

Rather than 'stealing the show' and trumping master-players in final acts, adolescent actors had roles that were designed to showcase their talents, as attested to by Shakespeare recurring construction of complex 'boy actor' parts across his plays. Such roles suggest that the performances of whole plays could be shaped around showing off the acting skills of precocious adolescent actors. Andrew Power's study of Shakespeare's female roles as boys' roles has suggested a training model that supported the development of boy actors so that an ability to perform complex roles was anticipated as the boys progressed. This means that the exhibition of adolescent talent was likely a planned move, and not a fortuitous opportunity based on one surprisingly good adolescent actor's skill (although this would no doubt add to the complexity achieved). Power notes a cyclical use of 'developmental' (2003: 229) and 'accompanied' (2003: 228) female roles that aided boys as they trained for more difficult roles in Shakespeare's company. Power's observations fit within the broader context of supportive structures of 'enskillment' that Tribble has observed in aiding the production of early modern theatre (2011: 111–50), highlighting how other boy actors' parts as well as adult parts could be used to support the professional development of adolescent actors. An adolescent who was part-way through his training, for example, might be capable of delivering Katherine's more supported role in *The Taming of the Shrew* and hope to move towards the less supported, and longer, part of Juliet in *Romeo and Juliet* (Power, 2003: 221). While the adults involved in producing *Antony and Cleopatra* would have had to have been willing to privilege the adolescent's skills on display in the performance, this occurrence becomes normative, rather than unusual, in the theatrical training model that was likely used in Shakespeare's company. The well-trained, adolescent actor can be seen to collaborate with fellow actors who readily acknowledge and enable the adolescent actor's key part in the theatrical illusion.

Dusinberre's formulation of the apprentice/master relationship in *Antony and Cleopatra* seems, therefore, to depend upon a misleading assumption that heralding the adolescent actor, above an adult master, was an atypical move in Shakespeare's drama: 'the apprenticed boy actor [...] is allowed, in theatrical terms, to supersede' his master (1996: 55). Dusinberre's influential reading of Katherine's final speech in *The Taming of the Shrew* (1993) uses a similar the hierarchical master/apprentice relationship to understand the play's gender politics. For Dusinberre, the adolescent player's relationship to his master can be mapped onto the wife/husband union. However, this reading invites some important rethinking in light of the cultural and theatrical value that was placed upon adolescent speakers. Indeed, Katherine's lengthy speech, offering obedience, has often been considered as a moment where the subservient boy and wife can both triumph over the comparatively silent master/husband. Lisa Jardine suggests that 'the dependent role of the boy player doubles for the dependency which is woman's lot, creating a sensuality which is independent of the sex of the desired figure' (Jardine, 1989: 24). Karen Newman agrees, suggesting that Katherine is empowered in her final scene and 'persists in her characteristic "masculine" exuberance while masquerading as an obedient wife' (1991:45). The readings of Dusinberre, Jardine, and Newman depend upon situating adolescent boys as similar to women in terms of their subjection to adult male power. In terms of social power, there is certainly scope to conflate the apprenticed boy with women in early modern society. Being 'in service' could, after all, carry sexual connotations for master–apprentice relationships, placing boys as objectified and eroticised by adults in the acting company and theatre audiences (Astington, 2012: 116; Johnston, 2017). The boy could find himself disempowered in social and sexual relationships that resemble the subordination of women in patriarchal systems.

Yet Katherine's 'masquerade' of wifely subservience in the last scene of *The Taming of the Shrew* is not so easily equated with the relationships between adolescent boys and master actors when the esteemed qualities of adolescent voices are evaluated in the scenario. Knowledge of 'the communal partnership of the actors in the work of preparing and presenting their plays' (Astington, 2012: 139) unsettles the basis of Dusinberre's reading. We will never know how individual theatregoers felt about Katherine's speech. However, if, as Dusinberre suggests, Katherine's wordy finale allows for the skill and versatility of the performer to be showcased, recognition of the master/student relationship in this moment might well have reminded theatregoers of the differences between the adolescent female character and adolescent male playing her. The training of boys' voices tracked a collaboration between masters and apprentices that saw boys expand vocal dexterities as part of their maturation, and in ways that sit in stark contrast to the way that a husband's authority might be understood through his wife's 'tamed' voice. Complicated by its inclusion of female impersonation, the apprentice actor still engaged with systems in place for training his voice for performance in ways modelled for young men. Indeed, Mulcaster, who is very clear about distinctions between the eventual dulling of girls' wits and boys' abilities to retain vocal and performative skill is known to have applied his methods in training actors (McCarthy, 2021). The boy who performs the role of Katherine in *The Taming of the Shrew* and 'upstages' his master can, after all, achieve recognition for an accomplished performance that has included the shrewishness that he has also adeptly performed, as well as the final scene's long speech, where both serve as evidence of his skill. From this perspective, the trajectory for taming the character of Katherine into speaking her husband's authority and the development of an accomplished speaker in an all-male cast is divergent. If we take the comparison of the play's sisters, this notion of an actor/character parallel comes under clear pressure. Bianca is the more 'virtuous' character who is praised by the men around her, and she achieves some navigated influence over gender relations in her marriage by the play's end (Maurer, 2001; Parker, 2007). Katherine, by contrast, is shrewish and outspoken, but must then perform (whether internalised or not) her subordination to her husband. As theatrical roles, the boy playing Katherine is far more prominent than the actor playing Bianca. Katherine is a physical role that demands an energetic and vocally nuanced presentation, as shrew becomes obedient wife. The adolescent actor can be commended for all these features of his controlled performance; the fictitious Katherine can only be applauded for control when articulating subservience. If *The Taming of the Shrew* encourages us to perceive the adolescent boy in the role of Katherine, which it may well do considering the play's Induction that identifies the shrew narrative as a fiction performed by players, then the performance of Katherine's 'shrinkage' across the taming plot (Bicks, 2021: 19) becomes part of the boy actor's own more expansive rite of theatrical passage.

When meta-theatrical aspects highlight the male adolescent's vocal abilities in performances of female speech on the early modern stage, parallels between fictive female characters and adolescent male actors can come under strain. As David Scott Kastan more broadly observes, theatrical contexts made the representation of women 'heavily mediated' by 'male actors, speaking words written by a male writer, enacting female roles' (1999: 151). Aspects of gendered adolescent voice can, for example, disrupt a model that conflates the adolescent male speaker with the figure of the early modern wife, where 'adult' codes of feminine behaviour become insistent in the construction of the fictional character. Seeing the talented boy behind the character in these moments seems to push out female voices rather than allying them with the boy who is, in fact, likely encouraged to supersede his master in the context of his training.

If we return to Cleopatra, we can view the Shakespearean character as a creation that especially sought to showcase a proficient adolescent actor's skill, what Hill articulates as 'what Shakespeare felt he could do with a great boy actor' (1986: 254). The metatheatre of *Antony and Cleopatra*, moreover, carries implications for the performance of Cleopatra today. If actor and fictitious part are easily conflated in Shakespeare's play, the boy performer and Egyptian Queen can both wield satisfying power over the men who surround them. However, while fictional femininity could inspire through palpable representations of female empowerment, the balance threatens to shift if a concern for representing womanhood is displaced by an emphasis upon the actor's visibility. Who plays Cleopatra's self congratulating role becomes crucial if, in playing the part, the actor perpetuates social injustices that continue to marginalise speakers whose voices do not feature in the theatrical production. The actor's voice and actions that are recognised and applauded through the play's metatheatre herald a performance that can implicitly undermine any empowerment for the character, which, in an early modern context, would be bound to the boy player's white-centred, male representation. The white boy player can quite literally be seen, and, in being seen, reiterates the play's narrative of colonisation and a black subject's subjugation to white, male authority (Hall, 1995: 160; Habib, 2000: 157). The original audience of *Antony and Cleopatra* was repeatedly asked to view Cleopatra – whether as temptress or as a mother – in terms of models of femininity that the boy actor could perform with dexterity. The actor is commended for being the master of that performance. Characterising Cleopatra as 'Shakespeare's most sensual and least boyish heroine' (Dusinberre, 1996: 46), therefore, seems to underplay how the play's original audience seem to have been continually directed towards the accomplished nature of the adolescent player's craft.

While Ania Loomba suggests how the unpredictability and contradictions of Cleopatra's character leave room to explore 'the contradiction that lies at the heart of race' (2002: 134), that potential depends on how the self-conscious role is performed. Sujata Iyengar, who has explored early modern racial identities in relation to the 'gypsy' figure, using Shakespeare's Cleopatra as a key example, highlights the need to confront how a perceived resemblance between actor and theatricalised persona plays a part in 'creating and occupying spaces of performance' (2004: 197). In occupying the space that the role of Cleopatra affords, the actor's own race and gender are especially apparent. As Carol Rutter notes in discussing Mark Rylance's performance of Cleopatra in 1999, potential to draw out and work with the black racial identity written into Shakespeare's Cleopatra becomes an example of 'cultural hijack' if a white actor persists in performing the role (2001: 88). However, early modern theatrical constructions of racial identities present roles that remain limited and limiting for actors of colour. As Noémie Ndiaye observes in relation to early modern constructions of black identity, such roles involve 'a type of racial impersonation that brings into being and fashions what it claims to mimic' (2022: 2). A model of 'Performative blackness rubs up against lived Blackness historically and politically in ways that have informed the lives of Black professional performers to this day' (Ndiaye, 2022: 3). In the case of Cleopatra, recognition and praise of the 'boy' Cleopatra is explicitly written into Shakespeare's play, in a way that seems to extend beyond the meta-theatrical moment of the last act. Modern performance contexts will need, therefore, to mitigate and self-consciously engage with how the part was constructed in ways that privileged the white, adolescent male's 'impressive' performance, and where the complexity of Cleopatra's character was, it seems, presented, at least in part, as his 'boyish' accomplishment.

Meta-theatrical moments in *The Taming of the Shrew* and *Antony and Cleopatra* indicate where distinctions between the adolescent male actor and his role could have emerged for early modern audiences in terms of performances of race and gender. However, theatrical strategies could play down cultural constructions of gender difference and play up age-related symmetries in the adolescent actor's performances of adolescent femininities. After all, as I have discussed in chapter one in relation to her linguistic 'generational' framing as a declining rose, Cleopatra is not an adolescent character. As I will examine in the next chapter, some aspects of metatheatre do not seem to trouble the symmetry upheld between adolescent male actor and his adolescent female role. Performances of esteemed, female adolescent vivacity that we saw, for example, in Rosalind, Portia, and Bianca, could, therefore, be understood as inspired by, and inspiration for, female subjectivities in early modern culture. Indeed, Codrington includes the recommendation that girls hear and learn from 'stage-playes' (1664: 28–30) in order to learn decency in women's conversation. Codrington does also advise against watching plays every day (which he suggests could be fatal!), and anti-theatrical writings clearly feared for the loss of female virtue; however, the engaged and responsive female adolescent is also understood to exist as a positive formulation on the stage and in Codrington's model of the girl as theatregoer. Engagement with plays could act to re-inscribe gender biases that I have noted in this chapter, but girls in early modern theatre audiences might also style themselves according to the more expansive femininities that they heard and saw in early modern drama. Like the early modern girl readers who found creative modes available to 'read as a virtuous woman', girl subjects could have included the vibrant modes of speech available through theatrical representations in their own self fashioning (Lamb, 2018: 165). Fictions of adolescent femininity that saw girls masquerade as lawyers or find liberty in the forest of Arden through 'sport', all contributed to the imagined ways in which girls' 'words do well' (*As You Like It* 3.5.110), and female speakers may have responded to these cues in their own lived experiences.

Notes

1 As Evans notes, 'fertility and virility underpinned the attainment of manliness' (2016: 312) for most men in early modern culture, and concerns around male infertility often focused on the situation and condition of the testicles (2016: 321).
2 For an overview of medical ideas that overlapped and competed in the seventeenth century, see Roger French and Andrew Wear (1989).
3 Mulcaster uses the same rationale that speaking encourages the expulsion of excess heat in his recommendation that it is best not to talk if you are bleeding: 'silence is a meane both to stay bleeding' (62).
4 Elyot, in *Castel of Health* identifies the 'not naturalls' that informed humoral disposition through daily management as the air and environment, food and drink, motion and rest, sleep and wakefulness, excretions and retentions, and 'Affects' of the mind (1539: 1).

5 Elyot does not advise abstaining from food completely; his advice focuses on moderating excess through regulated diet and behaviour (1539).
6 Critics debate the date for the first performance of *The Taming of the Shrew*. Dusinberre (1993) suggests a later date than most, proposing 1594/5, and identifying Burbage – who joined the Lord Chamberlain's Men around this time – as a likely Petruchio.
7 Portia is a key spokesperson for anti-Semitic sentiment in *The Merchant of Venice*, and it is worth noting that her adolescent, vocal freedoms promote 'mercy' that is not inclusive and empowering for all.

4

The maypole and the acorn: body growth and disparities in height in Shakespeare's plays

COKES [...]
What kind of actors ha' you? Are they good actors?

[*Enter*] *Leatherhead*

LITTLEWIT
Pretty youths, sir, all children, both old and young, here's the master of 'em – [...]

He [Leatherhead] *brings* [puppets] *out in a basket*

COKES
What, do they live in baskets?

LEATHERHEAD
They do lie in a basket, sir, they are o' the small players.

COKES
These be players minors, indeed. Do you call these players?

LEATHERHEAD
They are actors, sir, and as good as any, none dispraised, for dumb shows: indeed, I am the mouth of 'em all!
(Ben Jonson, *Bartholomew Fair*: 5.3.48–78)

HERMIA
'Puppet'? Why so? Ay, that way goes the game.
Now I perceive that she hath made compare
Between our statures; she hath urged her height,
And with her personage, her tall personage,
Her height, forsooth, she hath prevailed with him.
And are you grown so high in his esteem
Because I am so dwarfish and so low?
How low am I, thou painted maypole? Speak!
(Shakespeare, *A Midsummer Night's Dream*: 3.2.289–96)

Jonson's *Bartholomew Fair* (c. 1614) and Shakespeare's *A Midsummer Night's Dream* (c. 1595/6) include scenes where characters engage with the cultural implications of being small. Indeed, the zealous and easily fooled Cokes of Jonson's comedy and Shakespeare's Hermia – who finds herself subjected to height-based insults from both her childhood friend, Helena, and her enchanted suitor, Lysander – show a shared interest in what being a small 'puppet' particularly entails. The scene in *Bartholomew Fair* draws a direct parallel between children's companies and the miniature 'actors' of the puppet show, as Cokes mistakenly expects child actors to be brought onstage. Indeed, Cokes continues to associate the puppets with these child actors in his responses across the scene.[1] Allusions to a 'puppet' figure draws into view a theatrical context for considering the significance of the size of an actor and/or character, recalling, as we shall see, the ambiguities that were considered in the previous chapter in relation to child actor's voice and issues of agency. The puppet, after all, is controlled by his physically larger master, who animates and gives voice to the figure. In *Bartholomew Fair*, Leatherhead, as puppet master, boasts that the words and vocal skill of his small actors are to be understood as originating from him: 'I am the mouth of 'em all!'. The adult/manager directs how the 'players minor' speak and behave, and the adult appears to somewhat delight in this assertion of control.

However, although Leatherhead wields and exposes adult-centred power in theatrical contexts, Jonson's scene – and this chapter – examines how adolescent actors' body sizes were attributed meaning that made them distinct from 'small' puppets and, moreover, distinct from each other. Studies of boy companies have paid particular attention to the ways in which the size of child actors was understood in relation to the comparatively 'large' adults in early modern audiences. Early modern drama regularly draws attention to the height and physique of its young characters and actors, and a child/adult distinction has been shown to be a point of negotiating social, erotic, and theatrical power. For Michael Witmore, for example, the 'diminutive' size of boy actors plays a part in the process by which boys were objectified and attributed 'unthinking agency' in relation to the adults around them (2007: 41). Witmore's work expands upon more familiar approaches to the appeal of boy actors in adult or children's companies, where the boys' desirability, which is often erotic, is seen to hinge upon an adult/child, master/servant power relationship. A clear distinction in body size and physical strength might be seen to play into these binaries.

In *Bartholomew Fair*, Cokes certainly expresses his desire to meet the 'Pretty youths, sir, all children' that Leatherhead describes; Cokes 'would be glad [to] drink with' and become more familiar with the child actors (5.3.50, 55–6). Undeniably, even upon finding that the actors are wooden puppets rather than children, Cokes persists in his assumptions about the erotic accessibility of the players, stating 'I am in love with the actors' and he is keen to purchase and pocket them as 'my fairings' (gifts from the fair) (5.3.131, 133). Moreover, as Kristina Caton observes, 'both Cokes and the audience view Cokes's action of putting his hand in and out of the glove of the puppet as sexually charged' (2013: 66). Cokes's intention to use the puppets that he 'loves' as his hobbyhorse, fiddle, and fiddlestick are sexually suggestive, and Cokes's comments might well also be accompanied by suggestive actions, if the actor mimics such uses of the puppets onstage. For example, Cokes describes the puppet Hero as a 'fiddle', and the puppet Leander as a 'fiddlestick', and the implied lewd actions around the sexualised properties may have involved rubbing the puppets together. Puppets as childhood toys and children as erotic playthings merge in Cokes's uncomfortable desire to engage in childish 'play' that is suggestive of erotic activity with the would-be child actors.

The scene from Jonson, then, suggests awareness of the kind of objectification and eroticisation of boy actors that critics, including Lisa Jardine (1989), Mario DiGangi (1995), and Stephen Orgel (1996), have long established as part of early modern theatrical culture. Moreover, studies of how the eroticism associated with boy players may have included (adult) female theatregoers have suggested the significance of cultural perceptions of the actors' body sizes and, specifically, their sexual immaturity. For example, Mark Albert Johnston (2017) has argued that the perceived infertility of boy actors offered an unthreatening sexual fantasy where sexually capable adolescent bodies do not carry the risk of reproductive sex. Valerie Billing has similarly foregrounded female audience members' desires in her reading of productions by boy companies, arguing that pleasure 'revolves around a physical domination that specifically calls attention to the boy's diminutive body in relation to the ostensibly mature body' (2014: 1) of offstage characters and audience members.

Although adult/child interactions will also feature in my thinking in this chapter, I seek to rethink a static model that sets the 'small' child solely in opposition to the 'tall' or large adult. As I have shown across the chapters of this book, adolescents were primarily understood in the context of narratives of growth and maturation in early modern culture. Indeed, we find that allusions to physical smallness are regularly included in plays that compare the body sizes *between* boy players. The adolescent male player who performed the part of Hermia is, along with the girl he plays, constructed as 'dwarf-like' in opposition to the taller adolescent male player who is the comparative 'Maypole' of Helena. Adolescent boys on Shakespeare's stages, and often the girl characters that are being represented, can be seen to participate in energetic interactions that draw attention to the varied stature of *growing* adolescent bodies. In this chapter, therefore, I situate boy actors less as 'puppet' miniatures, when compared to adults, and approach boy actors as *growing* adolescents, in accordance with cultural and medical discourses about puberty. The boy actors' energised physicalities will be shown to largely set them apart from the small and motionless puppets that, as Leatherhead notes, simply 'lie' and do not 'live' in their tiring-house-basket. Set along a continuum of growth, boy actors and adolescent characters, can be compared to each other, as well as adult figures in ways that challenge more fixed interpretations of body size, power, and agency.

The argument between Helena and Hermia in *A Midsummer Night's Dream*, a scene that features heavily in my analysis for this chapter, sees each adolescent retaliate to the words and actions of the other, as assumptions about the physically small being subjected to the authority of the physically large become destabilised. Hermia rejects the disempowered state of being called 'small' and 'low', in a scene that consists of the dynamic exchange of words and which has the potential to be highly physical when performed.[2] The comparatively small and outnumbered Hermia threatens to inflict damage upon her childhood friend despite her small physique: 'I am not yet so low / But that my nails can reach unto thine eyes' (3.2.297–8). In drawing attention to a character's height, a play can make use of the physicality of the player, which pointedly becomes part of the stage presence of the character. As Billing observes, this construction of character in relation to physicality could be 'large' in terms of impact, even when a character is short. As Helena observes, voicing the wisdom that is often cited on modern t-shirts and baby-grows, it would be an error to underestimate someone who 'be but little' when they can also be 'fierce' (3.2.325).

In *Bartholomew Fair*, the joke is also on Cokes; he is wrong to take the puppets as direct substitutes for child actors. Indeed, the real child actors involved in the performance of *Bartholomew Fair* can be seen to carry much more theatrical (and literal) weight than the puppets that, in being included, also help draw attention to and celebrate the variety of young actors in the company. Performed by the Lady Elizabeth's Men in 1614, a year after this 'adult' company merged with the Children of the Queen's Revels, *Bartholomew Fair* is a busy play that takes advantage of the theatre company's swollen numbers and readily available boy actors. Jonson writes parts for women, men, and children to depict the crowd taking in the delights of the fair, no doubt largely *because* the boys in the company make this possible. The assumption that boy actors were 'diminutive' carries over Witmore's (2007: 41) observations for much earlier plays by children's companies and, as Greteman has observed, by the early 1600s, 'most children on the English stage […] were far from the diminutive boys often imagined' (2012: 136). The boys in children's companies were mostly adolescents, being in their late teens and early twenties (Greteman, 2012: 138–9; Munro, 2005: 39–42).

Although Lamb (2009) has shown how the cultural and institutional fashioning of actors from children's companies *as* children could function somewhat regardless of the actor's actual age and body size, direct references to body size in plays also invite attention to be paid to how physical stature is being used in constructions of theatrical character. Moreover, growth and physical development is the stuff of puberty, and references to characters' and actors' comparative heights can be seen to actively activate these narratives of maturation so that the mutability of adolescent bodies becomes a source of theatrical variety. Often in theatre studies, changes to the adolescent actor's height (as with voice, as we saw in the previous chapter) have been framed as marking a somewhat abrupt transition between boyhood and adulthood. The 'suddenly' tall and 'squeaking' boy player is imagined as having to discard feminine roles (though he may really also play 'boyish' roles), and assume an 'adult' status (Bloom, 2007: 20–2; Callaghan, 2000: 49–74). Hamlet's interaction with the actors at Elsinore suggests that some anxiety would accompany responses to growing boy players, as theatrical illusions of femininity came under strain: 'your ladyship is nearer to heaven than when I saw you last' (2.2.351). Yet Hamlet's concerns for the temporary nature of the tall boy's female impersonation should be contextualised alongside performances that celebrated height discrepancies between actors and, as we will see, used ideas about growth to shape play content and underpin dynamic performances. Playwrights and actors could make theatrical use of the adolescent growth of its actors, as they grew 'nearer to heaven'.

Changes in body size for child actors were neither all that sudden nor unpredictable. Early modern commentators, as we have seen across this book, anticipated bodily changes for adolescents during puberty, and mutable and growing bodies were incorporated in theatrical production. In the first section of this chapter, I contextualise early modern ideas about puberty in relation to body growth to establish how the humoral changes of puberty were understood in relation to changes in height. An alteration in stature will be shown to be connected to the wider 'ripening' of the adolescent body, specifically carrying connotations for the female body, where ideas about appropriate growth become aligned with anxieties about future fertility. I suggest how Hermia's insulted shortness is particularly poignant in this context, as Lysander evaluates and rejects his lover, citing her 'stunted' development as his rationale, to situate Hermia's undesirability in terms of ideas of dysfunctional fertility.

In the second section of the chapter, I develop a reading of body size and adolescence in *A Midsummer Night's Dream*, turning to the interaction *between* Helena and Hermia in the play. In contrasting the physicalities of two adolescent girls, and the players behind these roles, Shakespeare's play seems to delight in altering perspectives to recalibrate the singularity of a 'normative' measure for adolescent selves. My reading of the representation of the Athenian adolescents in *A Midsummer Night's Dream* suggests how the plight of Helena and Hermia (and, to a lesser extent, Lysander and Demetrius) intersects with the fairy narrative of *A Midsummer Night's Dream*, where concerns about childhood development and changeable body size are also prominent. Variety, growth, and physical mutability are celebrated in *A Midsummer Night's Dream* as a source of entertainment, theatrical illusion, and social continuation. We find, moreover, that it is a story about *growing* adolescents that sits at the heart of the play's celebrations.

In the final section of the chapter, I begin with a similar comparative framing of characters' girlhoods to that seen in *A Midsummer Night's Dream* by exploring the pairing of Celia and the 'more than common tall' (1.3.111) Rosalind in *As You Like It*. This relationship between girls is complicated, however, by the crossdressing of Rosalind's character and her performance of boyhood through the persona of Ganymede. Comparisons in representations of girlhood expand to include representations of male adolescence that move beyond the meta-theatrical glimpses of boy players in *A Midsummer Night's Dream*. The performances of adolescence again evoke comparative physicalities that become additionally complicated by Orlando's involvement in the Rosalind/Ganymede plot, when the adolescent character is performed by the adult Burbage. By having differentiated girl characters, Burbage's performance of male adolescence realises Orlando's distinction both from the girl characters and Rosalind's crossdressed persona of Ganymede. Burbage's 'adult' status, I suggest, informs how *As You Like It* presents its characters, but the implications do not simply underline distinctions between adult and child. Instead, we once again see an audience being encouraged to contemplate a group of adolescents and explore *degrees* of maturation across the party, often pointedly attending to the heights of the characters/actors in order to do so.

A Midsummer Night's Dream (c. 1595/6) and *As You Like It* (c. 1599) realise multi-layered and nuanced performances of adolescent characters that include reference to body size. Moreover, these plays offer suggestive examples of how a particular performative strategy that involved the comparative staging of adolescent heights could be reused and developed across Shakespeare's plays. In this chapter I suggest some of the ways in which Shakespearean drama seems to have embraced the theatrical possibilities that the changeable statures of the company's adolescent players allowed, viewing these actors as not simply 'small' but as growing and differentiated from each other.

Early modern attitudes towards shortness, tallness, and growing in stature

According to Bacon, 'to *Grow* in *Stature*' is one of the later alterations to take place during adolescence, coming 'thus long, and sometimes later' than the onset of menstruation and the growth of body and facial hair (1638: 370). Indeed, Bacon presents a clear order in which the physical developments of puberty take place, where it is only after a discernible change in height that an individual can be furnished with the final *'Strength and Agility'* that is accredited to adulthood, which Bacon describes as *'full years'* (1638: 369–70). Medical sources replicated similar observations about body growth, observing that the final completion of reproductive ability was achieved when the humoral heat that was needed for generation was no longer required to 'augment' the rest of the body (*Aristotle's Masterpiece*, 1684: 5–6). As we have seen across the chapters of this book, the lengthy process of puberty was understood to involve numerous bodily alterations that took place as the result of humoral heat and moisture. These other physical changes were thus set alongside, and to some degree measured against, the achievement of an appropriate 'stature'. In the trajectory used by Bacon, height is an indicator of promising or unpromising progress along the course to maturation.

Importantly, however, achieving full height indicated impending, but not achievement of, *'full years'*. Getting taller, set in Bacon's formulation, demonstrates that puberty is well underway, with menstruation and hair growth having begun, but the growth spurt that can supposedly be recognised as signalling stability in the achievement of full height is also not the end of puberty, where the 'ripening' of reproductive seed and broader qualities of *'Strength and Agility'* still require accomplishing. Therefore, when Hamlet observes that the boy player is 'nearer to heaven than when I saw you last' (2.2.351), measuring the growth of the actor against the height of the heel to a shoe (specifically a 'chopine'), he anticipates further signs of maturation still to come. The notable growth of the actor, who *is* still impersonating women, promotes thoughts about alterations to the voice, which Hamlet hopes 'be not crack'd' (2.2.452). Contemplating the adolescent within the context of a narrative of growth encourages consideration of other aspects of the 'ripening' processes of puberty and an evaluation of how much growing there is left to do.

However, height as a marker for assessing how and when further change will take place for an adolescent is a problematic signifier, as is calculating just when the impending adulthood that it suggested might be judged as achieved. When can we say that someone has stopped growing and are as tall as they will ever be? A study from Oxford University into 'Highs and

Lows of and Englishman's average Height over 2000 years' adopts 'the classification made by archaeologists that the age group 18–49 years represents adults who had achieved their mature heights' (Galofré-Vilà, 2017: n.p.) in order to create useable data about skeletal remains. However, the study also observes that it 'cannot control for the age at which mature height was reached' (Galofré-Vilà, 2017: n.p.). As we have seen, early modern commentators on physical development saw the ages of maturation as far less fixed than this categorisation by numeric age implies. Broad conclusions of studies about average heights are, therefore, limited in what they can tell us about the cultural framing of age and height, and these statistics tell us nothing of the specific meaning that height carried in signifying the complexities of being in a certain life stage. However, some sense of a measurable, average 'adult' height in early modern society can help contextualise the treatment of height in early modern texts for a modern reader, particularly for performance texts, where height parameters can help us imagine what height was considered tall or short. Data analysis across historical periods can also usefully identify factors upon which bodily development depends. For example, the Oxford study illuminates coinciding 'highs' in height and agricultural prosperity to reiterate scientific conclusions about body growth being 'reliant on good health', environmental conditions, and inherited characteristics (Galofré-Vilà, 2017: n.p.). The Oxford scholars conclude that 'From 1400 to the early 1650[s], mean height reached 173–174 cm' (Galofré-Vilà, 2017: n.p.), around five feet and seven inches.

An understanding of average heights proves useful when encountering some early modern attitudes about heights appropriate to adulthood. For example, we find the regularly cited and somewhat unhelpful notion that the ideal full height for an adult male is seven feet, because this was the height commonly ascribed to Hercules. Thomas Hill's treatise on physiognomy observes, for example, that seven feet is the desired height for the perfected body, offering 'perfite boundes of the length and largenesse of the bodie' (1571: 110). While the fact that it is very unlikely that individuals could have achieved this height might have in itself been useful in indicating the 'imperfect' state of postlapsarian man, such comments add to the uncertainty around the murky age and height markers used to measure maturation in early modern culture.

Perceptions of height clearly mattered in the theatrical fashioning of dramatic character on the early modern stage. As S. P. Cerasano's (1994) discussion of Edward Alleyn's towering stature in relation to his Marlovian roles of Tamburlaine and Doctor Faustus suggests, the physicality of an actor could be a powerful resource in theatrical representation. Cerasano debunks the more extreme accounts of Alleyn's height from historians, who use portraits to estimate that the actor was six feet, eight inches (175), literally ascribing the actor an almost Herculean stature. Yet Cerasano's calculations, using evidence from the size of Alleyn's signet ring, still situate Alleyn as taller than his contemporaries, with him being 'at the shortest possibility – approximately 5 feet and 9–10 inches' (1994: 178), and taller still in theatrical buskins. That Alleyn could *appear* Herculean, or 'like a giant to his audiences at the Rose' (1994: 171), a theatre with a small stage and building dimensions, is down to both an understanding of the significance that could be ascribed to bodies that are considered tall, or small, or growing, and the theatrical staging of that height in the context of a play's action and character. For example, we can also note that Burbage was commonly referred to as his company's Hercules (Stern, 2004: 16), something that more clearly alludes to the 'largeness' of his stage presence and theatrical feats than his actual size, although – as we will see – this could be manipulated through the comparative staging of actors' bodies.

Though I do not attempt to calculate the specific heights of the actors involved in theatrical representations in this chapter, a sense of scale and the cultural parameters regarding early modern height do inform an overall discussion of smallness, tallness, and ideas of growth. All boy players, and certainly the ones still performing female roles, would have been situated in a cultural context that understood the adolescent as 'growing' in stature. Moreover, the way in which adolescents handled their physical development was understood to carry significant consequences, and body growth during adolescence could be evaluated to indicate a promising or unpromising foundation for adulthood. Concerns for achieving appropriate growth during adolescence can be observed in the recommendations that early modern writers offered regarding diet and behaviour. For example, in *Sylva Sylvarum*, Bacon notes the potential need 'To *Accelerate Growth* or *Stature*' (1626: 354) during childhood and suggests two means of achieving the desired effects: nourishment and exercise. While Bacon broadly observes the logic of modern social and anthropological historians about good health supporting body growth, he also applies early modern humoral logic to his assessments. Bacon recognises that the quantity and humoral properties of the nourishment received by a child will contribute to growth, warning against excess 'For it maketh the Childe Corpulent; And Growing in Breadth, rather than in Heighth' (1626: 354). As Newton notes in her study of 'children's physic', greed was associated with children and understood as appropriate, to some degree, in supporting growing bodies in the provision of extra nourishment (2012: 32). Excess in quantity or particular humoral properties was, however, still considered unproductive in a humoral model that favoured moderation that accorded to the particular disposition of the individual in question (Newton, 2012: 58–9). Children's health was evaluated according to key physical features that included 'individual strength and weight and size' (Newton, 2012: 39), although weight – and, presumably, height – were not routinely measured in medical examinations (Toulalan, 2014: 70). Despite lacking specificity, ideas about timely and orderly growth were, therefore, part of early modern approaches to evaluating childhood health.

In adolescents, a malleability of form that enabled growth was understood to depend upon their naturally hot humoral disposition. Batman described '*Adolescentia*' as a stage of physical development that 'hath might and strength', but where 'members are softe and tender, and able to stretch: and therfore they grow by vertue of heate that hath masterye in them' (1582: 70). Humoral properties in food that inhibited the motion of hot humours in adolescent bodies could hinder development, especially if moisture, which worked with heat to create pliable bodies, became deficient. Bacon therefore uses humoral logic when he observes that 'an *Ouer-drie Nourishment* in Childhood putteth backe Stature' (1626: 94), as drying humours countered the quantity of moisture in the body (further diminished in adolescence) and impeded faculties of growth. Batman uses similar, more generalised reasoning about the significance of diet to humoral dispositions when he states that 'drinesse destroyeth and wasteth the humours' (1582: 26). Elyot, in *Castel of Helthe*, also makes use of humoral common sense about replenishing moisture when he encourages children to eat especially moist diets after the age of thirteen, suggesting 'meates more grosse of substaunce, colder and moyster' (1539: 41). While Elyot seems to prioritise moisture in adolescents' diets, along with broader ideas of tempering excess 'accordyng to their complexions' (1539: 41), Bacon goes further in advising that a heated disposition should be upheld, stipulating that overly cool foods should be avoided by growing children. Bacon warns against giving '*Children,* anything that is *Cold* in Operation', which 'doth hinder both *Wit,* and Stature' (1626: 94). Exercise, recommended by Elyot (1539: 41) and Bacon (1626: 94), is explained as beneficial to growth due to its heat-promoting properties. Bacon advocates physical activity, because it enables the '*Quickening* and *Exciting* of the *Naturall Heat*' (1626: 94). Mulcaster's instructions to his students likewise advise the use of exercises that 'increase, and encourage the natural heat' (1581: F3^r). Once again, we see how the humoral heat of the adolescent was much more than a potentially disorderly component of an adolescent disposition. Heat was necessary to adolescent development, enabling bodily growth and such character and cognitive traits as 'Wit'.

What is more, we can see from contemporary observations that some concern for how growth might be properly managed and achieved during adolescence was expressed. The 'heat' of adolescence could require some nurturing. In *Historie Naturall and Experimentall*, Bacon reiterates that if growth is not achieved during childhood, it will have significant repercussions for adult health: 'Men of a tall stature, proper, bigge, strong, and active, are long-liv'd; but a low stature, and slow disposition, are contrary signes' (1638: 122). Supporting growth during childhood, when remedial action to 'accelerate growth' may be taken, seems to be underpinned by the understanding that the 'natural heat' of the individual's life force will be perceptible in how 'well' the child grows. Evaluating the child's bodily development, therefore, includes assessing the foundational 'natural heat' that appears to be in place for life (where how long someone will live may be discernible), but where a degree of intervention is still possible to invigorate the heat of childhood growth.

For the adolescent body, the extremes of bodily changes that were more generally applicable to the wider category of 'childhood' come into sharper focus. With its increased heat and the life stage's association with achieving 'full' stature, adolescence presented an age where evaluations of body growth were especially pertinent to imagining impending adult futures. In particular, the progress that an individual was making could be measured against cultural expectations for appropriate sexual maturation. For example, Lysander's scathing verbal attack on Hermia, in *A Midsummer Night's Dream*, includes a list of insults for being small that culminates in her being called 'you bead, you acorn' (3.2.330). An acorn is clearly like the 'puppet' and 'bead' in being small, but the acorn also carries associations with physical immaturity because it is a seed, the earliest stage of the oak tree's life cycle. While Faircloth and Thomas identify acorns as 'a fertile symbol with the cup as the feminine and the acorn as the masculine parts' (2016: 'acorn'), the allusion in *A Midsummer Night's Dream* seems more appropriately framed as a comment about stunted growth: the short, adolescent girl is likened to the seed-state of a tree. Coupled with Lysander's derisory description of the creeping weed, knotgrass – 'You minimus of hind'ring knot-grass made' (3.2.329) – the acorn insult is aligned with another plant that grows 'low' to the ground and was 'widely thought to stunt growth if drunk in an infusion' (Thomas and Faircloth, 2016: 'knot-grass'). Horticultural metaphors of growth, budding, flowering, and ripening that we have seen to be commonplace in early modern descriptions of ageing are once again applied to Hermia in an allusion that places Hermia's maturation under scrutiny. The inclusion of the plant related imagery in Lysander's intimidation is, moreover, all the more threatening in a culture, and a play with its magical purple flower, where plants and their properties can be used to inflict alterations upon a person.

Lysander, Hermia's once-devoted suitor, reimagines Hermia to reject a future with the 'rose-like' girl, who, as I discussed in the first chapter of this book, has otherwise been described as the flourishing, albeit vulnerable, adolescent that early modern culture venerated. In Act 3, Scene 2, Lysander renounces his desires, characterising Hermia as an implausible love interest by using Hermia's short physique as a sign of physical immaturity and insufficient growth. Lysander fully utilises early modern prejudices about body size to frame Hermia as physically disproportioned when he calls her 'dwarf' (3.2.328), merging ideas of physical disability with constructions of normative physical development in relation to Hermia's age. As Laura Coker has observed of performances of 'disability drag' (2016: 6), where boy actors played dwarf characters in early modern theatre, a conflation of disability with the language and performance of physical immaturity forces embodied states into becoming 'only infantilizing labels' (2016: 6–7). Shakespeare has Lysander call Hermia a 'dwarf' to soundly convey a slur upon her bodily development. Hermia is denounced as a 'dwarf' in the same speech that includes Lysander's insults of 'acorn' and 'knot-grass', construing Hermia's small stature as non-normative and a permanently 'immature' state of existence. Indeed, Sara van den Berg recognises a tendency for early modern writers to liken the dwarf's body to 'a kind of child' (2013: 25). A similar insult is used in *Antony and Cleopatra*, where Cleopatra manipulates a messenger into providing a negative report of her rival, Octavia. In requesting a comparison based on height, 'Is she as tall as me?' (3.3.11), Cleopatra constructs an image of a 'dwarfish' (3.3.16) woman so that she can be satisfied that her own beauty is superior to that of Octavia. Cleopatra is no adolescent character but she, like Lysander, suggests that the sexual attractiveness of women is associated with evaluations of height. Likewise, the ableism of Lysander's insults set dwarfism as a state of underdevelopment that is disassociated from a normative, and so desirable, adult state.[3]

Indeed, Hermia's insulted smallness can be understood in relation to early modern ideas that connected desirability with reproductive fitness. Lysander's hurtful words of rejection play into what Toulalan observes as 'an erotic aesthetic in which sexually desirable bodies were bodies that were perceived as fertile' (2014: 67). Toulalan, who has examined representations of fat bodies as reproductively dysfunctional, has shown how early modern commentators perceived excess and deficiency in body sizes as a cause of infertility, albeit rarely 'quantifying what precisely would constitute too much' (2013: 70). Body size was identified as a crucial determinant in evaluating fertility, and physical stature was therefore used in cultivating the parameters by which an individual's desirability would be assessed as part of early modern culture's 'erotic aesthetic'.

It is worth pointing out that evaluations of age and body size, in terms of fatness and leanness, and height were also used in interpreting male fertility as well as female fertility (Toulalan, 2014; Evans, 2016). Phillip Barrough, for example, relates the idea that age 'too little, doeth let conception', stating that male bodies are unready for reproduction until thirty years – an especially late maturation, even by early modern standards – and female bodies are deemed unready before eighteen (1583: 157). However, while concerns about sexual maturity and fertility were a source of anxiety for early modern males (Evans, 2016: 312), medical historians have confirmed that female bodies received far greater attention in medical writings about infertility and 'barrenness', where 'infertility was more often seen as a woman's 'fault', even when there was evidence to the contrary' (Oren-Magidor, 2017: 87).

Although scholarly attention has begun to analyse the ways that adult female health and fertility were understood in early modern culture, little has been said about how the bodily alterations of puberty may have been viewed in relation to later experiences of fertility or barrenness. Hermia, who we saw threatened with the physical decline of old age and greensickness in the first chapter of this book, finds her sexual maturation scrutinised by another gendered attack that focuses on her height, which seems likewise bound to her sexual maturation. Early modern writers do not always make explicit connections between the bodies they describe as growing towards sexual maturity and the issues of fertility that are also explored. However, concerns about not growing 'enough' during puberty can clearly be linked to some regularly recounted concerns about women's fertility. In particular, the structural size of women's bodies was evaluated to assess the likelihood of successful conception and childbirth, where overall stature was associated with the size of the womb. For example, Jacques Guillemeau suggests the correlation between woman's small body size and the size and space in the womb, which, in turn, influences her ability to carry a child to term: 'when shee is eyther too small, or low of stature, which causeth that the child cannot grow in so little roome neither moue himselfe or breath (although he breath onely by the arteries of the mother) her breast beeing so straight that it cannot be stretched or inlarged' (1612: 71). Guillemeau observes that the child in the womb of a short woman will have too little space to grow, and the structural smallness of the woman's breast is also associated with restricting the child's access to air. Similar observations were made about fat bodies constricting the child in the womb and inhibiting the concoction of potent reproductive seed (Toulalan, 2014). Barrough includes shortness as 'an occasion to barennes' (1583: 157), describing how 'a woman, that is fertile, ought to haue a moderate stature & height of the body, breadth of the loynes and the share, buttocks sticking out, a handsome & conuenient greatnesse of the belly' (1583: 157–8). The subjective nature of Barrough's judgements of an 'uncomly and foolish shape and form' (1583: 157) is evident, here clearly linking 'comely' beauty to reproductive capability and using the female's height and body proportions in relation to his evaluations of fertility.

Female maturation was expected to entail an increase in body stature that was set in parallel with the developing size of the womb. The 'ripening' female body was regarded as readying reproductive seed *and* the reproductive environment of the womb in ways that distinguished male and female maturation. Sharp's midwifery treatise recognises how age is key in this body/womb size formulation of early modern thinking: 'Some womens wombs are larger than others, according to the age, stature, and burden that they bear; Maids wombs are small and less than their bladders; but womens are greater' (1671: 74). A normative trajectory of growth is suggested by Sharp's observations: the adolescent female's womb is smaller than the womb of an adult, and growth of the whole body and this organ is expected as a girl matures. However, the girl whose growth is treated as slow, where a small 'stature' continues as she approaches adulthood, could continue to be associated with the maidenly 'wombs [that] are small and less than their bladders', where the undersized nature of the womb would be thought to entail reproductive complications that would persist into adulthood. A small womb was, for example, thought to exacerbate pain during childbirth, and problems during delivery were anticipated. Guillemeau notes that where wombs are 'too little, [women] may likewise bee deliuered with much difficulty. And when this happeneth, it cannot be remedied, as one would desire' (1612: 106). Offering little consolation to women who may anticipate hard labour if they suspect that their wombs are small in correspondence to a small stature, Guillemeau also records attitudes that connected body size to miscarriage. Small wombs, deemed especially likely in bodies of small stature, were thought to make miscarriage more likely in providing inadequate space for a child to develop healthily. Here, Guillemeau does offer some advice to women who have previously miscarried due to 'the littlenesse or lownes of the mother [womb]', suggesting that 'Bathes, fomentations, and oyntments that may loosen and inlarge her belly, and Matrice [womb]' (1612: 73). Medical remedy for miscarriage, here, might well be seen to mimic the adolescent's heat-induced body growth, where parts of the body are 'ablee to stretch: and therfore they grow by vertue of heate', so that what is presented as physical underdevelopment in adulthood can be rectified to some degree (Batman, 1582: 70). As Evans has shown in her recent work on treatments for miscarriage found in recipe books, remedies that intended to support the womb's retention of the foetus and strengthen both mother and child were often recommended to women who were regarded as prone to miscarriage (2022: 518). While being judged as having a predisposition to miscarry during a pregnancy often involved consideration of the personal histories of women, medical writings, as with those from Guillemeau, demonstrate how such reasoning around preventative measures could also involve evaluating body shapes, sizes, and humoral temperaments.

An adult's 'too small' body stature presented more than structural complications in early modern humoral accounts of reproduction (Guillemeau, 1612: 71). The small 'space' provided by a small body was also understood to facilitate damaging excesses in humoral temperaments that could harm fertility. Small bodies that might be described as lacking the natural heat necessary to grow sufficiently during puberty were reimagined in terms of excessive heat once adulthood was thought to be achieved. Hot humours that were no longer directed towards increasing the growing adolescent's body size would have little space to be dispersed in a small, adult body. Hill's popular sixteenth-century treatise on physiognomy relays this humoral logic when he relates why small bodies result in witty personalities and heated, quick thinking:

> For in those (as the Physiognomer affirmeth) the bloude, the liuely spirite, and naturall heate hastily and swiftly procéede, and are moued from the heart vnto the braine, or vnto the cogitatiue vertues: in which such a motion is on the small, and short space: and euen the same is in very small persons, in as much as by the quantitie of the body. (1571: 111)

Here, Hill explains the humoral foundation for the early modern proverb that he uses later in his treatise: 'seldome anye séeth, the long and tall person wittie, nor the short person, méeke and pacient' (1571: 113). Hill clarifies that not all individuals who are small will be witty, their cool humoral disposition could significantly counter the effects of heated 'lively spirite' moving in the body. However, Hill observes how a small body size exacerbates the effects of humoral heat. Smallness facilitates the 'heated' personality trait of wit by enabling speedy movement of heated blood to the brain and providing a shorter journey that limits the cooling that will take place in the process. Short individuals were understood to possess a physique that lent itself to a heated humoral disposition, which enabled witty thoughts.

As we saw in the previous chapter, the adolescent's 'heated' brains could also enjoy associations with wit, but the person of short stature might also retain this quality into adulthood. While wit is generally a positive attribute ascribed to a small, heated body, similar ideas about restricted space in relation to intense heat also resulted in negative personality traits. Hill, for example, offers analogous logic about heated humours to explain the turbulent temper of choleric individuals who, he observes, are often small bodied. Hill explains how 'the small' are 'chollericke in quality [...] in whom a drinesses and superfluous hotnesse consisteth' because 'The motion of the spirits in them is ouer swift, and by reason of the smalnesse of the space' (1571: 111ʳ).

For women, in particular, physical smallness and its association with excess heat was associated with dysfunctional fertility, where observations about the whole body could again encourage scrutiny of the womb. Although, early modern writers do not always explicitly connect body size to their discussion of humoral excesses in the womb, as they do with discussions of womb size, the humoral rationale that used age and stature to assess overall humoral disposition, indicates that body size was a familiar component in evaluations of humours. For example, Barrough observes how the 'Heate of the matrice [womb] is known by the heate in the rest of the body' (1583: 158), and Barrough moves swiftly from an overall assessment of humoral disposition to an assessment of the internal workings of the female's reproductive body. Heat, though required for successful generation in early modern thinking, would destroy generative seed in a womb that was regarded as too 'hot and fiery' (Barrough, 1583: 157). Barrough notes, moreover, that menstruation is often absent in 'baraine women', where 'women of hote temperature, that be wilde, and doe use strong exercise, they purge out little or nothing' (1583: 157, 145). Meanwhile, Guillemeau connects any 'biting humors' in the womb with miscarriage, 'wherwith the Matrice [womb] beeing stirred, or prouoked, while it endeuours to expell them, may thrust out the child also' (1612: 71). The humoral parallel of body/womb is a central concern in early modern writings about infertility and miscarriage. With the humoral state of the womb being 'known by the heate in the rest of the body' (Barrough, 1583: 158), it is likely that early modern women could find the size of their bodies being used in evaluations of their reproductive health. Moreover, as the cold and 'straight' womb is also associated with bodily leanness in early modern writings, and, as humoral health was assessed through bodily proportions, tallness also seems implicated here (Barrough, 1583: 48). A woman, whether deemed too short, tall, fat, or lean, could anticipate having her stature included in an assessment of her erotic appeal and fertility, whereby her humoral heat, the size of her womb, and her experience of menstruation would all be suggested.

Although Evans's work on aphrodisiacs has shown that early modern culture understood that humoral excess or deficiency could be somewhat mediated by diet and exercise, Evans is also clear that the intense interest in fertility indicates anxieties within early modern culture and 'paints a picture of many men and women struggling to conceive and give birth to live children' (2014: 191). Ideas about growth during female adolescence may have carried negative connotations if projected constructions of an adult reproductive body were deemed at fault. The female life cycle presents a trajectory of growth that sets any notion of inappropriate growth during adolescence alongside the adulthood that the younger age anticipates. Therefore, the short-statured female adolescent might additionally be fashioned as a likely candidate for having hot humours in her womb if her height does not increase as she moves into adulthood.

When we connect changes central to adolescence to concerns that surrounded women's fertility, we see how conditions like greensickness not only stigmatise bodily changes linked specifically to girlhood, as scholars such as King (2004) and Potter (2013) have so proficiently explained, but the intrusive diagnostic approach to growing bodies also presents a template by which the sexual health of the female could become bound across her life cycle. Indeed, the ideological connections between greensickness, the 'virgin's' disease, and dysfunctional reproduction in female adulthood have material links. As I discussed in my analysis of Ophelia's botanics in Chapter 1, the same emmenagogues that were used to encourage menstrual bleeding to alleviate greensickness were also used to regulate menstruation in women wanting to conceive (Evans, 2014: 171–5). The 'ripening' girl's propensity for physiological disorder lays the groundwork for interrogating fertility in adult women. This may explain the anxiety that Read (2013) records in the tracing the experience of 'transitional bleedings' across accounts of the female life cycle. Likewise, Susan Broomhill's study of female correspondence in sixteenth-century France observes how family members could express concern over female physical development, specifically the importance of regular menstruation being established as girls became women (2002: 2–4). The correlation between the regulated, *growing* female body and its sexual maturation appear entwined with cultural pressures placed upon women who are expected to become wives and mothers.

The connection between attitudes towards sexual maturation in girls and their adult fertility seems a key part of Lysander's critique of Hermia's repugnant smallness in *A Midsummer Night's Dream*. As I have noted, the acorn is an underdeveloped form of the oak tree, and knotgrass was linked to stunted growth, so Lysander situates his exchange with Hermia in the context of cultural ideas about her maturation. However, knotgrass was also used in medical treatments for female reproductive health. Knotgrass, most likely due to 'drying' qualities that Bacon warned against in his recommendations for diets that encourage growth, was also prescribed for menstrual disorders. Barrough encourages use of 'juices of knotgrasse' as a means to reduce excessive menstrual flow, while binding the body with the weed was meant to remove excess moisture that was more broadly associated with infertility in women (1583: 148, 159). These properties of reducing bodily fluidity may also explain why knotgrass could also be recommended as a preventative for miscarriage (Evans, 2022: 522). Whether Lysander infers Hermia's own infertility and/or Hermia's effect on others *as* the small weed with drying properties associated with uterine and reproductive disorders, Lysander's words relate Hermia's stature to hostile images that contrast with idealised models of flourishing adolescence. Allusions to insufficient growth and infertility, underscored by references to excesses in humoral heat and dryness, help present Hermia's adolescence as incompatible with any life-giving, reproductive future that she might have as Lysander's wife and mother to their children.

While this rather bleak imposition of medical doctrine upon adolescent female bodies is part of the cultural fashioning of gendered experiences of adolescence, Hermia, and the bodies of early modern girls, are not quite the simple signifiers of medical meaning that the diagnostic and prescriptive writings of physicians can suggest. A state of embodiment also usually involves subjects who can articulate experiences, and – for all its misogynistic framing of female bodies – medical diagnosis in early modern society still depended heavily on how individuals described their bodies and how they acted. Physician and patient interactions involved social negotiations that did not necessarily place women's bodies solely at the mercy of the physician's authority and diagnosis. As a patient, a woman could make 'autonomous decisions regarding her medical diagnosis and treatment' and, as she could usually refuse physical examination, influence a diagnosis that would hinge largely on her behaviour and words (Churchill, 2013: 58, 76). Evans also observes evidence of female agency in the way women used preventative medicines as interventions against the threat of miscarriage, where such actions asserted some control over a bodily state that was often used to disempower female subjects, whose 'failure' to carry a child to term was understood in relation to 'broader spiritual concerns and a means to assess one's own behaviour' (2022: 514). Required navigations of hostile biases in medical discourse must have made seeking treatment a fraught experience for girls and women, and the nature of some illnesses (where, for example, speech may be difficult) would inhibit the ability to assert control over such situations (Churchill, 2013: 209). However, this negotiated position for female patients in early modern society offers a revised context for viewing the more isolated interpretations of bodies offered in medical texts. In medical practice and early modern social interactions, medical interpretations could be disputed, and processes of evaluating health would usually involve the individual whose body was being interpreted.

What is more, adolescent bodies were considered unfixed entities when compared to adult bodies. In being recognised as undergoing a process of growth and change, adolescent bodies were understood to be mutable in ways that could resist the attachment of fixed meaning. Although connected to the adult state that their adolescence foregrounded, the adolescent body was not yet a fully-grown form. As Hill observes in relation to age and physiognomy, the terms of interpreting the ageing body that is subject to change necessitates caution in readings that 'sometimes declare the matter rather past, than to come' (1571: 115). Bodies that change significantly due to a life stage cannot, according to Hill, be regarded as fully reliable in gauging a subject's personality or morality.

While bodies continue to change in various ways during adulthood, only the adult can explicitly be subjected to judgements regarding whether they have, in the end, achieved an acceptable 'full' height. The narrative of growth that underpins an understanding of adolescent bodies particularly resists a stable interpretation of a physiognomy. In Hill's 'Preface to the Reader', he insists upon the value physiognomy holds in making it possible to 'learne to know ourselues' and understand 'the naturall aptnesse vnto the affections, and conditions in men, by the outwarde notes of the bodie' (1571: 1). The adolescent body, however, presents a source of knowledge that is in motion, and subject to intense humoral influences, suggesting that any interpretation of self is also by necessity subject to reinterpretation. Children's bodies, as humorally hot and moist, were potentially more vulnerable to external impositions, and this could disrupt a trajectory of growth. However, children's bodies, understood as in motion and humorally malleable, could also be thought of as resilient. Newton's research into 'child's physic' again provides provocative observations, noting ambivalence in early modern attitudes towards children's bodies and their 'humid humours' (2012: 32), where 'fixed' states of illness could be navigated by children's mutable physicalities. Small and vulnerable, children were also associated with resistance to some diseases, where full recovery from an illness might even be achieved *because* a child's state of growth involved significant humoral change (Newton, 2012: 32). Newton cites records from the mid-sixteenth-century physician Isbrand van Diemerbroak as one example of this early modern thinking. Diemerbroak notes how 'the Strength and Age of the Patientt gave great hopes of a cure[,] For being but a Child, the very change of Youth out of one Age into another many times effects the Cure' (cited in Newton, 2012: 32). Here the child is not yet an adolescent, but the adolescent's proximity to adulthood likewise evokes the idea of still having capacity to *grow further* and experience humoral change that resituates interpretations of un/healthy bodies.

It is true that adolescence can be scrutinised as always 'falling short', as it were, of awaited adulthood, but contextualised as an age during which growth and significant change occurs, it invites acknowledgement of the child's active and mutable state where physical outcomes are hitherto not set. After all, even the 'short' adolescent can be imagined to resist being categorised as too short if Bacon's (1626: 354) recommendations for accelerating growth by increasing exercise and eating moist foods are taken on board. Lysander's insults are initially suggestive of a hostile perspective on adolescence, which frame Hermia's body as being not yet mature in a way that exaggerates comparative debility when the adolescent body is set in opposition to an adult state. However, shifting perspective to one that acknowledges a body in motion, where the adolescent body that is small is understood as still having further to grow, opens possibilities for the individual, possibilities that theatrical production could exploit. *A Midsummer Night's Dream*, as I suggest in the next section of the chapter, encourages such shifts in perspective by setting growing adolescent characters alongside each other, and by placing their stories of transformation at the heart of the play. Hermia is, after all, restored to her status as Lysander's desired love match in *A Midsummer Night's Dream*; her physical stature is resituated back in the context of a narrative of growth and continuation towards anticipated fruitfulness. In the next section, I suggest how Hermia's redeemed adolescence depends upon the way in which Shakespeare's play dismantles the familiar adult/child binary. Once adolescence becomes less about unattained future states, setting constructions of adolescence in dialogue with each other, *A Midsummer Night's Dream* focuses attention upon what the age of adolescence may itself entail.

Acorns and maypoles: Hermia, Helena, and staging comparative heights between girls

The audience of Shakespeare's *A Midsummer Night's Dream* would likely have understood the attitudes upon which the insults used to attack Hermia, in Act 3, Scene 2, depend. Theatregoers are asked to recognise Hermia's short stature and follow the logic of Lysander's insults, which associate that shortness with sexual immaturity and infertility. However, an audience of *A Midsummer Night's Dream* would also be aware of Hermia's previous position as an admired beauty in the plot of the play. This duality of admiring/mocking Hermia's physicality works, in part, because the staging of Hermia's height-based abuse involves more than just the verbal onslaught she receives. The construction of age-related height in *A Midsummer Night's Dream* draws upon a model of comparison that is used throughout the play. From the beginning of *A Midsummer Night's Dream*, Hermia is compared to her girlhood friend, Helena. This means that, although the hostile language of Act 3 Scene 2 insists upon Hermia's unpromising distance from 'adult' maturity, we find that the theatrical comparison is not only between an adult and child state but also a tussle that involves comparisons *between* adolescents, one short, one tall.

In this section, I examine how the argument scene, understood in the context of the narratives at work in *A Midsummer Night's Dream* as a whole, takes advantage of ideas about difference and degree that a comparative staging of girlhood heights allows. Here, contrasts between small and tall observe the mutability and variability of *growing* bodies and elicit meanings that repeatedly revel in the unfixed nature of the characters being observed. Individuated girls, I suggest, become recognised, albeit through conversations that are underpinned by misogynistic emphasis upon female reproductive 'purpose'. The interactions between Helena and Hermia seem to acknowledge that adolescence can be experienced differently by those who might otherwise be viewed as inhabiting the same life stage. Girls who 'grew together' (3.2.208) elicit recognition of difference and, what is more, a capacity to change and reimagine selves. Both Hermia and Helena can talk back to insults about body size, and each adolescent character offers a complementary dynamism in the argument scene, which utilises the body size and energetic performances of the actors involved. I suggest, therefore, that the 'big' impact of both characters acts to destabilise assumptions about the diminutive power of *growing* child actors, who, in being set across from each other, were evidently not always and only being compared to adults in early modern theatre.

Throughout *A Midsummer Night's Dream*, Helena and Hermia are compared in ways that draw attention to similarities and difference in social standing and behaviour, where physical comparisons are especially pronounced. As is typical of Shakespearean romantic comedy, the beauty of each girl and her desirability is paramount, with the childhood friends being positioned as comparable objects of male desire. Initially, Hermia is evidently favoured by Lysander and Demetrius, although Helena ponders why the comparison must leave one girl slighted when both girls have been acknowledged as possessing beauty: 'Through Athens I am thought as fair as she' (1.1.227). The issue of 'fairness' is a persistent point of contention in comparing the girls, and *A Midsummer Night's Dream* uses racially coded language to construct Hermia's darkness in opposition to Helena's whiteness (Erickson, 1993: 518; Hall, 1995: 1–24; Karim-Cooper, 2023: 250–1). Notably, these racialised comparisons most overtly surface in Lysander's language of rejection, where the insults levied at Hermia focus on her dark complexion: 'Away you Ethiope' (3.2.257); 'Out, tawny Tartar' (3.2.263). The racism within early modern constructions of beauty is included in Lysander's language of insult and works alongside hostile depictions of body size.[4]

To some degree, however, the play explores the instability of its constructions of girlhood beauty, as Hermia and Helena find themselves variously adored or rejected during the play. Specifically, ideas about the passing of time and processes of growth seem to shift the parameters for judging body size as beautiful, realising ambiguities around interpreting female maturation. As Hermia insists, 'I am as fair now as I was erewhile' (3.2.274). Nothing has changed in Hermia's appearance since Lysander's declarations of love were offered only a scene earlier. Hermia's statement of stable beauty would seem to provide reassurance after Theseus's threats of premature decay and withered blossoms that he insists await Hermia if she persists in disobeying her father, and which I discussed in Chapter 1 (1.1.77). Lysander's hurtful words stress, however, that stasis is not a feasible state for the early modern adolescent, perhaps particularly in a play where change is desirable, eroticised, and entertaining. Metamorphosis underpins all the action of *A Midsummer Night's Dream* and remaining what you were 'erewhile' becomes problematised by the focus that the play puts upon adolescence as a time for desired transformation.

It makes sense, at this stage in the analysis of Hermia and Helena's comparative adolescence, to consider the broader contexts in which *A Midsummer Night's Dream* situates the girls' maturation. Fairies in early modern culture and Shakespeare's play are associated with two key concerns that help illuminate the way in which *A Midsummer Night's Dream* centres upon adolescent growth narratives. Firstly, fairies, who are small enough to sleep in flowers and have names to indicate this miniature state in *A Midsummer Night's Dream* – for example, Mustardseed, Moth, Peasblossom – also have the ability to 'appear in human-like form and interact with humans' (Esra and Gibson, 2017: 79). We know that Shakespeare's fairies can alter their body sizes, because Titania takes Bottom as a human/ass lover, and Oberon is said to have masqueraded 'in the shape of Corin', a human shepherd, to court Phillida (2.1.66). Secondly, fairies were recognised as supernatural creatures that could interfere with human childhood development. As Titania's and Oberon's battle over the changeling boy recalls, early modern fairies were thought to steal, disfigure, and even kill human children (Lamb, 2000). Fairy children, substituted for stolen human offspring, were associated with physical ugliness, disability, and stupidity, whereby a child's 'supposed deficiency might be attributed to the fact that it was a fairy' (Esra and Gibson, 2017: 38). Perceived 'deficiency' in early modern ideas about childhood commonly involved allusions to fairy magic and involvement.

For Ben Wiebracht (2020), Titania's involvement in Shakespeare's play draws upon cultural associations of disrupted maturation, where male adolescence is specifically threatened by the fairy's influence. Wiebracht observes how Titania's interactions with Bottom suggest a re-enactment of her treatment of the changeling boy, where Titania's claim on the boy is that of 'an overwhelming adult lover' (2020: 341) who inhibits the adolescent's navigations towards manhood. Oberon's interventions, understood in this light, are required to remove (or become a substitute for) Titania's overbearing presence. For Wiebracht, Shakespeare reuses a model of adult/adolescent evident in Shakespeare's representation of Venus and the reluctant Adonis, and the allusion characterises Titania's erotic dominance over Bottom/the changeling boy as a threat to the 'entire maturation process' (2020: 341).

Links between fairies and body development are also suggested through Oberon's presence in *A Midsummer Night's Dream*. According to some early modern tales about fairies, Oberon's own childhood development was understood as having been subjected to supernatural interference. In these stories, Oberon receives a curse that stunted his growth when he was three years old (Hendricks, 1996: 46).[5] *Huon of Bordeaux* (1601) records this detail in Oberon's description, noting that, although Oberon would 'grow no more' after the age of three, the woman who cursed him regretted her curse and provided recompense by making Oberon attractive in all other ways. In *Huon of Bordeaux*, Oberon is presented as 'the fairest creature that euer Nature fourmed' (1601: Chapter 24). In Oberon's own backstory, ideas about disrupted growth and evaluations of how 'fairness' is evaluated are included. Early modern fairy narratives that carry striking associations with concerns about altering human bodies during childhood in changeling stories, and broader ideas about changes to body size contextualise the action between adolescents in *A Midsummer Night's Dream*. The inclusion of Oberon, who 'is a catalyst for change, for transformation in the human world' (Hendricks, 1996: 47), additionally helps set the scene for *A Midsummer Night's Dream* to tap into ideas about adolescence and its own associations with bodily transformation.

We hear, for example, that Titania and Oberon's dispute over the changeling boy has disrupted the human world of growth and development. The seasons have become confused, midsummer harvests have been ruined, and growth and continuation are disturbed by the fairies' discord:

> The seasons alter; hoary-headed frosts
> Fall in the fresh lap of the crimson rose,
> And on Hiems' chin and icy crown
> An odorous chaplet of sweet summer buds
> Is, as in mockery, set. The spring, the summer,
> The childing autumn, angry winter, change
> Their wonted liveries, and the mazèd world
> By their increase now knows not which is which. (2.1.107–14)

Thanks to the conflict between the fairy King and Queen, the natural rhythms of the world are in disarray and seasons have become indistinguishable for the humans who 'knows not which is which'. As I outlined in the first chapter, human lives were understood through mapping the life cycle onto the workings of the natural world, tracking growth, maturation, fruitfulness, and decline. Titania and Oberon's conflict creates discord that informs all human interactions in the play. This includes and moves beyond the influence of the purple flower, which is itself suggestive of the violet that is emblematic of youth (Faircloth and Thomas, 2016: 'Violet'). Oberon and Titania's disharmony is presented to the play's audience in a way that invites concern for that which is growing, whether crops or Athenian adolescents, in the play.

It is in this context of the fairies' disruptive influence that we understand the conflict between the adolescent Athenians in *A Midsummer Night's Dream*, particularly once the purple flower has been used. Yet it is also noteworthy that it is the play's adolescents who initiate contemplations about transformation in *A Midsummer Night's Dream*, and it is the story about adolescents that is set out before Titania and Oberon enter the play. The fairy plot and its components of metamorphoses are, therefore, also presented to be understood in relation to the adolescent plot within the play's structure. Linguistic echoes across the fairy and Athenian plots see fairy influence recall adolescent concerns. In the first scene of *A Midsummer Night's Dream*, for example, Helena confesses to Hermia that Demetrius's favouring of her friend's beauty means she yearns 'to be to you translated' (1.1.191). Helena speaks lines like those famously used by Quince to describe Bottom's bestial transformation through Oberon's magic: 'Thou art translated' (3.1.105). However, Quince's words repeat Helena's words, where a desire for metamorphosis is expressed in the play. To not be what you were 'erewhile' (3.2.274), for Helena, would enable romantic fantasies to be achieved.

The notion of being 'translated' primarily suggests a physical transformation for Helena (and Bottom); the adolescent girl yearns to assume the shape of her friend in order to appeal to Demetrius. However, 'translation' also carries additional meanings that relate to the word's recurring use in the play. As David Lucking observes of Bottom's 'translation', the term also meant 'to interpret, explain' (2011: 138) in a culture where acts of translation were a popular intellectual endeavour. Moreover, Lucking's findings offer helpful insight into Helena's wish for 'translation', which suggests both physical and discursive components. Translation of selves, bodies, or texts reworks the 'transformed' subject through an act of interpretation so that change is not solely rooted in a physical alteration but in how something is elucidated and given meaning: 'transformation is really a matter of how things are perceived' (Lucking, 2011: 138). Helena's 'translation' may not be quite the simple wish to be physically transformed into Hermia; Helena may express the desire to have her own body interpreted in the same way as Hermia's body and be perceived as beautiful.

In *A Midsummer Night's Dream*, the girlhoods of Helena and Hermia are set along parallel trajectories of growth. Helena offers a harmonious account, in which 'we grew together' (3.2.208) as 'Two lovely berries molded on one stem' (3.2.211). Yet the differences between Helena and Hermia offer a means of understanding adolescence as a life stage that presented variation of experience and bodily development. In Act 3, Scene 2, the comparative tall height of Helena is stressed to help situate the scathing comments that are made about Hermia's shortness. While Hermia is aligned with an acorn-like immaturity, the disparity in heights between the actors playing each girl is used by the adolescent male characters of the play to construct Helena's taller height as a comparative sign of positive growth and fertility. Demetrius's response to Helena eroticises her body and uses the familiar agricultural language of ripening to do so: 'how ripe in show / Thy lips, those kissing cherries, tempting grow' (3.2.139–40). The allure of Helena's 'ripe' form is sexualised in opposition to the sterility we see applied to Hermia's seed-like, short stature.

Hermia adopts a similar approach to Helena's tallness, aligning her height with sexual activity. However, Hermia converts Helena's tall form into a sign of sexual availability rather than admired sexual ripeness. Hermia's response to insults about her small size include describing Helena as a 'painted maypole' (3.2.296). The image fashions Helena as tall in a way that connects her height to the sexual awakenings associated with the mayday harvest. This allusion to a 'maypole' could, presented in isolation, simply re-inscribe an image of achieved 'ripeness', seeing as the maypole image offers a partner image for Hermia's unripe 'acorn' description. As we hear in a song from *The Two Noble Kinsmen*, 'Give us but a tree or twain / For Maypole, and again' (3.5.147–8): the maypole was made from a tree. However, as Philip Stubbes's zealous condemnations of 'The Fruits of may-games' suggest, mayday festivities could be associated with licentious sexual activity, where maids were unlikely to be 'returned home again undefiled' (1583: n.p.). While Shakespeare's adolescents observe relative sexual modesty in their behaviour in the woods, with Hermia asking Lysander to 'lie further off yet; Do not lie so near' (2.2.44) to retain a sense of decorum when the pair fall asleep in the forest, Hermia's retaliations in her exchanges with Helena align Helena with a compromised notion of the maypole's symbolism of fertility. Hermia pointedly makes Helena a '*painted* maypole' (emphasis added). In so doing, Hermia draws connections between Helena's appearance and the recurring image of 'the painted lady' in early modern culture (Garner, 1989: 123). As I discussed in detail chapter two, those who used cosmetics were often castigated as 'agents of seduction and deceit' in early modern culture (Garner, 1989: 125). Through Hermia's jibe, Helena's erotic appeal becomes associated with deceptive appearances and sexual looseness.

Hermia's insult, however, may do more than suggest Helena's sexual immodesty. Cosmetics were understood to falsify appearances and Hermia's comments invite the audience to notice the make-up on Helena's face. The allusion to cosmetics, therefore, seems to draw attention to the boy actor when the audience might otherwise accept the theatrical cosmetics as a sign of feminine, natural beauty. Indeed, Hermia's accusation of artifice and painted bodies especially seems to encourage awareness of the boy actors playing each girl in the scene, if we note that the exchange has invited us to realise that both girls are, in fact, painted. Hermia is implicitly identified as using cosmetics in Act 3, Scene 2, by being called a 'puppet'. While Hermia interprets the word as a comment about her stature, Helena more clearly uses the word to suggest that Hermia is performing false speech and presenting a misleading appearance: 'you counterfeit, you puppet' (3.2.288). Helena, viewing Hermia as a puppet, suggests that both her speech and her body should be regarded as inauthentic. The puppet, as Caton notes, is an unsettling object that takes on subjectivity and draws attention to 'shared borders' between fiction and reality (2013: 32). Describing a person as a puppet suggests that the person presents a fictitious presentation of selfhood. Women who used cosmetics were particularly associated with deceptive self-presentation akin to the puppet that was also usually painted. Joseph Swetnam's *The Arraignment of Lewd, Idle, Forward, and Unconstant Women* makes this connection explicit, describing women who use cosmetics as 'painting themselues [...] to pranck vp themselues, in their gaudies; like Poppets' (1615: 28).

References to puppetry and paint simultaneously draw attention to issues of female artifice and performance. Early modern attitudes towards female beauty that are implicated in allusions to cosmetic use by a character also seem to gesture towards the use of cosmetics in theatrical practice, making the artistry of the boy actors discernible in the scene's action. As this chapter's opening discussion of Cokes's encounter with puppets also suggests, comparisons between child actors and puppets may have been familiar. Indeed, Cleopatra's infamous meta-theatrical allusions to her own representations by a boy actor, which I discussed in the previous chapter, are preceded by concerns that Iras will be presented to a crowd as an 'Egyptian puppet' (5.2.206). Allusions to puppetry in Shakespeare and other early modern sources, often encourage evaluations of theatrical performance.

In *A Midsummer Night's Dream*, contrasts between adolescents can certainly include the girl characters in the play and the physically distinct boy actors performing the roles, who are likewise either short or tall. The scene's energetic interactions also work to distinguish between each character's disposition (and each actor's performance), although this distinction between girls notably comes at the cost of female friendship, which is dismantled in a scene that witnesses 'disruption of women's bonds with each other' in order to enable heteronormative couplings (Garner, 1989: 127). Hermia shows strength despite her abuse, and her 'fierce vein' (3.2.82), which is noted by Demetrius prior to his enchantment, is built upon in her dynamic exchanges with Helena. We get to know far more about Hermia and Helena in this scene's comparative framing of the girls in relation to each other compared to what we learn in thinking about the girls in relation to their male suitors. For example, from Helena we hear about a recalled past, which, in this scene, focuses on the girls' schooling, when Hermia was allegedly 'a vixen' (3.2.324). The lines from each boy actor help feed the energy of the scene, as Helena's descriptions cue Hermia's reactive responses so that verbal assault threatens to escalate into a physical one: 'not yet so low / But my nails can reach unto thine eyes' (3.2.297–8). The individuation of girl characters in the scene seems to work in parallel with individuating the boy players, as each actor orientates his performance of either Hermia's ferocity or Helena's pronounced fear, utilising their comparative body sizes (and so working together) in order to do so.

The cultural fashioning of the vocal accomplishments of adolescent speakers that we encountered in the last chapter often identified an appreciation for the adolescent's controlled physical movement that accompanied measured speech. For example, the exercises that Mulcaster recommends for adolescent learners regularly combine walking, gesturing, and talking. A model by which the adolescent male pronounced 'his orations alowd, as he walked vp against the hill' is deemed especially beneficial to the adolescent who 'strengthened his voice' (1581: 85) through these exertions. McCarthy's analysis of the repertoires of early modern boy companies, in his work with Edward's Boys in practical workshops, has, moreover, indicated how energetic play content was commonplace in productions designed for early modern boy actors (2020b). An expectation of vibrancy in an adolescent actor's performance fits neatly with the cultural constructions of adolescence that have been outlined in this book. While the complex group work of 'energetic', all-boy companies is not evident to the extent that McCarthy (2020b; 2022) reveals in works written solely for boys, Shakespeare's plays suggest a similar taste for the physical and linguistic dexterity attributed to adolescents. Shakespeare's Cleopatra, for example, is a role that would have required an energetic performance that matched vocal skill with physical dynamism, with collaboration between actors being require in staged action that includes the beating of messengers and the hoisting of Antony onto the Monument (see McCarthy, 2022: 147–53). The adolescent actor who performed the role of Cleopatra moves further away from the 'puny boy' once imagined when the physical and vocal demands of the role are considered (Dusinberre, 1998: 12).

In writing adolescent parts for adult actors, playwrights also seem to have kept these cultural attitudes about energetic physicalities in mind.

After all, Burbage, as Orlando in *As You Like It*, is a proficient, though 'tender' wrestler. Likewise, the allocation of physically demanding parts to adolescent actors indicates how these actors were considered especially able to pull off such displays. We might, for example, consider the ways in which a play like *Titus Andronicus* (c. 1594) foregrounds the physical performances of its young players, even if the plot itself sees violence somewhat relentlessly enacted upon adolescent characters who are placed at the mercy of political worlds controlled by adults (Knowles, 2013: 63–89). The original staging of *Titus Andronicus* would have depended upon the skills of the adolescent actors who performed the play's central acts of violence. For example, Chiron and Demetrius, who are certainly adolescent characters (Knowles, 2013), are also framed as young in comparison to numerous other child/son characters in the play's plot, and these characters are only older than the very Young Lucius and Aaron and Tamora's baby. This sense of age and degree across the male roles in *Titus Andronicus* makes it likely that, as 'boys' (2.1.38, 45) who are separated by 'the difference of a year or two' (2.1.31), Chiron and Demetrius, along with Young Lucius and the female roles of Tamora and Lavinia, would have been played by boy actors. Indeed, the physicality of the roles of Chiron and Demetrius in Act 2 suggest as much, as Chiron and Demetrius taunt and manhandle Lavinia (another boy actor), sometimes spurred on by Tamora (also a boy actor). Actors who were likely adults (Bassianus and Aaron) move in and out of the play's central 'forest' scenes, where the action is decidedly focused upon the interaction of boy players. Although these scenes are neither the beginning nor the end of the violence in *Titus Andronicus*, the structural centrality of the scenes in the play's Act/Scene framework, and the continued presence of Lavinia, whose mutilated state of embodiment demands further physical feats from the actor (who, despite having no lines, interacts with other characters and properties, such as books, a staff, and a basin) in a way that also recalls the violence of the forest, and sets the interplay of adolescent actors at the heart of the play's original staging.

In *A Midsummer Night's Dream*, allusions to puppets and paint draw particular attention to the adolescent performers behind the play's lively girl characters. Such allusions to adolescent actors, however, seem to complement the theatrical illusion, suggesting overlap between character/performer in terms of a paralleled adolescent age. The energetic performance, therefore, here appears appropriate to early modern constructions of both girlhood and boyhood, and, unlike the shift away from Cleopatra's womanly and racialised character that results from metatheatre that makes the part appear 'boyish', which I discussed in the last chapter, *A Midsummer Night's Dream* seems to celebrate connections between the adolescence of its actors and characters. What is more, the threatening nature of the scene is somewhat mollified (though the misogyny of its insults is not) when the physical humour of the scene's allusions to body size is considered. In the exchange between Helena and Hermia, with Lysander and Demetrius also present, it is the smaller actor/character who is outnumbered and faces the greater verbal attack from three other characters. As a group, the actors' words insist upon their greater physical statures, and the scene has the potential to make the group's hostility towards Hermia physically intimidating, something that modern performance may utilise. The script, however, makes it the taller actor, playing Helena, convey a sense of physical intimidation at the prospect of being harmed by the 'fierce' (3.2.325) Hermia. The scene, which can be powerfully tense and uncomfortable in modern representations of Hermia's position, seems, in its early modern incarnations (and, indeed, many modern ones), open to making jokes by setting small and big bodies in opposition.[6] As we have seen, cultural assumptions about tallness and shortness feed into the language of the scene, but the physical reactions of the girl characters (one small and ready to fight, the other tall and scared) somewhat undercuts the insults made about each girl. Ideas about stunted growth and the lack of vitality (usually due to inadequate 'natural heat') are paired with Hermia's self-assertion and fiery temperament, while Helena's alignment with painted harlots and insatiable desire is (mis)matched with a display of physical reticence. Helena offers the cue for the energised conclusion to the adolescents' interaction in the scene by making a joke about her longer legs being able to run fast: 'Your hands than mine are quicker for a fray / My legs are longer, though, to run away' (3.2.342–3). Therefore, the performance of adolescent character in *A Midsummer Night's Dream* remains utterly appropriate to early modern ideas about 'heated' adolescence, as are the overblown nature of the insults, but the scene also deconstructs the signification of body size, which becomes unfixed when applied to adolescent growing bodies that are understood to be, quite literally, in motion.

In *A Midsummer Night's Dream*, the adolescent character/actor is not, in this instance, primarily understood by being set in opposition to an adult. Helena's and Hermia's contrasted maturations help resist the interchangeability of girl identities that their enchanted lovers' confusion suggests. A story about bodily change and difference allows for creative possibilities and nuances in constructing adolescent subjectivities. That the actor playing Helena is tall and the actor playing Hermia is short enables these dynamic characterisations that drive *A Midsummer Night's Dream*. Adolescent transformation sits at the centre of Shakespeare's play, which seems to recognise and use the fact that adolescent bodies grow in height. *A Midsummer Night's Dream* provides a vibrant example of how a change in height, an unsurprising aspect of puberty, need not solely be a source of anxiety in a theatrical context. The physical changes of puberty, experienced at different times and to different degrees by many adolescent actors in a company, could clearly be a useful resource when collaborating with these actors to produce varied characterisations onstage.

Burbage as adolescent and the comparative heights of *As You Like It*

In the Athenian love plot of *A Midsummer Night's Dream*, it is the predicament of the girl characters, played by adolescent actors, which largely dominates the play's storytelling. The boys playing Helena and Hermia often seem to draw focus from the actors playing Lysander and Demetrius, characters who Grote, summarising the findings of critical tradition, suggests would originally have been played by key adult players: Burbage and Henry Condell, respectively (2002: 229). Lysander and Demetrius do have important lines and performance features to deliver (both characters being placed under the magical influence of Oberon's flower), but even the performances of bewitchment, which include Lysander's virulent insults about Hermia, are presented in a way that directs attention back to the adolescent girl characters. It is, after all, the actors playing the girls who must enact bewilderment in response to the change in the male characters and contribute to the lively antagonism that develops across the group in Act 3, Scene 2. The roles of Hermia and Helena appear indicative of what Power describes as 'accompanied' roles for adolescent players who are in training (2003: 228). Such roles demand some complex features from adolescent actors, but these remain supported by the presence of other actors. As Hermia and Helena are usually either onstage together or with the adult actors play Lysander or Demetrius, this suggests the collaborative processes at work in theatre companies, where support could be offered within and across the age categories of actors. Such supportive and collaborative structures, moreover, could act to privilege the position of the adolescent being trained in the scene's action.

Burbage's likely presence in the adolescent plot of *A Midsummer Night's Dream* (c. 1595/6) further attests to the play's initial framing of the adolescent transformations as being at the heart of its narrative. Early performances of the play would surely draw attention to the company's rising star player, in a role where Burbage may also have been beginning to cultivate his specialism for performing male adolescence. Burbage would perform the role of Romeo a couple of years after his representation of Lysander, and his Orlando would follow around two years after that. Considered in this light, Burbage's Lysander can also be regarded as formative in the context of his own theatrical career. According to Grote, Burbage would move from the role of Lysander to that of Oberon in 1605 (2002: 238). If this is true, the change would suggest a shift in the play's emphasis, possibly relocating the company's well-established star due to his own ageing, as Burbage would have been nearly forty in 1605. Burbage's presence in the fairy narrative would likely have placed greater emphasis upon this aspect of *A Midsummer Night's Dream* and signalled movement away from the prominence of adolescence in the play's storytelling in a way that tallies with later (including modern) productions of the play, which tend to stress the interactions of fairies over Athenian adolescents.

For a significant part of his career, Burbage was clearly considered adept at representing adolescent protagonists. Taking into account some debate over dates for first performances, Burbage's portrayals of Lysander, Romeo, Hamlet, and Orlando would all have been first performed when the actor was in his twenties and thirties. In this section, I consider how the modelling of adolescence that we saw at work in *A Midsummer Night's Dream* (c. 1595/6) is used and developed in *As You Like It* (1599), when Burbage (and Shakespeare writing for Burbage) had tested out several adolescent roles. Greater complexities emerge through the presence of the adult 'star' actor in the comparative staging of adolescence in *As You Like It* than is seen in *A Midsummer Night's Dream*. The presence of Burbage alongside the 'wide-ranging role' (McMillin, 2004: 240) of Rosalind, who receives cues from thirteen characters across the play, does not suggest a simple master/apprentice support system because the boy actor is clearly experienced enough to hold the stage without Burbage. Indeed, the adolescent actor playing the less-expansive role of Celia is accompanied by the Rosalind actor, except for Celia's non-speaking entrance with a group in the final scene (where Rosalind is soon onstage), indicating that the boy playing Rosalind was providing the primary support for another adolescent performing in the play. We may also note that Celia's part is significantly reduced from Lodge's source (1590), and this again suggests that a less experienced and probably younger player was in the role of Celia for *As You Like It*.

Although the parts are less evenly weighted, this comparative staging of girl adolescent characters of Rosalind and Celia realises similarities with the comparative staging of Hermia and Helena in *A Midsummer Night's Dream*. Once again, one girl is notably taller than the other. Rosalind, in devising her plot to crossdress as the adolescent male, Ganymede, draws attention to her height when she reasons that her disguise will be convincing because she is 'more than common tall' (1.3.111). The line reworks the wording of Lodge's *Rosalynde*, where Rosalynde says, 'I (thou seest), am of a tall stature, and would very well become the person and apparell of a page' (1590: 14ʳ). Lodge's Rosalynde, like Shakespeare's character, suggests that tallness in an adolescent female will support a performance of masculine adolescence, unlike smallness. However, by retaining Lodge's notion in his play, Shakespeare adds an allusion to real bodies on stage and specifically emphasises the tallness of the actor playing Rosalind. Celia, shorter than her childhood friend, will retain a female disguise in the forest, unlike her crossdressed companion. While there might well have been an age gap between the boy actors, the girls of *As You Like It* are fashioned as being the same age. Like Hermia and Helena, the girls have grown up together and reflect upon a shared upbringing, having 'learned, played […] together' (1.3.70). The paralleled narrative of maturation continues across *As You Like It*, as both girls finish the play with a marital partner as they move into adulthood.

Rosalind's partnering with Orlando adds another dimension to the comparative staging of age and gender in *As You Like It* that goes further than the more simplistic and supportive presence of Lysander and Demetrius as male adolescents in *A Midsummer Night's Dream*. Orlando, as we saw in the first two chapters of this book, is fashioned as a promising youth whose puberty is well underway, as shown by his growing beard, developing eloquence, and his demonstrations of physical strength. But where does Orlando's maturation, performed by Burbage, sit in comparison to Rosalind's or Ganymede's development? Much of the compelling scholarship about *As You Like It* draws upon the gender fluidity at play between Orlando and Rosalind/Ganymede (Howard, 1988; Jardine, 1989; Stallybrass, 1991; Orgel, 1996). How the interplay and eroticism between characters works depends, at least in part, on the physical presentation of the characters. Considering whether Orlando and Ganymede look alike and the handling of age and gender around the physicality of each character informs an understanding of the characters' relationship. In many ways, *As You Like It* makes Orlando and Ganymede similar, so that 'Rosalind in her disguise resembles Orlando' (Talbot van den Berg, 1975: 890), as both characters are associated with being 'furnished like a hunter' (3.2.226, 1.3.114). According to Kent Talbot van den Berg, 'The resemblance between the lovers was further marked for Elizabethan spectators by the fact that both of them, on Shakespeare's celibate stage, were played by young men' (1975: 890). In this reading, Burbage and the boy player are readily aligned because of their maleness and what is characterised as little distinction in age. Yet constructing the actors as similar in these ways would evidently entail theatrical efforts, from costuming decisions to efforts in manipulating beard growth. What is more, we have seen that these efforts seem to construct similarities in order to invite comparison between the male adolescent characters in terms of their degree of maturation. After all, the eroticism between Orlando and Ganymede works in relation to early modern understanding of Classical mythology, where Ganymede is the beautiful adolescent who is beloved by the adult Jupiter

(Orgel, 1996). As Wiebracht observes, the play gives Orlando 'the role of Jupiter – the most virile force in the classical universe', and 'One sure way to prove you are no longer a beautiful boy, after all, is to make love to one' (2020: 348). Wiebracht's observation is a useful one, although it takes Orlando's adulthood a little too for granted considering the performance cues that insist that the character is also an adolescent who is still developing towards adulthood. If the boy player is Ganymede, Orlando *aspires* to be Jupiter in his courtship.

The partnering of Orlando with Ganymede suggests far more subtlety in the staging of age, including degrees of maturation for adolescent characters, than is generally observed in discussions about the exchanges that the characters share. Margaret's Boerner Beckman's overview of the play's main characters still observes important and familiar distinctions: 'Rosalind is taller, braver, and more aggressive than Celia, just as she is shorter, more fearful, and less physically aggressive than Orlando' (1978: 48). How these differences were conveyed to suggest a trajectory of adolescent growth is rarely noted, but there seem to be some theatrical practicalities that appear to have been skilfully manipulated in the group's characterisations. At its basic formulation, the 'more than common tall' (1.3.111) actor who plays Rosalind in *As You Like It* is set in contrast with her shorter colleague who plays Celia. Rosalind is tall for a girl, but theatrical efforts are made to make the character not so very tall for a boy. Being paired with the thirty-year-old Burbage would likely help distinguish between performances of male adolescent characters, as do Phoebe's observations about Ganymede, which situate Ganymede's age in relation to his stature: 'He is not very tall, yet for his years he's tall' (3.5.117). The boy actor's physique is used, along with other theatrical interventions, to situate him as both the 'more than common tall' adolescent girl and a tall adolescent boy, but a boy who is still expected to have further to grow, especially when compared with Orlando. Rosalind/Ganymede is constructed as distinct from Orlando in terms of height as well as beards.

As You Like It, therefore, seems to stress aspects of physical similarity between Orlando and Ganymede in ways that reduce the age gap between the adult/child actor. However, the play also does not collapse age distinctions entirely in order to facilitate the representation of degrees of growth that remain loosely bound to the actors' physicalities. Having established a palpable age trajectory between Ganymede and Orlando *as* adolescents, moreover, the interplay between the characters often subverts the adult/child power relations that we might expect to be mapped onto the characters or the actors in a theatre company's hierarchy. That Burbage, star adult player of the Lord Chamberlain's Men by 1599, might be aligned with Jupiter when courting Ganymede is unsurprising. The model seems to uphold the master/servant, older/younger power relationships that have been observed in early modern male homosexual relationships (DiGangi, 1995). However, Ganymede is not the 'easily controlled subject' (Billing, 2014: 10) that is often imagined in thinking about objectified and eroticised boys on the early modern stage. Shakespeare's Ganymede seems to be set upon making Orlando (our would-be Jupiter) into the lover of his choosing, dictating where, when, and how interactions should take place. Orgel's more recent work on early modern Ganymede figures suggests that feisty adolescent characterisations were also a part of early modern thinking, where an account of Ganymede's 'further adventures' situates Ganymede sometimes as the active subject in his encounters with Jupiter (2017: 143–61). It is an assertive, if sometimes swooning, Ganymede that Shakespeare presents, and scenes that involve Orlando and Ganymede see the younger adolescent dominate the conversation. This does not mean that assertive adolescents cannot still be pressured by adult influence, but the assertiveness of Shakespeare's Ganymede resituates the template by which the staging of eroticism seems to work. Adolescent boys are presented as attractive not singularly for their passive and diminutive form but for the vitality and growth associated with their pre-adult state.

In *As You Like It*, the stage presence of the Rosalind/Ganymede actor was likely even larger than that of Burbage's Orlando in the scenes that they share; the boy actor at least seems to match the adult actor's impact in the play. Ultimately, it seems to be less a situation of rivalry, or adult vs child, but a play in which actors of different ages work together and with other stage partners (Rosalind and Celia, Orlando and Adam) to present an exploration of adolescent selves. Early modern theatrical culture was clearly very aware that children did not stay small or unchanged, and any sense of a 'diminutive' (Witmore, 2007: 41) state when viewing the feats of boy actors begins to look decidedly unfixed. In broader cultural attitudes, adolescence was defined by ideas of growth, physical change, and humoral mobility. It is in this context that this chapter has considered performances of adolescence that specifically allude to body size and height. While the adolescent's transformative state may well have incited anxiety about growing boys no longer being suited to perform a female part, the mutable qualities of adolescence were also highly valued for the creativity and energy that could be contributed to early modern theatrical productions. The idea of nearly being an adult and still growing was itself a theatrically compelling state.

Notes

1 In thinking about body size for this chapter, I have found myself thinking back to a conservation I had with Dr Shona McIntosh several years ago. I am thankful to Dr McIntosh who drew my attention to the puppet scenes in *Bartholomew Fair* as a possible commentary on the treatment of child actors.
2 For example, the size of actors and the potential physicality of the action in the scene was used in Propeller's *A Midsummer Night's Dream* (Dir. Edward Hall, 2014), where height differences between actors playing Hermia (Matthew McPherson) and Helena (Dan Wheeler) were exaggerated by having Hermia initially speak from a cowed position (she had been pushed to the floor by Lysander). Looking up to Helena, and speaking about the characters' respective heights, Hermia then launched herself at Helena, springing up from the floor.
3 Lysander's words may engage with broader early modern fascination with dwarfism as 'a stage effect, nothing more' when disabled bodies were put on display within early modern entertainments (Page, 2001: 87).
4 While this chapter focuses on the transformations that take place during adolescence, *A Midsummer Night's Dream* is underpinned by a concern with metamorphosis that has been shown to engage with early modern constructions of race and early imperialist thought. For a detailed discussion of early modern anxieties about miscegenation, constructions of race as a category for identity, and the mapping of these ideas onto a narrative about Oberon, fairyland, and an Indian boy as the changeling upon which the play depends, see Margot Hendricks (1996).
5 Although I focus on issues of body size, Margot Hendricks's (1996) observations about Oberon's associations with India in early modern narratives (45–6, 50–2) note that the magic and exoticism of fairyland in Shakespeare's play situate Oberon and the influence of his magic as an encounter with racial otherness.
6 Propeller's performance (Dir. Edward Hall, 2014) stressed the physical comedy of this scene, prompting laughter from the audience as the sudden movements of Matthew McPherson's Hermia were reciprocated with exaggerated squeals from Dan Wheeler's skittish Helena.

Conclusion – spot the difference: symmetry, difference, and gender in early modern constructions of adolescence

> In the fourteenth yeare proceedeth their strippling age. And betwixt that and the fifteenth yeare there falles out in the body a tumultuous whurly-burly or wambling commotion of humours, which in some breakes out into scabs or hote watry issues, in others into kindes of agues. (William Vaughan, 1612: 117)

In *Approved Directions for Health*, in his chapter entitled 'Which be the most dangerous yeares in mans life?', William Vaughan includes what, by now, is a recognisable description of early modern adolescence. An understanding of this life stage is bound to its associations with physical changes, which Vaughan depicts in a particularly expressive way as the 'whurly-burly or wambling commotion of humours'. In many ways, Vaughan's observations attest to a trend that we have seen across the chapters of this book: for early modern commentators, adolescence involved significant humoral change, and this change is often regarded as unsettling. The bodily alterations of puberty, we have seen, were regularly fashioned in this way, with cultural motifs somewhat insistently converting images of 'ripening' adolescent potential into visions of rotting decline. That adolescents could be seen as vulnerable to the changes taking place in their bodies, moreover, infers that the early modern adolescent was often contemplated as an individual who was unable to assert command over the humoral 'commotion' that puberty entailed. Certainly, the adolescent that Vaughan describes is subject to humoral disturbance that manifests itself through violent outbreaks of skin irritations. When responding to his question about the perils that may befall the adolescent, Vaughan has well-known humoral reasoning at his disposal as he offers an account of the adolescent's physical disturbance. Yet Vaughan's account is tellingly shaped by the question to which it responds. Dangers are identifiable in relation to puberty if early modern commentators looked to discuss them. Early modern culture articulated anxieties about harm befalling adolescents, but these descriptions of humoral change as unruly are somewhat misleading in casting adolescents as inevitably fragile individuals, who would almost certainly succumb to the dangers that their maturing humoral bodies encouraged.

Conclusion – spot the difference

As I have highlighted in each of the chapters of *Shakespeare's Adolescents*, the heat and moisture that could suggest unsettling changes during adolescence were also categorically understood to enable and enliven the body, activating physical and cognitive faculties that were considered necessary for the individual's development. In Elyot's *Castel of Helthe*, 'Adolescency' is described in more simplistic terms than in Vaughan's depiction, where the life stage is characterised by a 'hotte and moyst' humoral disposition that fundamentally facilitates the body's maturation: 'in the whiche tyme the body groweth' (1539: 11). This rudimentary narrative of humorally supported growth underpinned how early modern culture understood male and female adolescence. As such, pubescent humoral change may have required management, but it was also advised that the 'heat' that enabled growth, and an array of physical, mental, and vocal developments, should not be impeded. Indeed, the 'heat' of adolescence could be presented as something that should be actively encouraged and nurtured.

Adolescence was a stage of life that evidently fascinated early modern commentators. It was also a life stage that, in lasting over a decade in some formulations, was being experienced by many in early modern society. Shakespeare's plays register the degree to which adolescence was of interest, presenting stories and characters that explore the time in human life when the individual was thought capable of flourishing. The adolescent could be imagined as actively navigating the changes of puberty, where hazards were avoided and the mobility of humours could be harnessed in demonstrations of commanding speech, witty thoughts, and an energised physicality. Theatrical representations of adolescence involved careful management and use of commonly noted signs of puberty, which I have tracked across the chapters of this book, including the use of verbal cues, facial adornments, pronounced vocal skills, and allusions to body growth. Performances by adolescent actors were evidently thought to be worth these theatrical efforts in managing bodies that were undergoing change. Indeed, I have suggested how these mutable, rather than 'blank' (Dusinberre, 1998: 2), adolescents who were involved in performances of Shakespeare's plays enabled as many theatrical illusions as they troubled. As many of Shakespeare's adolescent characters show us, the early modern adolescent was regularly the hero of the story being told. Highly valued for qualities such as beauty, vitality, and creative ingenuity, adolescent features are represented as admirable through a host of Shakespearean characters, and such qualities were utterly entwined with an understanding of an unfixed humoral condition appropriate to age.

Vaughan's picture of the turbulent humoral state of the adolescent with inflamed skin is, we may note, somewhat unlike the theatrical representations of adolescence in Shakespeare's works. The result of excesses in heat and moisture, Vaughan offers familiar humoral thinking and describes ungendered alterations when commenting on the pubescent individual's skin. Vaughan's choice of skin complaints is probably unsurprising to the modern reader who is likely aware of links that are made between the hormonal changes of puberty and spots today. However, Vaughan is relatively unusual in isolating pimples and inflamed skin as a sign of early modern adolescence. In medical writings, observations about heat-induced blushes, beards, voices, and body growth repeatedly feature in early modern descriptions of the physical changes that take place in adolescent bodies. Spots and pimples, by comparison, are infrequently mentioned. I have found very few discussions of spots in relation to puberty across the extensive selection of medical and popular texts used in writing this book. Were early modern teenagers perhaps the rosy-complexioned, spot-free individuals that idealised models of adolescent beauty seem to promote? It seems unlikely, especially as Vaughan *does* make the connection.

It appears fitting, then, to draw out my findings from across *Shakespeare's Adolescents* by considering why it may be that so few writers make the connection that Vaughan makes between spots and puberty. That spots are not privileged as a sign of puberty (when, say, they might well be today) suggests that certain implications and emphases are inferred when particular signs of puberty are chosen over others in cultural constructions of adolescence. In being subject to excesses in humours, adolescents could certainly have been regarded as likely candidates for suffering from spots. However, pimples and skin irritations seem to have been common afflictions across age groups in early modern society. Numerous early modern writings offer home remedies for pimples and do not make any note of recommendations being age-specific. For example, one medical advice book simply suggests that pimples will be cured by using the blood of a newly killed hare, cinnamon, and honey (Ruscelli, 1569: Book 1, 31). The same book also suggests the somewhat more appealing routine of washing the face often with 'water that shall be distilled' (Ruscelli, 1569: Book 2, 5). Readily available ingredients feature in *A Closet for Ladies and Gentlewomen*, which advocates treatments for pimples that use roses, camphire, herbs, and mercury (1608: 162, 164, 189). Likewise, William Langham suggests an array of home-grown cures in his *Garden of Health* (1597: 14, 94, 223, 232, 291, 389, 416, 434). Spots and pimples seem to have been a common complaint and early modern cures seem directed towards general use.

Another reason why pimples may not be mentioned in many medical books that describe adolescence may be that spots were not regarded as an important sign in judging the body's sexual development. Pimples, though regarded as unsightly enough to warrant remedy, do not seem to have been thought to cause concern as long term health problems. Batman even notes how pustules and sores on the bodies of young children are generally a good sign, indicating that the body is expelling bad humours, and better health will follow the outbreak: 'In small children such blaines bée healthfull: and is a good token of health, that commeth afterwarde' (1582: 112). Indeed, Batman's concerns about childhood spots and sores primarily focus upon the scarring of faces with 'vnséemely and foule pittes' that may occur due to itching (1582: 112). As Batman's observations suggest, certain poxes and spots (as well as coughs and worms), were identified as diseases that were common in early childhood (Newton, 2012: 45–8). By comparison, the 'spottiness' of adolescence may well have seemed relatively mild, having fewer severe medical implications for the individual who might well be readying home remedies for pimples across the life cycle. Spots on an adolescent were, perhaps, neither desirable nor a cause for much concern.

Unlike 'poxes', skin alterations associated with puberty were understood to result from the necessary humoral disturbances of age, rather than disease. Normative models of the early modern life cycle that situated the humoral excesses of puberty as a requirement for growth and sexual maturation meant that such spots could be distanced from ideas of disease, which would solely be understood as a negative state for the body. However, the line between the age-related and disease-related humoral imbalance was not always fixed, as I examined in relation to the condition of greensickness in the first chapter. How and where crossovers take place between disease and age-related excesses is suggestive when considering the signs of puberty that do and do not preoccupy early modern commentators. Pimples that registered humoral change did not signal disease, perhaps *especially* in adolescents where demonstrations of 'whurly-burly' humoral changes were an expected sign of maturation.

Representations of adolescence in Shakespeare's plays do not promote skin complaints as a recognisable, age-specific sign. In Shakespeare's plays, reputations threaten to become blemished, but imagery, and certainly the stage make-up used on actors to signal a character's femininity, presented adolescents with rosy cheeks. This may present a practical, as well as cultural, reason for the idealised representation of adolescent skin on early modern stages, seeing as the application of artificial spots with theatrical make-up could well mar a signification of femininity and suggest disease rather than an adolescent age for a character. Of course, the adolescent boys who played girls and women may well have been spotty beneath their cosmetics. Indeed, the corrosive make-up could have made this very likely indeed, and adolescent actors may have had skin blemishes related to their occupation rather than their age. As Stevens contemplates, 'it is tempting to wonder whether actors were marked by their trade in the way that tanner bore the visual evidence of their profession' (2013: 10).

In early modern theatrical contexts, it seems that spots were not used in constructions of adolescent characters, and these representations would, in turn, contribute to emphases in cultural attitudes about adolescence. The signs of puberty that early modern culture identified as most important, and which have structured the content of this book, tend to be bound to the reproductive implications that the signifiers carry. Growing beards, glowing blushes, heated thoughts, and attention to body growth all repeatedly present bodily change as manifestations of heat that are specifically associated with developing seed, menstruation, wombs, and genitals. The language of ripening bodies, though applied broadly to adolescent endeavours, was underpinned by a model that framed human existence and ageing around a fertile, 'adult' centre. Allusions to signs of developing sexual maturity in Shakespeare's plays often promote thoughts of sexual acts in their eroticised representation. Beards and blushes on the face, as we saw in the second chapter, seem to easily convert to contemplations of 'beards' on heated genitals. Pimples, broadly undesirable symptoms of the humoral excess typical of adolescence, do not seem to have been treated as a primary sign of an individual's sexual maturation in this way. In being regarded as temporary, unsightly, and potentially ambivalent in its connection to a certain age, spots on adolescents were not selected as a favoured means of connecting external and internal developments in the adolescent body, at least where dominant narratives of sexual 'ripening' are emphasised.

As I have shown in the chapters of this book, for the adolescent female, the reproductive emphasis that is made in coding the more prominent signs of adolescence in early modern culture was key in ascribing restrictive features to girl subjectivities. Where we have seen more extensive limitations placed upon girls has demonstrated how the reproductive body is inscribed with meaning according to social futures that dominant discourses deem to be available or unavailable to certain individuals. Boys became men by following a trajectory of growth less emphatically bound to how their heated blood, or reproductive materials, would corrupt their body from within; a misdemeanour had social consequences but usually only with extreme and persistent action would the body become dysfunctional.[1] By contrast, as concerns about the adolescent girl's corrupting blood, irregular menstruation, and body stature/womb size indicate, girls had social navigations to perform in order to side-step being diagnosed as greensick and ensure that 'heated' adolescent behaviour was not seen to complicate the anticipated fecundity of 'womanhood'. Enigmatic possibilities, palpable during adolescence for girls and boys, appear most limited when feminine identities become rigidly bound to body parts that are ascribed a social, reproductive purpose as an adult, which then acts to intrude upon earlier states of the body and the experiences of the individual.

The insistent limiting of personal agency achieved by writing prescriptive reproductive value onto gender identities, through body parts, has been unpacked in my explorations of representations of adolescence in Shakespeare's plays. We have seen how aspects of adolescent symmetry between boys and girls supported expansive possibilities for individuals whose age allowed them to be associated with humoral pliability and dexterity (as with Rosalind/Ganymede's sport and conversation and Hermia and Helena's physical dynamism). We have also seen, repeatedly, how explorations of adolescent possibilities are counterbalanced by limiting assumptions about what sexual difference should entail, where the desires and even the thought processes of individuals become inhibited by the intrusive intervention of commentators who may claim to make the individual 'well' through their actions. External impositions of meaning upon adolescent bodies reveal the constructedness of such interventions, when components of a more 'fixed' bodily basis for gender identity in adulthood reveal tensions in light of age-related identities that are based on bodily mutability. During adolescence, when bodies are not yet seen as fixed, we can more readily see the traceable imposition of adult-centred cultural discourses about gender, which intrude upon constructions of adolescent identities. Adolescent states can be seen as reworked to begin to be read in line with prescribed understandings of what adult bodies 'should' entail. As we saw when exuberant, adolescent desires are converted into subdued submission to another's will, for characters such as Phoebe and Katherine, Shakespeare's plays include adolescent female characters who have prescriptive gendered meaning applied to their bodies in these ways. Individual agency is limited in order to steer girls towards their 'acceptable' adult fate as part of a heteronormative, and potentially 'fruitful', marriage. Today, we may well be wary of rehearsing similarly restrictive, genital-based models for imposing gender identity, as for example, in the hostility that has been directed towards the transgender community. Animosity towards an individual based on an interpretation of what their 'sexed' bodies 'should' do, which disregards what the individual themselves has to say, suggests the residual influence of unstable and prescriptive models about 'fixed' bodies and narrow assumptions about reproductive futures.[2] The mutability of bodies and minds imagined for early modern male and female adolescents opens a space where gender identities exist in ways that challenge seemingly absolute models about the reproductive efficacy of 'sexed' bodies. As early modern transgender studies have begun to illuminate, literary and dramatic representations that recognise the constructedness of rigid meanings being applied to 'sexed' bodies help deconstruct the myth that the idea of 'transition was unthinkable until the development of hormone therapies' (Simone Chess et al, 2019: 1). In *Twelfth Night*, for example, we value and celebrate the characters of Viola and Sebastian in a way that does not need each character to be categorised as reproductively 'ripe' to be male or female.

Looking to Shakespearean constructions of age-based identities help, therefore, realise the space, selves, and experiences that can exist around the artificial centre of reproductive 'ripeness' that early modern life cycles present.

Early modern adolescent identities were often gendered, as we have seen, but such gendering relied on an understanding of the body as being in a state of transformation. As I have shown across this book, adolescent boys shared age-specific features with adolescent girls, and these parallels could withstand meta-theatrical gestures because parallels in the character and actors' ages (although not necessarily their imagined futures) remain aligned. Recognising that Hermia and Helena in *A Midsummer Night's Dream* or Rosalind/Ganymede in *As You Like It* are boy actors does not seem to unsettle the age-specific, energised characteristics of the play's girl characters. However, as we have seen, girls and boys were not simply seen as the same, and adolescent boys were understood as very different from adult women. Seeing an adolescent male behind a role could threaten to shift beyond a complimentary dual consciousness and encourage an awareness of difference ascribed to an actor's age and/or gender in comparison to that of his character. As we saw in my readings of Katherine in *The Taming of the Shrew*, and Cleopatra in *Antony and Cleopatra*, acknowledging the boy actor entails acknowledging the character he performs as his skilful construction. These moments suggest how cultural reverence for the adolescent male player can sometimes become an obstacle in seeing accomplishments as those of a character. The character, who may not be understood as revelling in the same adolescent freedoms, seems displaced in the process of representation, as qualities of empowerment shift discernibly to the highly visible boy who wields control over an admired performance.

The erotic and commercial appeal of adolescents in theatrical cultures could, of course, make boy actors especially vulnerable to adult attention. In this book, I do not deny the complicated position of adolescents in early modern theatrical worlds. The vibrant allure of the adolescent is palpable in early modern constructions and likely featured in the processes of eroticisation at work. The prominence of adolescent stories and real adolescent actors in Shakespeare's plays, however, seems to suggest that playwrights wrote parts for adolescent company members that supported their professional progress and re-inscribed the wider cultural desires to see adolescents thriving and flourishing in the parts they played. Whether real adolescents flourished as a result of their profession will likely remain a point of contention, where individual experiences no doubt differed. The hypothesised cyclical training model that Power (2003) and McMillin (2004) suggest for changes in the Lord Chamberlain's/King's Men repertoires hinges, however, upon the development of boy actors' skills across their apprenticeships, which must have mapped onto their experiences of adolescence. McMillin notes rises and falls in 'restricted' and 'wide-ranging' (2004: 257) roles for adolescent actors performing female roles across the late 1590s and 1610s. Power and McMillin both find that Shakespeare reacted creatively to the life stages and professional development of company members in ways that planned for future performances. Therefore, the treatment of adolescent boys undergoing training, whether mercenary in intention or not, seems to have generally supported the individual's development and future standing in the theatre. Periods when less-expansive female roles were created, as in 1604 and 1610, are explained by McMillin as being when 'a new generation of leading boy actors was being trained and rehearsed by their master actors' (2004: 240). This cyclical training system indicates concern for the continual development of adolescent talent that does more than simply 'fill' a certain role, as the lulls in creative female parts could, theoretically, be sustained if there were not also a desire to write and include expansive female characters at the centre of play narratives.

I have suggested that interactions between adolescent actors in Shakespeare's plays were treated as a useable resource that shaped plots in ways that not only incorporated training systems, but also provided a selling point in early modern theatrical culture. The delight that seems to be taken in managing ideas about body growth in *A Midsummer Night's Dream* suggests that greater nuance shaped the position of boy players than is registered in more negative ideas about 'how these boys were valued, or devalued, when they grew up' (Wiebracht, 2020: 351). While observations about theatre hierarchies can suggest that boy players were 'fairly low on everyone's list of priorities' (Belsey, 2005: 53), and evaluating individual agency remains impossible, ambiguities around maturation fuelled many theatrical performances as the point of interest in itself. Adolescents do not seem to have been simply marginalised in adult-centred theatrical structures where even the adult 'star' of Burbage took on adolescent roles during his career, forging his stardom, at least in part, from such roles, and acting opposite precocious adolescent actors as love interests.

Performances from boy actors were clearly often memorable. Jackson's reflections on the 'celebrated Desdemona' from 1610, which I discussed in Chapter 2, showed appreciation for the actor's convincing 'countenance' in playing dead (cited in Neill, 2006: 9). Jackson's words also record admiration for how Desdemona 'pleaded her case very effectively throughout' the scene (cited in Callaghan, 1989: 90) to provide an overview of the actor's striking performance in the play's finale, where Desdemona's speech contributes to the impact of the character's death. As has been noted, the lasting impact of Desdemona's death invites evaluation of the gender politics of *Othello*, seeing as Jackson and modern commentators on Desdemona's death seem to suggest relief at the silencing of the 'unruly' female character who disobeys her father to pursue her desires (Aebischer, 2004: 132). Misogyny coincides with the most 'commendable' features of the performance. The 'impressive' boy players who performed such parts do, however, often emerge as individuated and valued adolescent subjects, as scholarly work that draws into focus the names, careers, and roles of boys in early modern theatrical cultures attests (Kathman, 2004; McCarthy, 2022: 2–3). What is more, reputations of esteemed actors during adulthood cannot neatly be distinguished from theatrical achievements that predate the actor's 'adult' status, as is clear in the example of Nathan Field, whose notoriety was achieved in a children's acting company (Lamb, 2009: 118–75). A long-serving actor's skill could well have been recognised 'in terms of their boyhood' and not simply as 'feats they achieved as adults' (McCarthy, 2022: 4). The memorable features of the celebrated early modern actor likely often included the lively and engaging roles performed during adolescence.

Adolescence remained a key topical concern in the plays Shakespeare wrote during his lifetime, and adolescent actors were always a part of the playing company for which Shakespeare wrote. However, there are some noteworthy changes in how adolescence is represented across the 1590s–1610s, which indicate responses to changing circumstances in the company. As I suggested in the first chapter in the analysis of Orlando's pairing with the elderly character of Adam in *As You Like It*, age on the early modern stage could be constructed through the use of cultural motifs and attitudes that helped contextualise an actor's performance of adolescence. A direct parallel between an actor's numerical age and theatrical one was not essential in early modern theatre, although parallels could be strategically drawn. However, Burbage's own age would have eventually made a change in roles appropriate, as certain adolescent roles became less viable for the actor whose own ageing would be informed by cultural attitudes and expectations. As Power has observed, 'the practicalities of an ageing company led to, or at least aligned neatly with, a trend for older protagonists to match with daughters in Shakespeare's late plays' (2003: 220). It seems no coincidence that, as the company's star actor neared forty, Shakespeare wrote Burbage roles that entailed his representation of adult, and even elderly, characters rather than adolescent ones.

In plays like *Macbeth*, *King Lear*, *Antony and Cleopatra*, *The Tempest*, and *The Winter's Tale* (which also requires its characters to age sixteen years across its plot), Burbage's altered roles can be seen to have implications for how adolescence is treated in Shakespeare's plays. Shakespeare's later plays seem to approach adolescent characters by placing an emphasis upon characters as daughter/sons, where their involvement in love plots is a secondary concern through which intergenerational relationships may be examined. Perdita in *The Winter's Tale* and Miranda in *The Tempest* have love plots that inform their styling as 'ripening' adolescents (as we saw with the flower-wielding and blushing Perdita in the first and second chapters), but these plays seem focused upon how adolescents navigate relationships with parents, and how their promising futures may redeem errors of the past. That Burbage likely played Leontes and Prospero, fathers to adolescents in these plays, offers a logical reason for resituating the treatment of adolescence (Power, 2003: 220).

In light of the findings of this book, one of the interesting implications of having a greater emphasis upon the intergenerational contexts surrounding adolescence (something that is also a component of earlier plays like *Romeo and Juliet*) is that girl characters in Shakespeare's later plays seem less tethered to love plots. This seems to present an opportunity for adolescent femininities to be imagined in ways that develop earlier works, where navigating the route to marital conclusions, as we have seen, was a key part of girls' stories. As Bicks has observed, Miranda's 'brainwork' in *The Tempest* (c. 1611) suggests her ability to manipulate her position as the precocious student attending Prospero's lessons and apply the empiricism of scientific observation to assert agency and command knowledge (2021: 105–26). Miranda's position as girl student who acknowledges the 'beating in my mind' (1.2.176) recognises development of Bianca's 'student' role in *The Taming of the Shrew*, performed nearly a decade earlier. While Bianca must use her 'lessons' to navigate future marital arrangements, Miranda, in contrast, begins *The Tempest* as her father's student, and her performances of intellectual enquiry exceed contemplations of a marital future. Miranda poses questions about her past, 'Wherefore did they not / That hour destroy us?' (1.2.38–9), and evaluates the world around her, responding both to the island she encounters while also navigating the formidable power of her sorcerer father: 'your reason / For raising this sea storm?' (1.2.176–7).

In this way, girl characters in Shakespeare's comedies, where love plots are decentred, seem to realise some space to be freed, or at least distanced, from the language that more emphatically scrutinises their bodily maturation in terms of a 'ripening' that insists upon the myth that girls are biologically determined to be future wives and mothers. Although it takes an island location (an even more remote form of isolation than that briefly contemplated in Hermia's convent in *A Midsummer Night's Dream*, c. 1595/6, 1.1.65–90), the early modern girl can be imagined to grow and develop beyond a reproductive context. Moreover, while boy actors played the intellectually engaged adolescent daughter figures of Shakespeare's later plays, it seems that the adolescent males, who acted opposite Burbage in his more senior roles, were still valued for their boyish energy. Women's roles that we see after 1605, as we saw with Cleopatra, seem to take up the dynamism of earlier girlish characters and include enigmatic and complex adult female roles (for example, in Lady Macbeth and Hermione), although, notably, these adult female characters do have their wombs scrutinised (Adelman, 1992).

Theatrical explorations of adolescent characters across more than two decades no doubt offered a rich store of adolescent identities for Shakespeare and other playwrights to work from by the 1610s. After all, Shakespeare was neither the starting point nor the end point for showing a fascination with adolescent characters. We might note, for example, that Francis Beaumont and John Fletcher's *Philaster* dates from around this period (c. 1608–10). In *Philaster*, the ambiguous gendering of Bellario makes evident an indebtedness to previous theatrical productions, where clear inter-theatrical gestures include the following components: nods to Shakespeare's *Twelfth Night* (c. 1602) in the play's 'girl' page/master plot; gentle ridicule of *Hamlet* (c. 1601) through the male protagonist's questionable behaviour and thoughts of ghosts; and inclusion of a character who shares the name of the titular figure from John Lyly's *Gallathea* (c. 1588). In *Gallathea*, two girls crossdress as boys and fall in love, with one girl being said to become a boy through divine intervention at the play's conclusion. The fluid gendering of characters and their love, in *Gallathea*, as critics have noted, make the offstage gesture to a change of sex, and the more fixed positioning of bodies, somewhat inconsequential in light of the intimate bond between the characters (Jankowski, 1996: 263; Dooley, 2001: 61; Bicks, 2021: 170–2). Inter-theatrical reference points presented playwrights of the 1610s with opportunities to develop and respond creatively to the adolescent identities that were consistently a vibrant feature of earlier theatrical production.

Of course, playwrights did not explore adolescence in a theatrical culture that was removed from wider influences. Revisions to theatrical constructions of adolescent subjectivities were not part of a never-ending process of breaking down restrictive gender models. Girlhood freedoms, we have seen, were always negotiated in relation to early modern contexts. Historical and cultural studies have begun to suggest, moreover, that negotiating age-related freedoms began to be especially hard for girls as the seventeenth century continued beyond Shakespeare's lifetime. This seems to be, in part, a result of medical changes that repositioned how female bodies were treated, both literally and discursively, in mid-late seventeenth-century medicine. For example, female health became a more broadly contested arena, as female and male medical practitioners vied for authority, and the male midwife/physician appropriated more of the areas of knowledge and medical practices that had traditionally been considered appropriate to female expertise (Donnison, 1988; Evenden, 2000). By the 1660s, Bicks also identifies 'some kind of shift in popular thinking about female adolescent cognition' (2021: 223). Specifically, the activity and heat of female minds appear to have become more narrowly focused on the reproductive function of maturing girls' bodies, as the humoral heat of puberty and the thoughts it incurred became more emphatically directed towards concerns about sex. Depictions of female adolescent thoughts seem to have become more singularly associated with lust, whereas early medical and educational writings also emphasised a girl's capacity for intellect, creativity, and wit (Bicks, 2021: 223). Changes in medical understanding, though slow, also began to connect female health and its association with wombs to ideas about the nervous system. Consequently, constructions of hysteria as a nervous condition that affected female brains began to emerge alongside older humoral ideologies (Peterson, 2010: 183–5). Energised thought in girls itself appears to have become more closely linked to a symptom of uterine/nervous disorder that left less scope for them to use dynamic action or speech in navigating ideas of chastity.

These changes in cultural attitudes towards adolescent bodies and minds are indicated in some of the alterations that we see in the print history of *The Taming of the Shrew*. As Maurer has suggested, 'Bianca says little, so much depends on the nuances of what she says and to whom' (2001: 191). Textual emendations across the play's editorial history notably play down the 'virtuous' sister's wit and 'sauciness' (Maurer, 2001: 191). Bianca, who expresses a non-committal stance to her suitors in the First Folio (1623), has her lines subtly revised to suggest a clearer preference for her future husband, Lucentio, across later editions of the Folio. Such alterations seem intended to ensure that the performance of Bianca's adolescence accords to what, presumably, would appear as a more 'orderly' version of female sexuality. The changes, as Maurer has explained, ensure that Bianca's thoughts no longer appear to evaluate possible suitors for an anticipated marital future, but remain more clearly fixed upon one man in engaging with the process (2001).

The social and religious upheavals of the civil war would also have influenced changes that are notable in cultural ideas about female bodies. As Bicks observes, the socio-historical uncertainties of civil war heightened 'the persistent anxiety (made more intense with the Protestant emphasis on marriage and procreation) over how to recognize the markers of virginity, chastity, pregnancy, and paternity' (2021: 6). Efforts to 'understand', identify, and then control bodies and individuals in states of medicalised 'disorder' seem part of a response to wider social and political disturbances. The afterlives of Shakespeare's plays, as seen in the editorial history for Bianca, record alterations to how girls could speak and still be considered virtuous, their bodies and minds more firmly viewed in a manner that anticipates reproductive and 'wifely' duty. The perceived liberties of adolescence, in this sense, contract to narrow the scope for exploring female subjectivities. While I have shown that concerns about girls' sexual futures are evident in

Shakespeare's plays, the room to circumnavigate these ideas seems to have tightened across the seventeenth century. As Dusinberre notes, 'It is easy to chart a very steady cleaning-up of the language of Shakespeare's heroines' (1998: 7) in the latter half of the seventeenth century, a move that no doubt also responded to female actors – with their bodies and voices – now being on the Restoration stage.

Although full exploration of later cultural, historical, and theatrical constructions of adolescence are beyond the scope of this book, shifts in the key medical and theatrical components that I have considered in this study may serve to indicate how later formulations of adolescence were also at work. Identifying aspects of symmetry and difference in early modern constructions of adolescence has especially helped identify slippage within processes that ascribe restrictive gendered meanings upon bodies. Across Shakespeare's career, the characters he produced offered explorations of adolescence that were varied and often vibrant. Motifs of adolescent change and vitality, as well as ideas about its disruption and feared loss, are key in the Shakespearean corpus and early modern cultural representations more generally. What is more, Shakespeare's plays offer a particularly complex engagement with broader, topical concerns relating to early modern adolescence due to the deep-rooted significance of adolescence to a theatrical culture in which adolescent players formed a key part of acting companies. Revisiting assumptions about adult/child interactions in early modern theatrical contexts reveals how models of comparison did not always set adult and child in clear opposition, and that the valued position of being an adolescent could even supersede concerns for how the child is understood in relation to the adult. Shakespeare's representations of adolescence help, perhaps most importantly, in illuminating positive approaches to ideas of bodily mutability in early historical periods. Through recognising narratives that attribute value to transformative features of the body, we can perhaps more readily deconstruct restrictive models of identity that insist upon bodily fixity in ways that can impose meaning upon an individual's own experience of embodiment.

Notes

1 Work that has discussed the 'waste' of reproductive potential for the lovely boy in Shakespeare's *Sonnets* has suggested, using early modern medical writings, how excessive masturbation was, for example, thought to damage male fertility (Brooks, 2011).
2 The influence of transgender studies in early modern scholarship is beginning to gather momentum, stressing, as Cáel M. Keegan observes, the individual's experience of self over meanings that get inscribed upon their body: 'transgender studies places high value on the embodied, speaking transgender subject as a producer of constant self-knowledge' (2020: 67).

References

Primary sources

Abbott, George (1600) *An Exposition on the Prophet Jonah*. London. Early English Books Online. Web. 1 Jun. 2018.

Abbot, Robert (1646) *Milk for Babes*. London. Early English Books Online. Web. 1 Jun. 2018.

The Ancient, Honorable, Famous, and Delighfull Historie of Huon of Bourdeaux (1601) London. Early English Books Online. Web. 6 Jun. 2021.

Aristotle (1910) *Historia Animalium*, trans. D'Arcy Wentworth Thompson. Clarendon Press: Oxford.

Aristotle's Masterpiece (1684) London. Early English Books Online. Web. 1 Jan. 2015.

Bacon, Francis (1623) *Historia Vitae & Mortis*. London. Early English Books Online. Web. 3 Jun. 2015.

Bacon, Francis (1625) 'Of Youth and Age', *The Essays*. London. Early English Books Online. Web. 3 Jun. 2018.

Bacon, Francis (1626) *Sylvia Sylvanum*, London. Early English Books Online. Web. 28 Jun. 2015.

Bacon, Francis (1638) *Historie Naturall and Experimentall*. London. Early English Books Online. Web. 1 Jan. 2015.

Bancroft, Thomas (1658) *Time's Out of Tune*. London. Early English Books Online. Web. 10 Mar. 2015.

Barrough, Philip (1583) *The Method of Physick*. London. Early English Books Online. Web. 12 May 2022.

Batman, Stephen (1582) *Batman Upon Batholome*. London. Early English Books Online. Web. 18 Aug. 2018.

Burton, Robert (1621) *Anatomy of Melancholy*. Oxford. Early English Books Online. Web. 18 Aug. 2023.

Cary, Elizabeth (2002) *The Tragedy of Mariam*, in David Bevington, Lars Engle, Katherine Eisamann Maus, and Eric Rasmussen (eds), *English Renaissance Drama*. W. W. Norton: New York and London.

Castiglione, Baldassarre (1588) *The Book of the Courtier*. London. Early English Books Online. Web. 18 Aug. 2020.

Chamberlain, Peter (1665) *Dr Chamberlain's Midwifes Practice*. London, 1665. Early English Books Online. Web. 5 Jan. 2015.

Chaucer, Geoffrey (1996) 'The Miller's Tale', in *The Canterbury Tales*. Penguin: London.

A Closet for Ladies and Gentlevvomen (1608) London. Early English Books Online. Web. 21 Jun. 2021.

Codrington, Robert (1664) *The Second Part of Youths Behavior, of, Decency in Conversation Amongst Women*. London. Early English Books Online. Web. 24 Jun. 2021.

Crossman, Samuel (1665) *The Young Mans Monitor*. London. Early English Books Online. Web. 10 Mar. 2017.

Crooke, Helkiah (1615) *Microcosmographia*. London. Early English Books Online. Web. 22 Jun. 2021.

Cuffe, Henry (1607) *The Different Ages of Man*. London. Early English Books Online. Web. 16 May 2015.

Cuffe, Henry (1633) *The Different Ages of Man*. London. Early English Books Online. Web. 16 May 2015.

Cuffe, Henry (1640) *The Different Ages of Man*. London. Early English Books Online. Web. 16 May 2015.

Cuffe, Henry (1653) *The Different Ages of Man*. London. Early English Books Online. Web. 16 May 2015.

Dupleix, Scipion (1635) *The Resoluer; or Curiosities of Nature*. London. Early English Books Online. Web. 5 May 2015.

Elyot, Thomas (1539) *Castel of Health*. London. Early English Books Online. Web. 22 Jun. 2020.

Evelyn, John (1664) *Kalendarium Hortense, or, The Gard'ners Almanac*. London. Early English Books Online. Web. 30 Mar. 2019.

Ferrand, Jacques (1640) *Erotomania*. London. Early English Books Online. Web. 23 May 2017.

Ford, John (2008) *'Tis' Pity She's a Whore*, Marion Lomax (ed), *'Tis' Pity She's a Whore and Other Plays: The Lover's Melancholy; The Broken Heart; 'Tis' Pity She's a Whore; Perkin Warbeck*. Oxford World Classics: Oxford.

Gosson, Stephen (1579) *The School of Abuse*. London. Early English Books Online. Web. 27 May 2018.

Gouge, William (1622) *Of Domesticall Duties*. London. Early English Books Online. Web. 23 Jun. 2017.

Gracián (1640) *Galenteo Espagnos*. London. Early English Books Online. Web. 23 Jun. 2017.

Greene, Robert (1583) *Mamillia*. London. Early English Books Online. Web. 20 Jul. 2018.

Greenwood, Will (1657) *Apographe Storges*. London. Early English Books Online. Web. 6 May 2015.

Guillemeau, Jacques (1612) *The Happy Delivery of Woman*. London. Early English Books Online. Web. 12 Nov. 2022.

Hawkins, Francis (1646) *Youths Behaviour, or, Decency in Conversation Amongst Men*. London. Early English Books Online. Web. 24 Jun. 2021.

Herrick, Robert (1648) 'To a Gentlewoman Objecting to Him His Gray Hairs', in *Hesperides*. London. *Luminarium*. Web. 8 Oct. 2018.

Herrick, Robert (1648) 'To the Virgins, to Make Much of Time', in *Hesperides*. London. *Luminarium*. Web. 8 Oct. 2018.

Hill, Thomas (1571) *The Contemplation of Mankinde*. London. Early English Books Online. Web. 3 Jan. 2015.

Huarte, Juan (1698) *Examen de Ingenios, or, The Tryal of Wits*. London. Early English Books Online. Web. 11 Jul. 2018.

Jonson, Ben (1616) *The Workes of Benjamin Johnson*. London. Early English Books Online. Web. 5 Sep. 2018.

Jonson, Ben (1620a) *Epicœne, or The Silent Woman*. London Early English Books Online. Web. 5 Sep. 2018.

Jonson, Ben (1620b) *The Silent Woman*. London. Early English Books Online. Web. 5 Sep. 2018.

Jonson, Ben (1919) 'On Salathiel Pavy', in Arthur Quiller-Couch (ed), *The Oxford Book of English*. Clarendon: Oxford.

Killigrew, Henry (1653) *Pallantus and Eudora*. London. Early English Books Online. Web. 23 Jun. 2021.

Langham, William (1597) *The Garden of Health*. London. Early English Books Online. Web. 20 Jun. 2021.

Lemnius, Levinus (1576) *Touchstone of Complexions*. Trans. Thomas Newton. London. Early English Books Online. Web. 9 May 2015.

Lemnius, Levinus (1592) *The Sanctuarie of Salvation*. London. Early English Books Online. Web. 20 May 2015.

Lemnius, Levinus (1658) *Secret Miracles*. London. Early English Books Online. Web. 9 May 2015.

Lodge, Thomas (1590) *Rosalynde*. London. Early English Books Online. Web. 25 Jan. 2018.

Lupton, Donald (1636) *Emblems of Rarities*. London. Early English Books Online. Web. 12 Jun. 2017.

Milton, John (2003) *A Masque Presented at Ludlow Castle [Comus]*, in Stephen Orgel and Jonathan Goldberg (eds), *John Milton: The Major Works*. Oxford University Press: Oxford, pp. 44–71.

Mulcaster, Richard (1581) *Positions Wherein Those Primitiue Circumstances be Examined, which are Necessarie for the Training vp of Children*. London. Early English Books Online. Web. 2 Feb. 2017.

Novembris Monstrum (1641). London. Early English Books Online. Web. 11 May 2015.

Paré, Ambroise (1665) 'Of the Generation of Man', in Thomas Johnson (trans), *The Workes of that Famous Chirurgion Ambrose Parey*. London. Early English Books Online. Web. 5 May 2015.

Peacham, Henry (1622) *The Compleat Gentleman*. London. Early English Books Online. Web. 10 Mar. 2017.

La Perrière, Guillaume de (1614) *The Theater of Fine Deuices*. London. Early English Books. Web. 18 Jun. 2017.

The Problemes of Aristotle (1595) Edinburgh. Early English Books Online. Web. 21 Jan. 2015.

Raynalde, Thomas (2009) *The Birth of Mankinde, Otherwise Named, The Woman's Book*. Elaine Hobby (ed). Ashgate: Farnham.

The Resoluer; or Curiosities of Nature (1635) London. Early English Books Online. Web. 12 May 2015.

Rich, Barnabe (1615) *The Honestie of This Age*. Edinburgh. Early English Books Online. Web. 5 Apr. 2020.

Riverius, Lazarus (1655) *The Practice of Physick*. London. Early English Books Online. Web. 5 May 2015.

Ruscelli, Girolamo (1569) *A Verye Excellent and Profitable Booke Conteining Sixe Hundred Foure Score and Odde Experienced Medicines*. Early English Books Online. Web. 18 Aug. 2023.

Sandys, George (1632) *Ovid's Metamorphosis Englished*. London. Early English Books Online. Web. 5 May 2016.

Sennert, Daniel (1661) *The Art of Chirurgery*. Vol. 5. London. Early English Books Online. Web. 5 May 2015.

Shakespeare, William (2016) *All's Well That Ends Well*, in Stephen Greenblatt, Walter Cohen, Suzanne Gossett, Jean E. Howard, Katherine Eisaman Maus and Gordan McMullan (eds), *The Norton Shakespeare*. Norton: London.

Shakespeare, William (2016) *Antony and Cleopatra*, in Stephen Greenblatt, Walter Cohen, Suzanne Gossett, Jean E. Howard, Katherine Eisaman Maus and Gordan McMullan (eds), *The Norton Shakespeare*. Norton: London.

Shakespeare, William (2016) *As You Like It*, in Stephen Greenblatt, Walter Cohen, Suzanne Gossett, Jean E. Howard, Katherine Eisaman Maus and Gordan McMullan (eds), *The Norton Shakespeare*. Norton: London.

Shakespeare, William (1997) *The Comedy of Errors*, in Stephen Greenblatt (ed), *The Norton Shakespeare Comedies*. Norton: London.

Shakespeare, William (1997) *Coriolanus*, in Stephen Greenblatt (ed), *The Norton Shakespeare Tragedies*. Norton: London.

Shakespeare, William (2016) *Hamlet*, in Stephen Greenblatt, Walter Cohen, Suzanne Gossett, Jean E. Howard, Katherine Eisaman Maus and Gordan McMullan (eds), *The Norton Shakespeare*. Norton: London.

Shakespeare, William (2008) *Henry IV, Part Two*. René Weis (ed). Oxford University Press: Oxford.

Shakespeare, William (1997) *King Lear*, in Stephen Greenblatt (ed), *The Norton Shakespeare Tragedies*. Norton: London.

Shakespeare, William (2016) *Measure for Measure*, in Stephen Greenblatt, Walter Cohen, Suzanne Gossett, Jean E. Howard, Katherine Eisaman Maus and Gordan McMullan (eds), *The Norton Shakespeare*. Norton: London.

Shakespeare, William (2016) *The Merchant of Venice*, in Stephen Greenblatt, Walter Cohen, Suzanne Gossett, Jean E. Howard, Katherine Eisaman Maus and Gordan McMullan (eds), *The Norton Shakespeare*. Norton: London.

Shakespeare, William (2016) *A Midsummer Night's Dream*, in Stephen Greenblatt Walter Cohen, Suzanne Gossett, Jean E. Howard, Katherine Eisaman Maus and Gordon McMullan (eds), *The Norton Shakespeare*. Norton: London.

Shakespeare, William (2016) *Much Ado About Nothing*, in Stephen Greenblatt, Walter Cohen, Suzanne Gossett, Jean E. Howard, Katherine Eisaman Maus and Gordan McMullan (eds), *The Norton Shakespeare*. Norton: London.
Shakespeare, William (2016) *Othello*, in Stephen Greenblatt, Walter Cohen, Suzanne Gossett, Jean E. Howard, Katherine Eisaman Maus and Gordan McMullan (eds), *The Norton Shakespeare*. Norton: London.
Shakespeare, William (2016) *Romeo and* Juliet, in Stephen Greenblatt, Walter Cohen, Suzanne Gossett, Jean E. Howard, Katherine Eisaman Maus and Gordan McMullan (eds), *The Norton Shakespeare*. Norton: London.
Shakespeare, William (1977) *Shakespeare's Sonnets*. Stephen Booth (ed), Yale University Press: New Haven and London.
Shakespeare, William (2016) *The Taming of the Shrew*, in Stephen Greenblatt, Walter Cohen, Suzanne Gossett, Jean E. Howard, Katherine Eisaman Maus and Gordan McMullan (eds), *The Norton Shakespeare*. Norton: London.
Shakespeare, William (2016) *The Tempest*, in Stephen Greenblatt, Walter Cohen, Suzanne Gossett, Jean E. Howard, Katherine Eisaman Maus and Gordan McMullan (eds), *The Norton Shakespeare*. Norton: London.
Shakespeare, William (2016) *Titus Andronicus*, in Stephen Greenblatt, Walter Cohen, Suzanne Gossett, Jean E. Howard, Katherine Eisaman Maus and Gordan McMullan (eds), *The Norton Shakespeare*. Norton: London.
Shakespeare, William (2016) *Twelfth Night*, in Stephen Greenblatt, Walter Cohen, Suzanne Gossett, Jean E. Howard, Katherine Eisaman Maus and Gordan McMullan (eds), *The Norton Shakespeare*. Norton: London.
Shakespeare, William (2016) *The Two Gentlemen of Verona*, in Stephen Greenblatt, Walter Cohen, Suzanne Gossett, Jean E. Howard, Katherine Eisaman Maus and Gordan McMullan (eds), *The Norton Shakespeare*. Norton: London.
Shakespeare, William (2016) *The Two Noble Kinsmen*, in Stephen Greenblatt, Walter Cohen, Suzanne Gossett, Jean E. Howard, Katherine Eisaman Maus and Gordan McMullan (eds), *The Norton Shakespeare*. Norton: London.
Shakespeare, William (1996) *The Winter's Tale*. Stephen Orgel (ed), Oxford University Press: Oxford.
Sharp, Jane (1671) *The Midwives Book*. London. Early English Books Online. Web. 11 May 2018.
Sharp, Jane (1999) *The Midwives Book*. Elaine Hobby (ed). Oxford University Press: Oxford.
Stubbes, Phillip (1583) *The Anatomie of Abuses*. London. Early English Books Online. Web. 24 May 2016.
'A Surprize' (1674) in *The Complaisant Companion, or New Jests*. London. Early English Books Online. Web. 1 May 2015.
Swetnam, Joseph (1615) *The Arraignment of Lewd, Idle, Forward, and Unconstant Women*. Early English Books Online. Web. 24 Jun. 2022.
Tanner, John (1659) *The Hidden Treasures of the Art of Physick*. London. Early English Books Online. Web. 25 Aug. 2015.
Vaughan, William (1612) *Approved Directions for Health*. London. Early English Books Online. Web. 2 Jul. 2022.

Wanley, Nathaniel (1673) *The Wonders of the Little Word*. London. Early English Books Online. Web. 20 Jul. 2018.

Whitney, Geoffrey (1586) *A Choice of Emblemes*. London. Early English Books Online. Web. 30 Aug. 2017.

Willis, Thomas (1681) *An Essay of the Pathology of the Brain*. London. Early English Books Online. Web. 24 Jun. 2021.

Woodward, Ezekiah (1640) *A Childe's Patrimony*. London. Early English Books Online. Web. 22 Jun. 2021.

Secondary sources

Adelman, Janet (1992) *Suffocating Mothers: Fantasies of Maternal Origins in Shakespeare's Plays, Hamlet to Tempest*. Routledge: London.

Aebischer, Pascale (2004) *Shakespeare's Violated Bodies: Stage and Screen Performance*. Cambridge University Press: Cambridge.

Aebischer, Pascale (2008) 'Silence, Rape and Politics in *Measure for Measure*: Close Readings in Theatre History', *Shakespeare Bulletin*, 26:4, pp. 1–19.

Archer, Jayne Elisabeth, Elizabeth Goldring and Sarah Knight (eds) (2011) *The Intellectual and Cultural World of the Early Modern Inns of Court*. Manchester University Press: Manchester.

Astington, John (2012) *Actors and Acting in Shakespeare's Time: The Art of Stage Playing*. Cambridge University Press: Cambridge.

Bailey, Courtney (2020) *Spectrums of Shakespearean Crossdressing: The Art of Performing Women*. Routledge: London.

Balizet, Ariane (2019) *Shakespeare and Girls' Studies*. Routledge: London.

Bamber, Linda (1982) *Comic Women, Tragic Men: Study of Gender and Genre in Shakespeare*. Stanford University Press: Stanford, CA.

Beckman, Margaret Boerner (1978) 'The Figure of Rosalind in *As You Like It*', *Shakespeare Quarterly*, 29:1, pp. 44–51.

Belsey, Catherine (2005) 'Shakespeare's Little Boys: Theatrical Apprenticeship and the Construction of Childhood', in Bryan Reynolds and William N. West (eds), *Rematerializing Shakespeare: Authority and Representation on the Early Modern Stage*. Palgrave Macmillan: Houndmills, pp. 53–72.

Ben-Amos, Ilana Krausman (1994) *Adolescence and Youth in Early Modern England*. Yale University Press: London and New Haven, CT.

Bicks, Caroline (2016) 'Incited Minds: Rethinking Early Modern Girls', *Shakespeare Studies*, 44, pp. 180–202.

Bicks, Caroline (2021) *Cognition and Girlhood in Shakespeare's World: Rethinking Female Adolescence*. Cambridge University Press: Cambridge.

Billing, Valerie (2014) 'Female Spectators and the Erotics of the Diminutive in *Epicœne* and *The Knight of the Burning Pestle*', *Renaissance Drama*, 42:1, pp. 1–28.

Bloom, Gina (2007) *Voice in Motion: Staging Gender, Shaping Sound in Early Modern England*. University of Pennsylvania Press: Philadelphia, PA.

Bly, Mary (2009) 'The Boy Companies 1599–1613', in Richard Dutton (ed), *The Oxford Handbook of Early Modern Theatre*. Oxford University Press: Oxford, pp. 136–50.

Boose, Lynda (1991) 'Scolding Brides and Bridling Scolds: Taming the Woman's Unruly Member', *Shakespeare Quarterly*, 42:2, pp. 179–213.

Bristol, Michael (1991) 'In Search of the Bear: Spatiotemporal Form and the Heterogenity of Economics in *The Winter's Tale*', *Shakespeare Quarterly*, 42:2, pp. 243–63.

Brooks, Charles (1960) 'Shakespeare's Romantic Shrews', *Shakespeare Quarterly*, 11:3, pp. 351–6.

Brooks, Jason (2011) '"Tired with All These, for Restful Death I Cry": Autoeroticism and Decadence in Shakespeare's Sonnets 62–75', *Orbis Litterarum*, 66:5, pp. 388–408.

Broomhill, Susan (2002) '"Women's Little Secrets": Defining the Boundaries of Reproductive Knowledge in Sixteenth-Century France', *Social History of Medicine*, 15:1, April, pp. 1–15.

Brown, David Sterling (2019) 'Remixing the Family: Blackness and Domesticity in Shakespeare's *Titus Andronicus*', in Farah Karim-Cooper (ed), *Titus Andronicus: The State of Play*. Bloomsbury, The Arden Shakespeare: London, pp. 111–34.

Brown, Pamela Allen (2014) 'Dido, Boy Diva of Carthage: Marlowe's Dido Tragedy and the Renaissance Actress', in Robert Henke and Eric Nicholson (eds), *Transnational Mobilities in Early Modern Theater*. Ashgate: Farnham, pp. 113–30.

Brown, Steve (1990) 'The Boyhood of Shakespeare's Heroines: Notes on Gender Ambiguity in the Sixteenth Century', *Studies in English Literature, 1500–1900*, 30:2, pp. 243–63.

Brown, Sylvia (1999) *Women's Writing in Stuart England. The Mother's Legacies of Elizabeth Joscelin, Elizabeth Richardson, and Dorothy Leigh*. Sutton: Stroud.

Buck, Anne and Phyllis Cunningham (1965) *Children's Costume in England: From the Fourteenth to the End of the Nineteenth Century*. Barnes and Noble: New York.

Bushnell, Rebecca (2003) *Green Desire: Imagining Early Modern English Gardens*. Cornell University Press: Ithaca, NY.

Busse, Clare (2006) '"Pretty Fictions" and "Little Stories"', in Andrea Immel and Michael Witmore (eds), *Childhood and Children's Books in Early Modern Europe, 1550–1800*. Routledge: New York, pp. 75–102.

Callaghan, Dympna (1989) *Women and Gender in Renaissance Tragedy: A Study of King Lear, Othello, The Duchess of Malfi and The White Devil*. Harvester Wheatsheaf: London.

Callaghan, Dympna (1993) '"And All is Semblative a Woman's Part": Body Politics and *Twelfth Night*', *Textual Practice*, 7:3, pp. 428–52.

Callaghan, Dympna (2000) *Shakespeare Without Women: Representing Gender and Race on the Renaissance Stage*. Routledge: London and New York.

Caton, Kristina E. (2013) 'Shared Borders: The Puppet in Ben Jonson's *Bartholomew Fair*', *Early Theatre*, 16:1, pp. 51–73.

Cerasano, S.P (1994) 'Tamburlaine and Edward Alleyn's Ring', *Shakespeare Survey*, 47, pp. 171–80.

Charney, Maurice (2002) *Shakespeare on Love and Lust*. Columbia University Press: New York.

Chedgzoy, Kate (2013) 'Did Children Have a Renaissance?', *Early Modern Women*, 8 (Fall), pp. 261–73.

Chedgzoy, Kate (2019) 'Other Maids: Religion, Race and Relationships Between Girls in Early Modern London', in Naomi J. Miller and Diane Purkiss (eds), *Literary Cultures and Medieval and Early Modern Childhoods*. Palgrave: Basingstoke, pp. 187–201.

Chedgzoy, Kate, Susanne Greenhalgh, and Robert Shaughnessy (eds) (2007) *Shakespeare and Childhood*. Cambridge University Press: Cambridge.

Chess, Simone, Colby Gordon, and Will Fisher (2019) 'Introduction: Early Modern Trans Studies', *Journal for Early Modern Cultural Studies*, 19:4, pp. 1–25.

Churchill, Wendy (2013) *Female Patients in Early Modern England*. Ashgate: Aldershot.

Ciraulo, Darlena (2014) 'Flower Imagery and Botanical Illustration: Health and Sexual Generation in *Romeo and Juliet*', in Sujata Iyengar (ed), *Disability, Health, and Happiness in the Shakespearean Body*. Routledge: London, pp. 158–75.

Coker, Lauren (2016) 'Boy Actors and Early Modern Disability Comedy in *The Knight of the Burning Pestle* and *Epicoene*', *Journal of Dramatic Theory and Criticism*, 31:1, pp. 5–21.

Cole, Herbert (1988) *Heraldry: Decoration and Floral Forms*. Bracken Books: London.

Collington, Philip D. (2006) 'Sans Wife: Sexual Anxiety and the Old Man in Shakespeare', in Erin Campbell (ed), *Growing Old in Early Modern Europe*. Ashgate: Aldershot, pp. 185–207.

Crawford, Patricia (1981) 'Attitudes Towards Menstruation in Seventeenth-Century England', *Past and Present*, 91, pp. 47–73.

Crawford, Patricia (2004) *Blood, Bodies and Families in Early Modern England*. Pearson Longman: Harlow.

Crawford, Patricia and Laura Gowing (1999) *Women's Worlds in Seventeenth-Century England: A Sourcebook*. Routledge: London.

Cressy, David (1997) *Birth, Marriage and Death: Ritual, Religion and the Life-Cycle in Tudor and Stuart England*. Oxford University Press: Oxford.

Crystal, David and Ben Crystal (2002) *Shakespeare's Words: A Glossary and Language Companion*. Penguin Books: London.

Dawson, Lesel (2008) *Lovesickness and Gender in Early Modern English Literature*. Oxford University Press: Oxford.

De Grazia, Margreta (1993) 'The Scandals of Shakespeare's Sonnets', *Shakespeare Survey*, pp. 35–50.

de Sousa, Geraldo U. (1999) *Shakespeare's Cross-Cultural Encounters*. Palgrave: Houndmills.

DiGangi, Mario (1995) 'Asses and Wits: The Homoerotics of Mastery in Satiric Comedy', *English Literary Renaissance*, 25:2, pp. 179–208.

Dolan, Frances (1993) '"Taking the Pencil Out of God's Hand": Art, Nature, and the Face-Painting Debate in Early Modern England', *PMLA*, 108:2, pp. 224–39.

Dollimore, Jonathan (1994) 'Transgression and Surveillance in *Measure for Measure*', in Jonathan Dollimore and Alan Sinfield (eds), *Political Shakespeare: Essays in Cultural Materialism*. Manchester University Press: Manchester, pp. 72–87.

Donnison, Jean (1988) *Midwives and Medical Men: A History of the Struggle for the Control of Childbirth*. Historical Publications: New Barnett.

Dooley, Mark (2001) 'Inversion, Metamorphosis, and Sexual Difference: Female Same-Sex Desire in Ovid and Lyly', in Goran V. Stanivukovic (ed), *Ovid and the Renaissance Body*. University of Toronto Press: Toronto, pp. 59–76.

Dusinberre, Juliet (1993) 'The Taming of the Shrew: Women, Acting, and Power', *Studies in the Literary Imagination*, 26:1, pp. 67–84.

Dusinberre, Juliet (1996) 'Squeaking Cleopatras: Gender and Performance in Antony and Cleopatra', in James C. Bulman (ed), *Shakespeare, Theory and Performance*. Routledge: London and New York, pp. 46–67.

Dusinberre, Juliet (1998) 'Boys Becoming Women in Shakespeare's Plays', *Shakespeare Studies*, 36, pp. 1–28.

Eisenbichler, Konrad (ed) (2002) *The Premodern Teenager: Youth in Society 1150–1650*. Centre for Reformation and Renaissance Studies: Toronto.

Elam, Keir (1996) 'The Fertile Eunuch: *Twelfth Night*, Early Modern Intercourse, and the Fruits of Castration', *Shakespeare Quarterly*, 47, pp. 1–36.

Erickson, Peter (1993) 'Representation of Blacks and Blackness in the Renaissance', *Criticism*, 35:4, pp. 499–527.

Evans, Jennifer (2014) *Aphrodisiacs, Fertility, and Medicine in Early Modern England*. Boydell & Brewer: Woodbridge.

Evans, Jennifer (2016) '"They Are Called Imperfect Men": Male Infertility and Sexual Health in Early Modern England', *Social History of Medicine*, 29:2, pp. 311–32.

Evans, Jennifer (2022) '"A Toste wett in Muskadine": Preventing Miscarriage in Early Modern English Recipe Books c.1600–1780', *Women's Writing* 29:4, pp. 514–32.

Evans, Jennifer and Victoria Sparey (2024) 'The Perils and Promise of Puberty', in Sarah Toulalan (ed), *Early Modern Bodies*. Routledge: London.

Evenden, Doreen (2000) *The Midwives of Seventeenth-Century London*. Cambridge University Press: Cambridge.

Everett, Barbara (1989) *Young Hamlet: Essays on Shakespeare's Tragedies*. Clarendon Press: London.

Findlay, Alison (2010) *Women in Shakespeare: A Dictionary*. Bloomsbury, Arden Shakespeare Dictionaries: London.

Fisher, Kate and Sarah Toulalan (2013) 'Introduction', in Kate Fisher and Sarah Toulalan (eds), *The Routledge History of Sex and the Body, 1500–Present*. Routledge: London, pp. 1–20.

Fisher, Will (2001) 'The Renaissance Beard: Masculinity in Early Modern Culture', *Renaissance Quarterly*, 54:1, pp. 155–87.

Fisher, Will (2002) 'Staging the Beard: Masculinity in Early Modern English Culture', in Jonathan Gil Harris and Natasha Korda (eds), *Staged Properties in Early Modern English Drama*. Cambridge University Press: Cambridge, pp. 230–57.

Fisher, Will (2006) *Materializing Gender in Early Modern English Literature and Culture*. Cambridge University Press: Cambridge.

Fissell, Mary (2004) *Vernacular Bodies: The Politics of Reproduction in Early Modern England*. Oxford University Press: Oxford.

Foakes, R. A. (ed) (2002) *Henslowe's Diary*. Second Edition. Cambridge University Press: Cambridge.

French, Anna (2015) *Children of Wrath: Possession, Prophecy and the Young in Early Modern England*. Ashgate: Farnham.

French, Roger and Andrew Wear (eds) (1989) *The Medical Revolution of the Seventeenth Century*. Cambridge University Press: Cambridge.

Frick, Carole Collier (2011) 'Boys to Men: Codpieces and Masculinity in Sixteenth-Century Europe', in Naomi J. Miller and Naomi Yavneh (eds), *Gender and Early Modern Constructions of Childhood*. Ashgate: Aldershot, pp. 158–80.

Galofré-Vilà, Gregori (2017) A study from Oxford University into 'Highs and Lows of and Englishman's Average Height over 2000 Years', Department of Sociology, University of Oxford. Web. 23 Jul. 2021.

Garber, Majorie (1997) *Coming of Age in Shakespeare*. Routledge: London.

Gibson, Marion and Jo Ann Esra (2017) *Shakespeare's Demonology: A Dictionary*. Bloomsbury Arden Shakespeare: London.

Gowing, Laura (1996) *Domestic Dangers: Women, Words and Sex in Early Modern London*. Oxford University Press: Oxford.

Gowing, Laura (1997) 'Secret Births and Infanticide in Seventeenth-Century England, *Past and Present*, 156:1, pp. 87–115.

Gowing, Laura (2003) *Common Bodies: Women, Sex and Reproduction in Seventeenth-Century England*. Yale University Press: New Haven, CT, and London.

Green, Monica (2005) 'Flowers, Poison and Men: Menstruation in Medieval Western Europe', in Andrew Shail and Gillian Howe (eds), *Menstruation: A Cultural History*. Palgrave Macmillan: Houndmills, pp. 51–64.

Greenblatt, Stephen (1988) *Shakespearean Negotiations: The Circulation of Social Energy in Renaissance England*. University of California Press: Berkeley, CA.

Greg, Walter W. (ed) (1904) *Henslowe's Diary*. A. H. Bullen: London.

Greteman, Blaine (2012) 'Coming of Age on Stage: Jonson's "Epicoene" and the Politics of Childhood in Early Stuart England', *ELH*, 79:1, pp. 135–60.

Greteman, Blaine (2013) *The Poetics and Politics of Youth in Milton's England*. Cambridge University Press: Cambridge.

Griffith, Paul. *Youth and Authority: Formative Experiences in England, 1560–1640*. Clarendon Press: Oxford.

Grote, David (2002) *The Best Actors in the World: Shakespeare and His Playing Company*. Greenwood Press: Westport, CT.

Gurr, Andrew (1992) *The Shakespearean Playing Companies, 1574–1642*. Oxford University Press: Oxford.

Habib, Imtiaz (2000) *Shakespeare and Race: Postcolonial Praxis in the Early Modern Period*. University Press of America: Lanham, MD.

Hall, Edward (Dir) (Mar. 2014) *A Midsummer Night's Dream*. By William Shakespeare. Propeller. Everyman Theatre: Plymouth.

Hall, Kim (1995) *Things of Darkness: Economies of Race and Gender in Early Modern England*. Cornell University Press: Ithaca, NY.

Hammersmith, James P. (1982) 'The Serpent of Old Nile', *Interpretations*, 14:4, pp. 11–16.

Harris, Johanna (2011) '"But I Thinke and Believe": Lady Brilliana Harley's Puritanism in Epistolary Community', in Johanna Harris and Elizabeth Scott-Baumann (eds), *The Intellectual Culture of Puritan Women, 1558–1680*. Palgrave: Basingstoke, pp. 108–21.

Harvey, Karen (2002) 'The Substance of Sexual Difference: Change and Persistence in Representations of the Body in Eighteenth-Century England', *Gender and History*, 14:2, pp. 202–23.

Hendricks, Margot (1996) '"Obscured Dreams": Race, Empire, and Shakespeare's *A Midsummer Night's Dream*', *Shakespeare Quarterly*, 47:1, pp. 37–60.

Higginbotham, Jennifer (2013) *The Girlhood of Shakespeare's Sisters: Gender, Transgression, Adolescence*. Edinburgh University Press: Edinburgh.

Higginbotham, Jennifer and Mark Albert Johnston (eds) (2018) *Queering Childhood in Early Modern English Drama and Culture*. Palgrave: Basingstoke.

Hile, Rachel E. (2009) 'Disability and the Characterization of Katherine in Taming of the Shrew', *Disability Studies Quarterly*, 29:4, electronic copy.

Hill, James L. (1986) 'What, Are They Children?: Shakespeare's Tragic Women and the Boy Actor', *Studies in English Literature, 1500–1900*, 26:2, pp. 235–58.

Hobby, Elaine (1988) *Virtue of Necessity: English Women's Writing, 1649–1688*. Virago: London.

Howard, Jean E. (1988) 'Crossdressing, the Theatre, and Gender Struggle in Early Modern England', *Shakespeare Quarterly*, 39:4, pp. 418–40.

Hull, Suzanne (1982) *English Books for Women, 1475–1640*. Huntington Library: San Marino.

Immel, Andrea and Michael Witmore (eds) (2006) *Childhood and Children's Books in Early Modern Europe, 1550–1800*. Routledge: New York.

Ingram, Martin (1987) *Church Courts, Sex and Marriage in England, 1570–1640*. Cambridge University Press: Cambridge.

Iyengar, Sujata (2004) *Shades of Difference: Mythologies of Skin Color in Early Modern England*. University of Pennsylvania Press: Philadelphia, PA.

Jankowski, Theodora (1996) '"Where There Can Be No Cause of Affection": Redefining Virgins, Their Desires, and Their Pleasures in John Lyly's *Gallathea*', in Valerie Traub, M. Lindsay Kaplan and Dympna Callaghan (eds), *Feminist Readings of Early Modern Culture: Emerging Subjects*. Cambridge University Press, Cambridge, pp. 253–74.

Jardine, Lisa (1989) *Still Harping on Daughters: Women and Drama in the Age of Shakespeare*. Columbia University Press: Columbia.

Jenson, Ejner J. (1972–3) 'The Changing Faces of Love in English Renaissance Comedy', *Comparative Drama*, 6:4, pp. 294–309.

Jewell, Helen (1999) *Education in Early Modern England*. Palgrave Macmillan: Houndmills.
Johnston, Mark Albert (2011) *Beard Fetish in Early Modern England: Sex, Gender and Registers of Value*. Ashgate: Farnham.
Johnston, Mark Albert (2017) 'Shakespeare's *Twelfth Night* and the Fertile Infertility of Eroticized Early Modern Boys', *Modern Philology*, 114:3, pp. 573–600.
Kahn, Coppélia (1978) 'Coming of Age in Verona', *Modern Language Studies*, 8:1, pp. 5–22.
Karim-Cooper, Farah (2006) *Cosmetics in Shakespearean and Renaissance Drama*. Edinburgh University Press: Edinburgh.
Karim-Cooper, Farah (2023) *The Great White Bard: Shakespeare, Race and the Future*. Oneworld Publications: London.
Kastan, David Scott (1999) *Shakespeare After Theory*. Routledge: New York.
Kathman, David (2004) 'Grocers, Goldsmiths, and Drapers: Freemen and Apprentices in the Elizabethan Theater', *Shakespeare Quarterly*, 55:1, pp. 1–49.
Kathman, David (2005) 'How Old Were Shakespeare's Boy Actors?', *Shakespeare Survey*, 58, pp. 220–46.
Keegan Cáel M. (2020) 'Transgender Studies, or How to Do Things with Trans', in S. Somerville (ed), *The Cambridge Companion to Queer Studies*. Cambridge University Press: Cambridge, pp. 66–78.
King, Helen (1998) *Hippocrates' Woman: Reading the Female Body in Ancient Greece*. Routledge: London.
King, Helen (2004) *The Disease of Virgins: Green Sickness, Chlorosis and the Problems of Puberty*. Routledge: London.
King, Helen (2013) *The One-Sex Body on Trial: The Classical and Early Modern Evidence*. Routledge: London.
Knowles, Katie (2013) *Shakespeare's Boys: A Cultural History*. Palgrave Macmillan: Houndmills.
Lamb, Edel (2009) *Performing Childhood in the Early Modern Theatre: The Children's Playing Companies (1599–1613)*. Palgrave Macmillan: Houndmills.
Lamb, Edel (2018) *Reading Children in Early Modern Culture*. Palgrave Macmillan: Cham.
Lamb, Mary Ellen (2000) 'Taken by the Fairies: Fairies Practices and the Production of Popular Culture in *A Midsummer Night's Dream*', *Shakespeare Quarterly*, 51:3, pp. 277–312.
Laqueur, Thomas (1990) *Making Sex: Body and Gender from the Greeks to Freud*. Harvard University Press: Cambridge, MA.
Larson, Katharine (2011) *Early Modern Women in Conversation*. Palgrave Macmillan: Basingstoke.
Laslett, Peter (1965) *The World We Have Lost*. Methuen: London.
Lerer, Seth (2012) 'Devotion and Defacement: Reading Children's *Marginalia*', *Representations*, 118:1, pp. 126–53.
Lerer, Seth (2017) 'Hamlet's Boyhood', in Richard Preiss and Deanne Williams (eds), *Childhood, Education and the Stage in Early Modern England*. Cambridge University Press: Cambridge, pp. 17–36.

Loomba, Ania (2002) *Shakespeare, Race, and Colonialism*. Oxford University Press: Oxford.
Lublin, Robert (2011) *Costuming the Shakespearean Stage: Visual Codes of Representation in Early Theatre and Culture*. Ashgate: Farnham.
Lucking, David (2011) 'Translation and Metamorphosis in *A Midsummer Night's Dream*', *Essays in Criticism*, 61:2, pp. 137–54.
Luscombe, Christopher (Dir) (2 Oct. 2010) *The Merry Wives of Windsor*. By William Shakespeare. Shakespeare's Globe: Shakespeare's Globe Theatre, London.
Martin, Christopher (2012) *Constituting Old Age in Early Modern English Literature, from Queen Elizabeth to King Lear*. Massachusetts University Press: Amherst, MA.
Maurer, Margaret (2001) 'Constering Bianca: "The Taming of the Shrew" and "The Woman's Prize, Or The Tamer Tamed"', *Medieval and Renaissance Drama in England*, 14, pp. 186–206.
McCarthy, Harry (2018) 'Men in the Making: Youth, the Repertory, and the "Children" of the Queen's Revels, 1609–13', *English Literary History*, 85:3, pp. 599–629.
McCarthy, Harry (2020a) 'The Circulation of Youthful Energy on the Early Modern London Stage: Migration, Intertheatricality, and "Growing to Common Players"', *Shakespeare Survey*, 73, pp. 43–62.
McCarthy, Harry (2020b) *Performing Early Modern Drama Beyond Shakespeare: Edward's Boys*. Cambridge University Press: Cambridge.
McCarthy, Harry (2021) '"M[aster] Monkesters Schollars": Richard Mulcaster, Physical Education, and the Early Modern Boy Companies', *Early Modern Theatre*, 24:2, pp. 31–54.
McCarthy, Harry (2022) *Boy Actors in Early Modern England: Skill and Stagecraft in the Theatre*. Cambridge University Press: Cambridge.
McManus, Clare (2015) '"Sing It Like Poor Barbary": *Othello* and Early Modern Women's Performance', *Shakespeare Bulletin*, 33:1, pp. 99–120.
McMillin, Scott (2004) 'The Sharer and His Boy: Rehearsing Shakespeare's Women', in Peter Holland and Stephen Orgel (eds), *From Script to Stage in Early Modern England*. Palgrave Macmillan: Basingstoke, pp. 231–45.
Mendelson, Sara, and Patricia Crawford (eds) (1998) *Women in Early Modern England: 1550–1720*. Oxford University Press: Oxford.
Miller, Naomi J., and Diane Purkiss (eds) (2019) *Literary Cultures and Medieval and Early Modern Childhoods*. Palgrave Macmillan: Houndmills.
Miller, Naomi J., and Naomi Yavneh (eds) (2011) *Gender Constructions of Early Modern Childhood*. Ashgate: Farnham.
Montrose, Louis (1983) '"Shaping Fantasies": Figurations of Gender and Power in Elizabethan Culture', *Representations*, 2, pp. 61–94.
Munro, Lucy (2005) *Children of the Queen's Revels: A Jacobean Theatre Company*. Cambridge University Press: Cambridge.
Munro, Lucy (2017) 'Speaking Like a Child', in Richard Preiss and Deanne Williams (eds), *Childhood, Education and the Stage in Early Modern England*. Cambridge University Press: Cambridge, pp. 81–99.

Munson Deats, Sara (2005) 'Shakespeare's Anamorphic Drama: A Survey of *Antony and Cleopatra* in Criticism, On Stage, and on the Screen', in Sara Munson Deats (ed), *Antony and Cleopatra: New Critical Essays*. Routledge: New York, pp. 1–94.

Ndiaye, Noémie (2022) *Scripts of Blackness: Early Modern Performance Culture and the Making of Race*. University of Pennsylvania Press: Pennsylvania, PA.

Neely, Carol (1991) 'Documents of Madness: Reading Madness and Gender in Shakespeare's Tragedies and Early Modern Culture', *Shakespeare Quarterly*, 42:3, pp. 315–38.

Neill, Michael (1997) *Issues of Death: Mortality and Identity in English Renaissance Tragedy*. Oxford University Press: Oxford.

Neill, Michael (2006) 'Introduction', in Michael Neill (ed), *Othello*. By William Shakespeare. Oxford University Press: Oxford.

Nelles, William (2009) 'Sexing Shakespeare's Sonnets: Reading Beyond Sonnet 20', *English Literary Renaissance*, 39:1, pp. 128–40.

Nelson Garner, Shirley (1989) '"Let Her Paint an Inch Thick": Painted Ladies in Renaissance Drama and Society', *Renaissance Drama*, 20, pp. 123–39.

Nelson Garner, Shirley (1998) 'A Midsummer Night's Dream: "Jack Shall Have Jill / Nought Shall Go Ill"', in Dorothela Kehler (ed), *A Midsummer Night's Dream: Critical Essays*. Garland: London, pp. 127–43.

Newman, Karen (1989) 'City Talk: Women and Commodification in Jonson's *Epiceone*', *ELH*, 56:3, pp. 503–18.

Newman, Karen (1991) *Fashioning Femininity and English Renaissance Drama*. University of Chicago Press: Chicago, IL.

Newman, Lucile (1979) 'Ophelia's Herbal', *Economic Botany*, 32:2, pp. 227–32.

Newton, Hannah (2012) *The Sick Child in Early Modern England, 1580–1720*. Oxford University Press: Oxford.

Oren-Magidor, Daphna (2017) *Infertility in Early Modern England*. Palgrave: London.

Orgel, Stephen (ed) (1970) *Ben Jonson: Selected Masques*. Yale University Press: New Haven, CT, and London.

Orgel, Stephen (1996) *Impersonations: The Performance of Gender in Shakespeare's England*. Cambridge University Press: Cambridge.

Orgel, Stephen (2017) 'The Further Adventures of Ganymede', in Richard Preiss and Deanne Williams (eds), *Childhood, Education and the Stage in Early Modern England*. Cambridge University Press: Cambridge, pp. 143–61.

Packard, Bethany (2019) 'Inducting Childhood: The Scripted Spontaneity of Self-Referential Child Players', in Naomi J. Miller and Diane Purkiss (eds), *Literary Cultures and Medieval and Early Modern Childhoods*. Palgrave Macmillan: Houndmills.

Page, Nick (2001) *Lord Minimus: The Extraordinary Life of Britain's Smallest Man*. St. Martin's Griffin: New York.

Park, Katherine (2002) 'The Substance of Sexual Difference: Change and Persistence in Representations of the Body in Eighteenth-Century England', *Gender and History*, 14:2, pp. 202–23.

Parker, Patricia (2007) 'Construing Gender: Mastering Bianca in *The Taming of the Shrew*', in Dympna Callaghan (ed), *The Impact of Feminism in English Renaissance Studies*. Palgrave Macmillan: New York, pp. 193–209.

Paster, Gail Kern (1993) *The Body Embarrassed: Drama and the Disciplines of Shame in Early Modern England*. Cornell University Press: Ithaca, NY.

Paster, Gail Kern (2004) *Humoring the Body: Emotions and the Shakespearean Stage*. University of Chicago Press: Chicago, IL.

Peterson, Kaara (2010) *Popular Medicine, Hysterical Disease and Social Controversy in Shakespeare's England*. Ashgate: Farnham.

Pollock, Linda (2001) 'Adult-Child Relations', in David I. Kertzer and Marzio Barbagli (eds), *Family Life in Early Modern Times, 1500–1789*. Yale University Press: New Haven, CT, and London.

Pomata, Gianna (2001) 'Menstruating Men: Similarity and Difference in the Sexes in Early Modern Medicine', in Valeria Finucci and Kevin Brownlee (eds), *Generation and Degeneration in Early Modern Europe*. Dulce University Press: Durham, NC, pp. 109–52.

Potter, Ursula (2002) 'Greensickness in *Romeo and Juliet*: Considerations on a Sixteenth-Century Disease of Virgins', in Konrad Eisenbichler (ed), *The Premodern Teenager: Youth in Society 1150–1650*. Centre for Reformation and Renaissance Studies: Toronto.

Potter, Ursula (2013) 'Navigating the Dangers of Female Puberty in Renaissance Drama', *Studies in English Literature*, 53:2, pp. 421–39.

Power, Andrew J. (2003) 'Boy Parts in Early Shakespeare', in Rory Loughnane and Andrew J. Power (eds), *Early Shakespeare, 1588–1594*. Cambridge University Press: Cambridge, pp. 220–34.

@ProfFarahKC (10 April 2020) 'it's not unlikely that make-up was used in degrees to signal different states: woman, painted woman/lady, prostitute, etc. so i do believe that Cesario and Ganymede would have had a light application to signal "sex"', *Twitter*. twitter.com.

Rackin, Phyllis (1972) 'Shakespeare's Boy Cleopatra: The Decorum of Nature, and the Golden World of Poetry', *PMLA*, 87:2, pp. 201–12.

Rackin, Phyllis (1987) 'Androgyny, Mimesis, and the Marriage of the Boy Heroine on the English Renaissance Stage', *PMLA*, 102:1, pp. 29–41.

Read, Sara (2013) *Menstruation and the Female Body in Early Modern England*. Palgrave Macmillan: Houndsmills.

Richards, Jennifer (2019) *Voices of Books in the English Renaissance: A New History of Reading*. Oxford University Press: Oxford.

Roberts, Sasha (1998) *Writers and Their Works: Romeo and Juliet*. Northcote House: Plymouth.

Roth, Stephen (2009) *Hamlet: The Undiscovered Country*. Open House: Seattle, WA.

Rutter, Carol Chillington (1999) 'Introduction', in Carol Chillington Rutter (ed), *Documents of the Rose Playhouse*. Manchester University Press: Manchester.

Rutter, Carol Chillington (2001) *Enter the Body: Women and Representation on Shakespeare's Stage*. Routledge: London.

Rycroft, Eleanor (2019) *Facial Hair and the Performance of Masculinity*. Routledge: London.
Schiffer, James (ed) (2000) *Shakespeare's Sonnets: Critical Essays*. Garland: London.
Schoenfeldt, Michael (1999) *Bodies and Selves in Early Modern England*. Cambridge University Press: Cambridge.
Scott, Charlotte (2017) 'Incapable and Shallow Innocents: Mourning Shakespeare's Children in *Richard III* and *The Winter's Tale*', in Richard Preiss and Deanne Williams (eds), *Childhood, Education and the Stage in Early Modern England*. Cambridge University Press: Cambridge, pp. 58–77.
Scott, Charlotte (2018) *The Child in Shakespeare*. Oxford University Press: Oxford.
Semenza Colo'n, Gregory M. (2011) '"Second Childishness" and the Shakespearean Vision of Ideal Parenting', in Noami J. Miller and Naomi Yavneh (eds), *Gender and Early Modern Constructions of Childhood*. Ashgate: Aldershot, pp. 222–35.
Shapiro, James (2005) *A Year in the Life of William Shakespeare: 1599*. Harper Collins: New York.
Shapiro, Michael (1982) '"Boying Her Greatness": Shakespeare's Use of Coterie Drama in *Antony and Cleopatra*', *The Modern Language Review*, 77:1, pp. 1–15.
Shepard, Alexandra (2003) *Meanings of Manhood in Early Modern England*. Oxford University Press: Oxford.
Simpson, Anna-Claire (2019) 'The Child on Display in Ben Jonson's *Bartholomew Fair*', in Noami J. Miller and Diane Purkiss (eds), *Literary Cultures and Medieval and Early Modern Childhoods*. Palgrave Macmillan: Houndmills, pp. 119–33.
Skuse, Alanna (2014) 'The Worm and the Flesh: Cankered Bodies in Shakespeare's Sonnets', in Sujata Iyengar (ed), *Disability, Health, and Happiness in the Shakespearean Body*. Routledge: London, pp. 240–59.
Skuse, Alanna (2015) *Constructions of Cancer in Early Modern England: Ravenous Natures*. Palgrave Macmillan: Houndmills.
Smith, Lisa Wynne (2008) '"An Account of an Unaccountable Distemper": The Experience of Pain in Early Eighteenth-Century England and France', *Eighteenth-Century Studies*, 41, pp. 459–80.
Smith, Lisa Wynne (2011) 'The Body Embarrassed? Rethinking the Leaky Male Body in Eighteenth-Century England and France', *Gender and History*, 23:1, pp. 26–46.
Smith, Nathaniel B. (2014) 'Speaking Medicine: A Paracelsian Parody of the Humors in *The Tamining of the Shrew*', in Sujata Iyengar (ed), *Disability, Health, and Happiness in the Shakespearean Body*. Routledge: London, pp. 195–211.
Snyder, Susan (1999) 'Mamillias and Gender Polarization in *The Winter's Tale*', *Shakespeare Quarterly*, 50:1, pp. 1–8.
Sofer, Andrew (2003) *The Stage Life of Props*. University of Michigan Press: Michigan, MI.
Sparey, Victoria (Fall, 2015) 'Performing Puberty: Fertile Complexions in Shakespeare's Plays', *Shakespeare Bulletin*, 33:3, pp. 441–67.
Stallybrass, Peter (1991) 'Transvestism and the "Body Beneath": Speculating on the Boy Actor', in Valerie Wayne (ed), *The Matter of Difference: Materialist Feminist Criticism of Shakespeare*. Harvester Wheatsheaf: London, pp. 64–81.

Stallybrass, Peter (2000) 'Worn Worlds: Clothes and Identity on the Renaissance Stage', in Margreta de Grazia, Maureen Quilligan and Peter Stallybrass (eds), *Subject and Object in Renaissance Culture*. Cambridge University Press: Cambridge.
Stern, Tiffany (2000) *Rehearsal from Shakespeare to Sheridan*. Clarendon: Oxford.
Stern, Tiffany (2004) *Making Shakespeare: From Stage to Page*. Routledge: London and New York.
Stevens, Andrea Ria (2013) *Inventions of the Skin: The Painted Body in Early English Drama*. Edinburgh University Press: Edinburgh.
Stewart, Alan (2008) *Shakespeare's Letters*. Oxford University Press: Oxford.
Stolberg, Michael (2003) 'A Woman Down to Her Bones: The Anatomy of Sexual Difference in the Sixteenth and Early Seventeenth Centuries', *Isis*, 94:2, pp. 274–99.
Stott, Annette (1992) 'Floral Femininity: A Pictorial Definition', *America Art*, 6:3, pp. 60–77.
Talbot van den Berg, Kent (1975) 'Theatrical Fiction and the Reality of Love in *As You Like It*', *PMLA*, 90:5, pp. 885–93.
Taunton, Nina (2006) 'Time Whirligig: Images of Old Age in *Coriolanus*, Francis Bacon and Thomas Newton', in Erin Campbell (ed), *Growing Old in Early Modern Europe*. Ashgate: Aldershot, pp. 21–38.
Taylor, Gary and John Lavagnino (eds) (2010) *Thomas Middleton: The Collected Works*. Oxford University Press: Oxford.
Thomas, Vivian and Nicki Faircloth (2016) *Dictionary of Shakespeare's Plants and Gardens*. Bloomsbury, Arden Dictionaries: Ebook.
Toulalan, Sarah (2013) '"Age to Great, or to Little, Doeth Let Conception": Bodies, Sex and the Life Cycle, 1500–1750', in Kate Fisher and Sarah Toulalan (eds), *Routledge History of Sex and the Body, 1500–Present*. Routledge: London, pp. 279–95.
Toulalan, Sarah (2014) '"T[o] Much Eating Stifles the Child": Fat Bodies and Reproduction in Early Modern England', *Historical Research*, 87:235, pp. 65–93.
Traub, Valerie (2002) *The Renaissance of Lesbianism in Early Modern England*. Cambridge University Press: Cambridge.
Tribble, Evelyn (2011) *Cognition in the Globe*. Palgrave Macmillan: Houndmills.
Van den Berg, Sara (2013) 'Dwarf Aesthetics in Spenser's *Faerie Queene*', in Allison P. Hobgood and David Houston Wood (eds), *Recovering Disability in Early Modern England*. Ohio State University Press: Columbus, OH, pp. 23–42.
Van Es, Bart (2017) 'Shakespeare versus Blackfriars: Satiric Comedy, Domestic Tragedy, and the Boy Actor in *Othello*', in Richard Preiss and Deanne Williams (eds), *Childhood, Education and the Stage in Early Modern England*. Cambridge University Press: Cambridge.
Wall, Wendy (1993) *The Imprint of Gender: Authorship and Publication in the English Renaissance*. Cornell University Press: Ithaca, NY.
Wiebracht, Ben (2020) 'Adonis in Fairyland: The Hazards of Boyhood in *A Midsummer Night's Dream*', *Shakespeare*, 16:4, pp. 340–55.

Wilder, Lina Perkins (2008) 'Stage Props and Shakespeare's Comedies: Keeping Safe Nerissa's Ring', in Heather Hirschfield (ed), *The Oxford Handbook of Shakespearean Comedy*. Oxford Academic: Electronic Book, pp. 377–94.

Williams, Deanne (2014) *Shakespeare and the Performance of Girlhood*. Palgrave Macmillan: Houndmills.

Williams, Deanne (2017) 'Chastity, Speech and the Girl Masquer', in Richard Preiss and Deanne Williams (eds), *Childhood, Education and the Stage in Early Modern England*. Cambridge University Press: Cambridge, pp. 162–83.

Winston, Jessica (2018) *Lawyers at Play: Literature, Law and Politics at the Early Modern Inns of Court, 1558–1581*. Oxford University Press: Oxford.

Witmore, Michael (2007) *Pretty Creatures: Children and Fiction in the English Renaissance*. Cornell University Press: Ithaca, NY.

Wilson-Floyd, Mary (2003) *English Ethnicity and Race in Early Modern Drama*. Cambridge University Press: Cambridge.

Index

Note: 'n.' after a page references indicates a note on that page.

ableism 168
acorn 157, 167–8, 173, 176, 181
adolescence
   terminology used 24, 32, 43, 57, 84
ageing 19, 25–6, 29, 30, 32, 40–2, 52, 54, 56, 58, 62, 67, 81, 83–4, 167, 174, 196
   of Richard Burbage 187, 200
   see also life cycle; old age
Alleyn, Edward 143–4, 164–5
aphrodisiacs 47, 172
apprenticeships 6–7, 11, 141–2, 145, 198
Aristotelian 14, 16–17, 24–5, 30
Aristotle 17, 23–4, 75, 108, 117
Aristotle's Masterpiece 31, 163

Bacon, Francis 26–7, 30–1, 36, 53, 105–6, 108–9, 111, 138, 163, 165–6, 173, 175
barrenness 47, 169
   see also fertility
Barrough, Phillip 168–9, 172–3
Batman, Stephen 24, 26, 47, 83, 166, 170, 194–5
beard 21, 26, 27, 31, 34–5, 74–88, 90, 97–100, 109, 111–12, 188, 189, 194, 196
   false 78–9
beardlessness 77–8, 80, 87, 96, 98
Beaumont, Francis 202
bed trick 70–1
Beeland, Ambrose 145
blush 34, 74–5, 84–5, 90–8, 100n.5
body size 158–62, 168–72, 177–9, 183, 185, 190, 191n.1, 191n.5
   see also height; stature

boy actors 11, 13–14, 35, 36, 90, 92, 139–44, 146–7, 149, 151, 158–60, 168, 182–4, 188, 190, 198–9, 201
   collaboration between 183–4
   eroticisation of 17, 98, 101n.7, 158–9, 190
boyhood 7–8, 15, 18, 78, 114, 145, 161–2, 184, 200
breasts 30–2, 74, 83
breeching 15–16
Burbage, Richard 12–13, 34, 37, 56, 61, 62, 85, 86, 92, 98–100, 116, 145, 150, 162, 165, 184, 186–90, 200–1

cancer 54
   see also canker
canker 63–4, 69–70
Cary, Elizabeth 125–6
   The Tragedy of Mariam 126
Castiglione, Baldassarre 96, 110, 114, 116
   [*The Book of*] *The Courtier* 96, 110, 114, 116, 118
caterpillar 54
   see also canker
chastity 7, 28, 35, 65, 69, 71–2, 108, 119, 125, 128, 203
Chaucer, Geoffrey 82
   'The Miller's Tale' 82
chemical medicine 113
childbirth 22, 169–70
childcare 15
childhood diseases 5–6, 8, 28, 31, 43, 64–6, 173, 195
   see also greensickness; pica; spots

childhood studies 7, 35, 103
children's companies 10–11, 141, 158, 160–1
    Children of the Queen's Revels 10–11, 145, 160
Codrington, Robert 120–1, 126, 131, 145, 155
comedy 4, 42, 57, 70–1, 87–8, 129–30, 158, 177, 191n.6
Condell, Henry 186
conversation
    and gender 119–21, 126, 128, 131–6, 155
    skills in 110, 112, 114, 116–17, 190, 197
cosmetics 78, 92–4, 96–9, 181–2, 195
    see also make-up
costume 67, 78, 99, 143
counsel 116, 127, 131–2
Crooke, Helkiah 106, 107, 124, 138
Crossman, Samuel 44, 63–4, 118
cue-script 95
Cuffe, Henry 17, 23–5, 32, 43, 60, 81, 84
Culpeper, Nicholas 30, 39n.9, 39n.10

death 49, 51, 54, 58, 67, 69, 84, 129, 133, 199
desire
    as sign of puberty 31, 47, 50–1, 64–5, 69–71, 83, 85–6, 91, 115–16, 123, 130, 133–4, 197, 200
    and speech 115–16, 123, 130, 133–4, 137
    see also humoral heat
diet 156n.5, 165–6, 172–3
    see also pica
dwarf 157, 159, 168, 191n.3

education 7, 9, 35, 46, 55–7, 63, 103, 110, 113–14, 117, 119–21, 145, 203
Edward's Boys 140–1, 183
Elyot, Thomas 25, 124, 155n.4, 156n.5, 166, 193
emblem 45, 57, 60, 62, 66–7, 147
emblematic staging 60–1
eunuch 105–8
exercise
    physical 165–6, 172, 175, 183
    vocal 113–14, 117, 183

fairy 70, 110, 162, 178–80, 187
Ferrand, Jacques 20, 31–2, 74, 84, 93, 115
fertility 6, 22, 42, 47, 49–50, 81, 84, 90, 105, 107, 155n.1, 161, 168–9, 171–3, 181, 204n.1
    see also infertility
Field, Nathan 144–5, 200
Fletcher, John 202
    The Two Noble Kinsmen 181
flowers 42–6, 48–9, 53–4, 56, 63–4, 85, 94, 178
    as menstruation 43–4, 64
    as stage properties 49
    see also rose; violet
friends 114, 129, 131, 177

Galenic 30, 124
Germain, Marie 19
girlhood 6–9, 28, 32–3, 67, 70, 91, 104, 119–26, 130–1, 135, 162, 173, 176–7, 180, 184, 202
The Globe 61, 101n.8
Gouge, William 27
Greene, Robert 65
greensickness 5–6, 28, 36, 47, 64–8, 120, 138, 169, 173, 195
Greenwood, Will 17, 75, 79, 113
Guillemeau, Jacques 169–72
gypsy 148–9, 154

Hawkins, Francis 114, 118, 120, 122
height 26–7, 32–8, 98, 157–8, 160–6, 168–9, 172, 175–6, 181, 185–6, 189–90, 191n.2
    see also body size; stature
Henslowe, Richard 142–4
Herrick, Robert 84, 149
Hill, Thomas 75, 164, 171, 174–5
Hippocrates 107
Hippocratic 21, 30
Huarte, Juan 19
humoral heat 30–3, 39n.7, 42, 64–6, 75, 83, 163, 203
    and gender 10, 18, 23
    of minds and voices 102–7, 111, 113, 124, 166, 171–2
    see also desire

impressment 10, 141
infertility 75–6, 107, 155n.1, 159, 168–9, 172–3, 176

see also barrenness
Inns of Court 140

Jackson, Henry 92–4, 199
Jonson, Ben 103, 146, 149
   Bartholomew Fair 157–60
   Epicœne 78–9, 100n.2, 126
   'On Salathiel Pavy' 144

Killigrew, Henry 139
King's Men 10–12, 145, 198
knotgrass 167–8, 173

lactation 22
Lady Elizabeth's Men 11, 145, 160
Laqueur, Thomas 14, 18–20, 22, 90, 100n.4
   see also one-sex model
Leigh, Dorothy 119
Lemnius, Levinus 24–5, 27, 29, 81, 111–12, 115, 122
letters 126, 136
life cycle 22–3, 25–6, 29–33, 167, 179, 195, 198
   and gender 14, 17, 22, 30–3, 43, 70, 107–8, 120, 172–3
   stages of 23–6, 29, 40–1, 52, 55, 57, 59–62, 111, 115
   see also ageing
Lodge, Thomas 45, 59, 67, 130, 187
Lord Chamberlain's Men 10–12, 37, 61, 145, 156n.6, 198
   see also King's Men
love melancholy 64
Lupton, Donald 66
Lyly, John 202

make-up 81, 88, 92–8, 101n.9, 182, 195
   see also cosmetics
marriage 3, 71, 77, 88, 121–2, 125–6, 129, 137, 152, 197, 203
   age of 27–8
   as cure for greensickness 65–6, 125
masques 93
maypole 157, 159, 176, 181
menstruation 5–6, 9, 21–2, 28–32, 43–4, 46, 64, 77, 82, 107, 125, 163, 172–3, 196
metatheatre 11, 14, 36, 105, 147, 150, 153, 155, 184

Middleton, Thomas 70
   The Changeling 70
   see also Rowley, William
Milton, John 35, 103
mirth 129–30, 133, 135
   see also sport
miscarriage 170, 172–4
Mulcaster, Richard 55–6, 63, 113, 116–17, 120–1, 124–6, 128, 132, 145, 152, 155n.3, 166, 183

old age 23–4, 41–2, 48, 52, 56–63, 67, 111, 169
   see also ageing; life cycle
one-sex model 14, 18–22, 90, 100n.4

Paré, Ambroise 19, 21, 24, 26
Peacham, Henry 40–1, 43–4, 53, 57, 63
penis 19–20, 72n.2, 76–7
physiognomy 164, 174–5
pica 28
Pig, John 143–4
The Problemes of Aristotle 77, 83
prodigal 68, 123
Propeller 191n.2, 191n.6
puberty 1, 4–9, 36, 86, 106, 111–13, 117, 160–1, 163, 171, 185–6, 188, 192–6
   and gender 5–8, 16–17, 21–3, 28–34, 38, 40, 42–4, 63–6, 71, 74–5, 81–3, 85, 87–91, 96–9, 102, 104, 108–9, 111, 120, 125, 139, 169, 196, 203
pubic hair 9, 82–3, 87, 100n.6
puppet 157–60, 167, 182, 184, 191n.1
Pythagorean 23, 25

race 39n.7, 154, 191n.4
   and beauty 94, 137
   and metatheatre 105, 148, 154, 184
   and puberty 28–9, 137
Restoration 204
Rich, Barnabe 93
rose 40, 45–54, 56, 66, 68, 72n.3, 84, 90, 94, 97, 133, 155, 167, 179, 194
The Rose 165
Rowley, William 70
   The Changeling 70
   see also Middleton, John
rue 46–9, 65
Rylance, Mark 154

seed
  as growth metaphor 40–1, 43, 45, 50, 53, 72n.2, 167, 181
  for human reproduction 21, 24, 26–7, 29–31, 38n.4, 43, 50, 67, 72n.2, 74–7, 81–5, 107, 113, 134, 163, 169–70, 196
'sexed' bodies 16–18, 29, 32–3, 44, 82, 88–90, 125, 197
Shakespeare, William 56–7, 61
  All's Well That Ends Well 51, 70–1
  Antony and Cleopatra 51–2, 105, 148–9, 151, 153–4, 168, 198, 200
  As You Like It 18, 34, 37–8, 40–2, 45, 50, 56–7, 59, 61–3, 67, 69, 85–7, 89–90, 97–8, 102, 104–5, 115–16, 118, 121, 129–31, 135, 137, 155, 162, 184, 186–90, 198, 200
  Coriolanus 86
  Hamlet 45–9, 55, 72, 114
  King Lear 58, 200
  Macbeth 200
  Measure for Measure 3, 34, 38n.1, 70–1, 84, 90, 94–5
  The Merchant of Venice 60, 89, 109, 111, 127, 129, 131–2, 156n.7
  A Midsummer Night's Dream 34, 37–8, 42, 49, 66, 68–72, 84, 104, 157–8, 160–2, 167, 173, 176–80, 182, 184–8, 191n.2, 198–9, 201
  Much Ado About Nothing 34, 95
  Othello 49, 92, 199
  Romeo and Juliet 45, 55, 60, 71, 84, 109–10, 125, 132–3, 148, 151, 201
  The Sonnets 53–4, 68–9, 72n.6
  The Taming of the Shrew 39n.5, 121–8, 130, 135, 137, 151–4, 156n.6, 198, 201, 203
  The Tempest 200–1
  Titus Andronicus 110, 184
  Twelfth Night 18–19, 34, 86–7, 99–100, 197, 202
  The Two Gentlemen of Verona 55
  The Two Noble Kinsmen 181
  The Winter's Tale 1, 4, 31, 48, 85, 91, 110, 112, 130, 200
Sharp, Jane 5, 20, 30, 39n.9, 39n.10, 43, 47, 64, 72n.2, 81–3, 170
sighing 115–16
silence 7, 35, 54, 95–6, 108, 116, 119–20, 126, 131, 155n.3
social status 91, 137
sport 69, 129–30, 136–7, 155, 197
  see also mirth; wit
spots 194–6
stature 26, 36, 159, 161, 163–73, 176, 181–2, 187, 189, 196
  see also body size; height

Tanner, John 75
transgender studies 197, 204n.2
Trapnel, Anna 119

university 44, 55, 63, 114

Vaughan, William 192–4
violet 46, 48, 180
virginity 43, 71, 90, 203
voice 27, 35–6, 87–9, 103–8, 110–12, 115–16, 132, 134, 139, 144, 194, 204
  and agency 109, 114, 118, 140, 145–7, 149, 158
  breaking of 13, 31–2, 35, 102, 105, 108–9, 139, 146–7, 149, 161, 163
  of girls 119–22, 125–7, 129, 131, 135–9, 152–3
  training of 113–14, 117, 152–3, 183

Wanley, Nathaniel 19
Whitney, Geoffrey 60, 62
wig 78
Wight, Sarah 119
Willis, Thomas 112–13
willow 49
wit 55, 76, 124–5, 129, 171, 203
  see also mirth; sport
womb 19–20, 47, 202–3
  size of 169–70, 172, 196
Woodward, Ezekiah 129
wrestling 86